The Spirits Of Bowen Downs

Compiled by

Louise Moloney

Second Edition

First published by Louise Moloney

Second edition published by Boolarong Press, 2014

National Library of Australia Cataloguing-in-Publication entry
Creator: Moloney, A. Louise, author.
Title: The spirits of Bowen Downs / Louise Moloney.
Edition: 2nd edition
ISBN: 9781925046793 (paperback)
Subjects: Frontier and pioneer life--Queensland--Bowen Region.
Death--Queensland--Bowen Downs--History.
Death--Queensland--Mount Cornish--History.
Burial--Queensland--Bowen Downs--History.
Burial--Queensland--Mount Cornish--History.
Bowen Downs (Qld.)--History.
Bowen Region (Qld.)--History.
Mount Cornish (Qld.)--History.
Dewey Number: 390.099435

Cover image: Stockmen at Mount Cornish sheep station near Muttaburra, Queensland, 1898. John Oxley Library.

Published by Boolarong Press, Salisbury, Brisbane, Australia.
www.boolarongpress.com.au

Printed and bound by Watson Ferguson & Company, Salisbury, Australia

Acknowledgement

Lesley Cowper contacted me enquiring if I had any information on graves on Bowen Downs for their one hundred and fiftieth year [2012]. This set me into research mode and the number kept growing. Helen Marsh who was a great source of information about the history of the area. Also great thanks to Judith McClymont who every time I thought I was finished, would e-mail me and say 'What about this bloke?'

Most of the information included in this book is from transcripts, from articles included in the old newspapers: http://www.nla.gov.au/ndp/selected_newspapers, which as of the 27 April 2012 has 6,930,534 pages consisting of 68,159,834 articles available to search containing some interesting articles. Queensland Birth, Deaths and Marriages were also used extensively to cross reference date, persons and family information. The reference or insert footnote are related to the Queensland Birth, Death and Marriages reference number. 'Early Days In North Queensland' by The Late Edward Palmer (Sydney: Angus & Robertson: Melbourne: Angus, Robertson & Shenstone: 1903) was also used as a reference.

Thanks must go to Duncan Leask, Senior Museum Assistant, Qld Police Museum, Qld Police Service who trawled through the *Queensland Police Gazettes* showing tables which include *'Deaths reported to Police'* relating to Bowen Downs and Mt Cornish, also Greg Swan, Senior Land Officer, State Land Asset Management for help retrieving information from the Government Gazettes from 1859-1900.

My mother who proofed it for me complaining about the bad grammar, and my husband Chris who I feel is getting used to me now trawling through information looking for '*my dead-uns*'.

Dedication

To all those who ventured to Western Queensland to follow their dreams and to open up this grazing country — men, women and children — many gave their lives.

Editors' Note

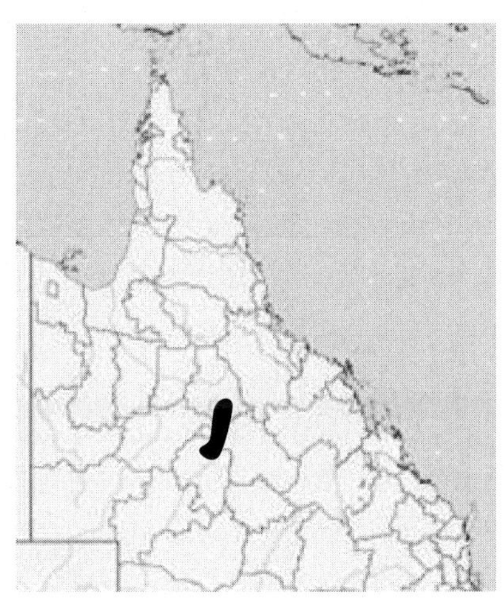

Approximate location of Bowen Downs 1870s

In 1860 William Landsborough and his team ventured into this region of western Queensland looking for good grazing lands. This was the region they called, Bowen Downs. They found new exception grazing land and so Landsborough returned to the Land's Office and selected a vast area of this region. Along with Nat Buchanan they set up a grazing enterprise but needed a bigger partner – the Scottish Australian Company to help with the stocking of it. In November 1861, Nat Buchanan set out from Port Denison [Bowen] to find a route from the sea to Landsborough Runs. The first cattle, 5,000 head, arrived in October 1862 from Landsborough's Fort Cooper station near Nebo driven by two colonists and eight aborigines, with Nat Buchanan acting as guide. Another three thousand cows walked from Narran, NSW in May 1863. Twenty-five thousand young sheep from Glengallan Stud near Warwick completed the early stocking of Landsborough Run, which eventually covered 3,683 square miles or some 2.36 million acres which eventually became Bowen Downs. Nat Buchanan was the first manager and in 1863, when a cluster of bark huts and fewer than twelve people made up the settlement of Bowen Downs.

During the research, I really did feel '*The Spirits of Bowen Downs*' looking down on me and helping along the way. What amazing people these pioneers were, venturing out into an unknown country — imagine travelling this country as Edward

Brooking Cornish did from the 1850s until his death in 1866. Edward was the man who encouraged the Scottish Australia Company to take the gamble on this great tract of land.

Most of the content of this book is transcribed from media, Queensland Birth Deaths and Marriages [Qld BDM], or Police and Government Gazettes. Some of the names are spelt differently either in the heading or the actual articles from different papers. Also, some the actual date of death in my heading and the information below may be different. The heading is what is recorded in Queensland Birth, Deaths and Marriages, and even they may be spelt differently in different events. Also, these are newspaper articles so there could be discrepancies with the actual truth or other records.

Every care has been taken to acquire the information contained within this book, but as most of it is over 100 years old, it may contain errors. Some people may be missing, I am sorry for this but it was not an easy matter to work out who was where and when.

It was difficult to sort out when actual blocks were resumed off Bowen Downs and Mt Cornish. All individuals related to Bowen Downs have been included but those found after about 1908 relating to Mt Cornish or Mt Cornish blocks were not included as these selections were no longer a part of the Scottish Australia Company. Mt Cornish was sold in 1903, but actually began to be resumed in the late 1880s as did Bowen Downs.

In this second edition, I have widened my scope to include the region first called Bowen Downs. I have found many more individuals who died in the area, and members of the public have come forward with graves, and like the rest they are not registered in any other cemetery or register. You will notice a few buried in the Aramac Cemetery. These are before the earliest records at the moment relating to that cemetery and the individuals came in from Bowen Downs for medical attention.

Most of the people listed in this book either worked, passed through or had a relationship with Bowen Downs and Mount Cornish, and are buried within its boundaries. There are some who died in other places but they had strong links to both Bowen Downs and Mount Cornish and have been included. The ones included in this book are the forgotten ones – the ones buried more or less where they died and most will not appear on any other Cemetery Register.

Some of the information about individuals included in this edition has been taken only from their death certificates. As I read these death certificates it is sad that some so young and others not so young have been buried in what was at this era, a harsh environment – some so far from home and without next of kin listed. Maybe their family never really knew what happened to their loved ones far away in this 'new colony'.

As you peruse each entry, think of these people, many who came from overseas and ventured straight to this western district. I hope you enjoy these entries, find them informative and remember these individuals who opened up our great Central Western Queensland.

Table of Contents

William Landsborough's Headstone

In Memory of William Landsborough
The Explorer
Born in Stephenstone Manse
Saltcoast Scotland
21st Feb 1825
Died at Caloundra
16th March 1886
He traced several rivers in Queensland to their sources and crossed Australia from the Gulf of Carpentaria to Melbourne

Maria Theresa Landsborough
Died 7th Nov 1912
Aged 86 Years
Also Her Son
Sydney Luttrell
Died at the Boar War
16 June 1900

Toowong Cemetery – Portion 12 Section 55 Grave 3

Nat Buchanan's Headstone

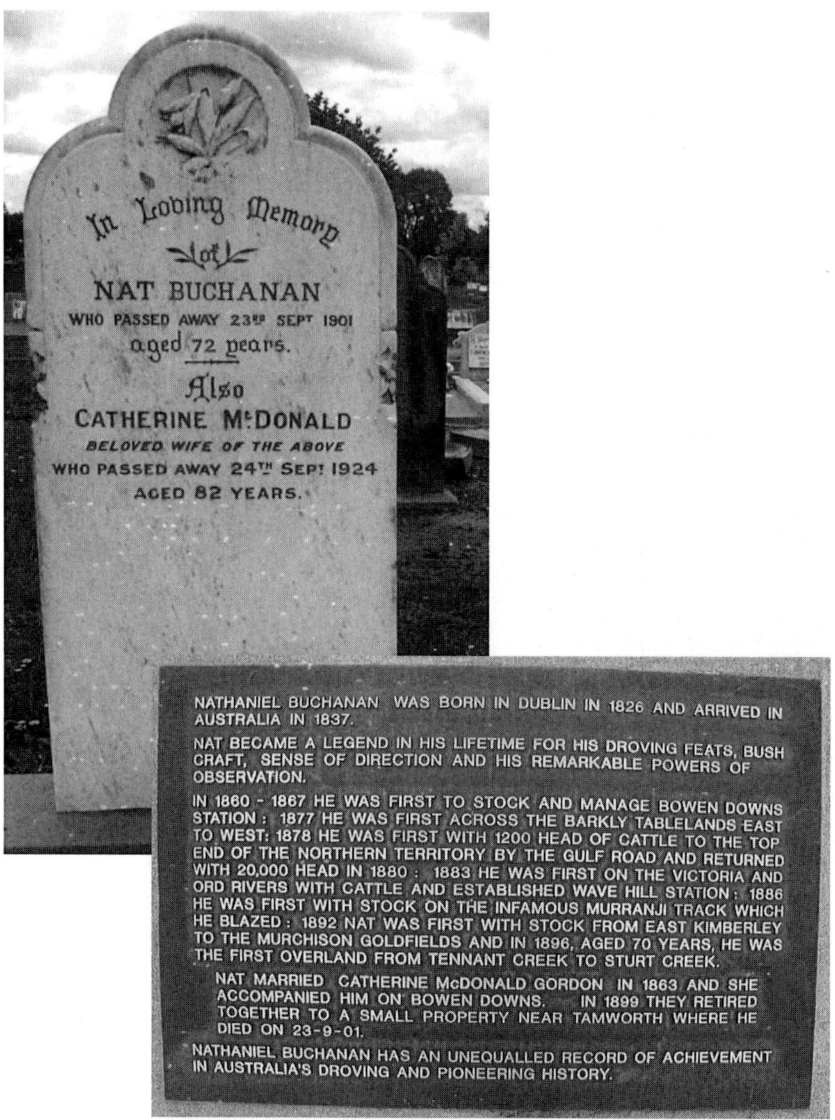

http://en.wikipedia.org/wiki/Nathaniel_Buchanan

Introduction

THE BOWEN DOWNS, FROM A SKETCH BY LANDSBOROUGH.

BOWEN DOWNS, the name given to an immense plain discovered by Landsborough, and so named by him in honour of the present Governor of Queensland, lies beyond the extreme boundary of the settled districts (settled in the squatting sense only) between Carpentaria and the Darling River. Bowen Downs, we understand, presents features in many respects common to much of the recently explored territory in the interior of Australia. Extensive open plains, with few trees to shade the traveller from the scorching rays of a tropical sun, watercourses like deep ruts worn in the ground, occurring at inconsiderable distances, with here and there a clump of timber, are the characteristic features of this portion of the country. In the accompanying sketch, the foreground presents a view of these watercourses or creeks, with the tops of the trees which grow on its margin scarcely reaching the level of the surrounding plain; while a distant view of some peculiarly shaped hills, like artificial mounds, relieves the monotony of the landscape. Landsborough describes Bowen Downs as a fine tract of country, and well adapted for pastoral purposes. With the exception of the north-west portion, to the left, of Stuart's tract, the interior, of Australia has now been pretty well explored. To Burke and Wills is due the honor of having first crossed the continent from shore to shore; but this they achieved at the sacrifice of their lives. Landsborough and others have shown how this feat may be accomplished with ease and safety. Landsborough's journey occupied him over three months and a half, having left Albert River on the 10th February and arrived at Baunaranah, on the Darling on the 1st June. During the period he travelled a distance of 1500 miles (according to dead reckoning), being at the rate of 15 miles per day, including Sundays; and during the last month the distance travelled was greater than in any month previous. In fact, from the time he started till the termination of his journey, he gradually increased the average distance. For instance, the daily average distance travelled was – in February 10¾ miles; March 11¾ miles; April 13 miles; May 16½ miles. And to show that he did not tax his animals beyond their strength, he mentions the singular fact that the foal dropped by his mare, shortly after leaving the Albert River, kept up with him at this speed the whole way, a distance of 1382 miles. It is worthy of notice, that Landsborough's travelling hours were between 8 a.m. and 3 p.m. and that he invariable rested on Sunday.

THE BOWEN DOWNS, FROM A SKETCH BY LANDSBOROUGH. (1866, March 16). Illustrated Sydney News (NSW: 1853 - 1872), p. 8. Retrieved April 30, 2012, from http://nla.gov.au/nla.news-article63512872

THE EXPLORER

A Few Interesting Facts.

AMONGST the answers to correspondents in our issue of 30th ultimo was one to a question put by "Muttaburra" as to whether the present Mount Cornish station should have been called Bowen Downs and the Bowen Downs station named Mount Cornish. Oar reply was that we were not aware that such was the case. It seems, however, that "Muttaburra" had some ground for questioning the correctness of the existing nomenclature, and we congratulate him upon the circumstance that his query has had the effect of eliciting from the man best qualified to speak upon the subject the exact state of matters.

The following interesting memorandum has been kindly forwarded to us by Mr. W. Landsborough:— "It may be interesting to 'Muttaburra' and others for me to say, that Bowen Downs was the name I gave to the whole of that part of the country. "The name was given in this way: Soon after Separation from New South Wales, the late Mr. E. B. Cornish and I called on the first Governor of Queensland, Sir George Bowen. I told him that Mr. N. Buchanan and myself had found an unlimited extent of the finest sheep country a long way inland on the southern watershed, and that with his leave I would name it Bowen Downs, to which he graciously assented. Hence the name, which, however, has only been retained for a small portion of the country for which I intended it.

"Now perhaps you will allow me to tell you about the discovery and settlement of this country. A reference to the maps of 1860 will show that beyond Mr. A. C. Gregory's furthest north in his expedition in search of Dr. Leichhardt in 1858 all was blank.

"In about 1859, Mr. N. Buchanan (who I may say here was a most skilful bushman, so much so that, for instance, he used after looking at his compass to travel for hours straight without consulting it again) and I were exploring in the unsettled country for about four months. Starting we went northward; we stopped a night or so at Marlborough, which was then the farthest out station, about sixty miles beyond Rockhampton. In the end of April we were on the Bowen River, then named the Bonar, at a point about seventy miles from Bowen, which was not then settled. The country was flooded; travelling northward was impracticable, so we went inland, and at Tower Hill, on the water-shed of what is now called the Landsborough River, we reached as fine pastures as any we had ever seen. Thence we travelled down the river to beyond the junction of the Aramac. Our path in doing so traversed an uninterrupted stretch of good country. The Aramac, as many wrong reasons for the name have been given, I may say here I named, in honor of the late Sir R. R. Mackenzie,' Ar-ar-mac,' who was so well known in Queensland, and who had acted in a very friendly way to me at Clifton, in New England, some years previously.

"It is seldom that the pioneers derive advantage from their discoveries. The stocking and settling of the Bowen Downs country was such an expensive affair that three of the partners, Messrs. Cornish and Buchanan and I, had to give it up at the end of five years. Good as the pastures proved themselves to be there was not anyone sufficiently tempted by them to take up country for settlement beyond the Bowen and Mount Cornish runs until comparatively recently, although it was well known for years that the country beyond them was of the most fattening description."

THE EXPLORER. *(1879, September 20). The Queenslander (Brisbane, Qld.: 1866 - 1939), p. 372. Retrieved March 25, 2014, from http://nla.gov.au/nla.news-article20328589*

1860s

Crown Lands Office, Brisbane, 29th July, 1862.

IT is hereby notified for general information, as provided in the 4th clause of the Unoccupied Crown Lands Occupation Act, 24th Victoria, No. 11, that Licenses for One Year to Depasture under the provisions of the said Act, have been issue to the respective Parties in the Pastoral Districts mentioned below.

Ditto	... ...	Kubbine	... ...	ditto ...	30	15 0 0
Wm. Landsborough	... ...	Bowen Downs	... ...	ditto ...	86	43 0 0
Ditto	... ...	Betawong	... ...	ditto ...	76	38 0 0
Ditto	... ...	Crossmore	... ...	ditto ...	66	33 0 0
Ditto	... ...	Balang	... ...	ditto ...	96	48 0 0
Ditto	... ...	Piewic Goshen	... ...	ditto ...	96	48 0 0
Ditto	... ...	Horsehalt	... ...	ditto ...	96	48 0 0
Ditto	... ...	Goodberry	... ...	ditto ...	96	48 0 0
Ditto	... ...	Longway	... ...	ditto ...	96	48 0 0
Ditto	... ...	Rio Downs	... ...	ditto ...	96	48 0 0
Ditto	... ...	Kateroy	... ...	ditto ...	96	48 0 0
Ditto	... ...	Bramoil	... ...	ditto ...	56	28 0 0
Ditto	... ...	Rayban	... ...	ditto ...	60	30 0 0
Ditto	... ...	Oatway	... ...	ditto ...	55	27 10 0
Ditto	... ...	Hadagoodin	... ...	ditto ...	40	20 0 0
Ditto	... ...	Beinbar	... ...	ditto ...	40	20 0 0
Ditto	... ...	Tablederry	... ...	ditto ...	48	24 0 0
Ditto	... ...	Overton	... ...	ditto ...	75	37 10 0
Ditto	... ...	Demeron	... ...	ditto ...	75	37 10 0
Ditto	... ...	Yan Adams	... ...	ditto ...	25	12 10 0
Ditto	... ...	Mundale	... ...	ditto ...	40	20 0 0
Ditto	... ...	Armida	... ...	ditto ...	56	28 0 0
Ditto	... ...	Aboyna	... ...	ditto ...	56	28 0 0
Ditto	... ...	Bolton	... ...	ditto ...	50	25 0 0
Ditto	... ...	Denwick	... ...	ditto ...	60	30 0 0
Ditto	... ...	Rympledon	... ...	ditto ...	70	35 0 0
Ditto	... ...	Houragan	... ...	ditto ...	100	50 0 0
Ditto	... ...	Ringby	... ...	ditto ...	70	35 0 0
Ditto	... ...	Buggeraga	... ...	ditto ...	76	38 0 0
Ditto	... ...	Gillah	... ...	ditto ...	76	38 0 0
Ditto	... ...	Jobell	... ...	ditto ...	96	48 0 0
Ditto	... ...	Boxdale	... ...	ditto ...	96	48 0 0
Ditto	... ...	Ingberry	... ...	ditto ...	48	24 0 0
Ditto	... ...	Bellabad	... ...	ditto ...	96	48 0 0
Ditto	... ...	Illmore	... ...	ditto ...	50	25 0 0
Ditto	... ...	Bangall	... ...	ditto ...	50	25 0 0
J. M. Dillon	... ...	Greendale	... ...	ditto ...	49	24 10 0
Ditto	... ...	St. John's	... ...	ditto ...	49	24 10 0
A. Morris		Malinginal		ditto	64	32 0 0

Maurice Donohue – 1862
October 12, 1862

(Extract) The discovery of the fine pastoral country on the Barcoo by the Mitchell expedition was soon followed by occupation. On October 12th, 1862, the first mob of cattle arrived on the Thomson River, for Mount Cornish and Bowen Downs. The Thomson River was at that time supposed to be the Barcoo, but Mr. N Buchanan found out that it was the same river that had been named the Thomson by Kennedy in 1847. The first station was named Bowen Downs, and the first stock arrived on these waters were the cattle started from Fort Cooper, where they had been depasturing for some time. The mob consisted of five thousand head, and the route followed was by Lake Elphinstone on to Suttor Creek, down the creek to the Belyando, following that river up a short distance, then across by Bully Creek, crossing the range at the Tanks by Lake Buchanan on to Cornish Creek, and down that creek to their destination.

Suttor Creek station then belonged to Kirk and Sutherland, and was the farthest out station in that direction. On arriving at Bully Creek, a dry stage ahead of forty-five miles, caused the leader to leave 1,500 head behind him, the balance arriving at their destination on October 12th 1862. Mr. R Kerr was in charge, with four white stockmen, one blackboy, three gins, and a white man named Maurice Donohue, who died before he had been there very long, and was doubtless the first man buried in the district.

In the following year, 1863, a drought occurred on the Thomson, the plains were left destitute of grass, and the waterhole, on the banks of which the station was formed, was reduced to two feet in depth. When full there would be about eighteen feet of water in it, and it was afterwards found that it took eighteen months without rain to bring it down to that level. In about March of this year, Messrs. Rule and Lacy, and also Mr. Raven, arrived on Aramac Creek with sheep, the former taking up and stocking the country now known as Aramac Station. Mr. Raven first settled down higher up the creek, afterwards returning to Stainburne, taking up and stocking the present Stainburne Downs. At the same time that these sheep arrived at the Aramac, three thousand cows from Narran (NSW) arrived on Bowen Downs, Messrs. Hill and Bloxham in charge; all these stock went out by the Barcoo, and the cattle suffered severely from the drought, one thousand being lost on route.

Early Days In North Queensland by The Late Edward Palmer; Sydney: Angus & Robertson: Melbourne: Angus, Robertson & Shenstone: 1903

Editor's Note – The Mr. R Kerr mentioned in the above article may be the man who was manager of Bowen Downs from 1871 to 1875.

Landsborough River Company – January 1863

A company has recently been formed in Sydney, called the "Landsborough River Company", whose object is to stock a large section of our newly-opened territory. The manager has arrived in this colony, en route for the North; and he is to take on 20,000 sheep, besides horned stock, horses, and supplies

http://nla.gov.au/nla.news-article3161223 WEEKLY EPITOME. (1863, January 31). The Courier (Brisbane, Qld: 1861 - 1864), p. 2.

Marriage:

On the 19th instant, at the Royal Hotel, Maryborough, by the Rev. G. M. Reed, Nathaniel Buchanan, Esq., Squatter, Bowen Downs, to Catherine McDonald, second daughter of Mr. John Gordon, Ban Ban.

Family Notices. (1863, August 28). Queensland Times, Ipswich Herald & General Advertiser (Qld.: 1861 - 1908), p. 2. Retrieved March 25, 2014, from http://nla.gov.au/nla.news-article123605260

Shepherd Killed – 1864

[Extract] The first white man known to have been killed by the blacks on the Thomson was one of the shepherds with Kirk and Sutherland's sheep. He was killed on Duck Pond Creek, a tributry of Cornish Creek. After he was buried, the blacks dug the body up at night and drove a stake through it, pinnng it to the ground. Kirk and Sutherland must have reached the Flinders about April, and then occupied and stocked Marathon.

Early Days In North Queensland by The Late Edward Palmer; Sydney: Angus & Robertson: Melbourne: Angus, Robertson & Shenstone: 1903

George Jonathon Jennings Nicholls – May 1964
Ethel Maria Nicholls – May 1864

During the year of 1864, a man maned G. Nicol[1], and his wife[2], both of whom had been employed at Bowen Downs, and had left with the intention of going to Rockhampton, were found dead between Bowen Downs and Stainburn. They had been offered quiet horses for the journey, but they preferred to walk. As they did not turn up at Stainburn, a search was instituted, and they were found on one of the branches of Bullock Creek, both dead. The woman had been dead much longer than the man, as portions of her corpse were missing, while the body of the man was whole; the woman had a hole in her skull; the man had a revolver with two chambers empty. She was the first white woman on the Thomson, and was a very kind decent little body. The story remains one of the mysteries of the bush that will never be solved.

Early Days In North Queensland by The Late Edward Palmer; Sydney: Angus & Robertson: Melbourne: Angus, Robertson & Shenstone: 1903

Editor's Note – These two bodies were found in the bush on Bowen Downs, on the 5 June 1864 and burried where they were found, by A S Holmes from Bowen Downs. There was no actual date of death registered for George and Maria. George, born in

[1] *Qld Ref: 1865/C596*
[2] *Qld Ref: 1865/C597*

England, was about 33 years old and Maria was about 40 years old. They had been married at St James' in Sydney. George had £83 9s 6d in credit in his estate on 4 March 1867 when it was wraped up.
As was the case in many of these deaths these were not registered in Rockhampton until the 30 January 1865.

Qld BDM – Death Certificate

Llewellyn A Meredith – 20 November 1864

and

Robert McNeely – 20 November 1864

A DOUBLE MURDER BY THE BLACKS. —Another double murder! Late last night news was brought to town of the murder of a gentleman named Meredith and his man. It appears that he was going forward with a horse team and one man, when he was surrounded by the blacks and murdered. No tidings having been heard of him for ten days a party went in search, and having rushed a native camp in the vicinity, they found everything belonging to the deceased gentleman, except his watch and one revolver. The horses were also found, hobbled and quite wild, but not a trace of the bodies, and the blacks could not or would not explain where they were. We say no more by way of expostulation, but if the Government do not send us assistance, and that speedily, the Kennedy District runs a good chance of being deserted. — P. D. Times, Jan. 7th.

No title. (1865, January 21). The Darling Downs Gazette and General Advertiser (Toowoomba, Qld.: 1858 - 1880), p. 3. Retrieved November 29, 2012, from http://nla.gov.au/nla.news-article75514583

MEREDITH. - On or about November 20, 1864, killed by Queensland natives, at Tower-hill, Llewellyn A. Meredith, aged thirty years.

Family Notices. (1865, February 14). Launceston Examiner (Tas.: 1842 - 1899), p. 4 Edition: MORNING. Retrieved October 26, 2012, from http://nla.gov.au/nla.news-article38658003

Murdered, in Northern Queensland, by the natives on the night of November 20th, 1864. Llewellyn Meredith, third son of the late John Meredith, Esq., Of Burning Farm, England.

Family Notices. (1865, February 18). The Cornwall Chronicle (Launceston, Tas.: 1835 - 1880), p. 9. Retrieved October 26, 2012, from http://nla.gov.au/nla.news-article66461019

MURDER BY THE BLACKS IN QUEENSLAND OF MR. LLEWELLYN MEREDITH

The sad intelligence which lately reached this colony of the murder of Mr. Llewellyn Meredith in Queensland; is now only too certainly confirmed, by the accounts received by his relative, the Hon. Charles Meredith. Mr. Jas. B Poynter, who has for the past two years resided on Mr. Harvey's station, near Tower Hill, North Queensland with Mr. L. Meredith, verifies the terrible report, after a brave and persevering search for his lost companion. A dray loaded with supplies for the station was on its way from the port, accompanied by Mr. Meredith, who rode on home alone, when within three days' journey, he found a number of blacks encamped near the road, who followed him for some distance in a threatening manner. When he reached the station; he heard that they had attempted to surprise another train of drays a short time before. As he had to return and guide the supply-dray home, he took a man with him, and both were well armed. On the night of November 20th, they camped on the creek where the blacks were; and, it is now certain, were murdered.

The non-arrival of the dray, and continued absence of Mr. Meredith was beginning to cause anxiety, if not alarm at the station, when a person passing, informed Mr. Poynter that the dray were waiting for a guide, and wondering that no one had come to pilot then on. Mr. Poynter immediately set out in search of Mr. Meredith, taking with him two men, and a black native boy. They found the horses of the missing hobbled in the bush near the creek, and in following up the search the next day discovered the saddles, bridles, rifles, &c belonging to Mr. Meredith and his servant in a deserted black's camp, overtaking them about twenty miles down the creek, and in the camp they had formed there, were the revolvers, quart pots, blankets and all else that the white men had with them, even to their clothes. Every endeavour was made to ascertain how the bodies had been disposed of, and the black boy tried to converse with the other natives, but owing to the diversity of dialect among different tribes, they could not understand each other, and no information could be obtained.

The party in search were occupied for more than a week in making every possible investigation, and endeavoring to discover the remains of the murdered men, but without learning any more of the circumstances of this terrible and melancholy calamity, by which a brave enterprising young man, whose excellent qualities of mind and heart endeared him to all who knew him, had been cut off in the outset of a promising career.

MURDER BY THE BLACKS IN QUEENSLAND OF MR. LLEWELLYN MEREDITH. (1865, February 18). The Cornwall Chronicle (Launceston, Tas.: 1835 - 1880), p. 10. Retrieved January 4, 2013, from http://nla.gov.au/nla.news-article66461013

MURDER OF MR. LLEWELLYN MEREDITH

The following letter has been kindly forwarded to us by a correspondent at Jerusalem for publication. It will give our readers some insight into the position of Tasmanians in Queensland:

Queensland, January 18th, 1865.

DEAR BROTHER:-I write to you in case you should see by the papers that we had some men killed by the blacks, and you might think I was one of the unfortunates. I must be thankful that I was not one; being in charge at the same place the whole of last year with only one man, everybody expected to hear of us being killed by the niggers, but I must say I knew how to manage them by never allowing them to stop on the station if I knew they were on it, and if they attempted to come up to the huts by letting drive at them. When the proprietor came down to manage with seven men, myself, and a black boy, he took very little notice of them. The blacks came straight from another station 40 miles distant, where they had just killed the hut-keeper while he was putting a damper in the fire, and left him on it. It appears they killed one man and threw him into a large lagoon, as his body has not yet been found. A portion of his sheep came home in the evening without him; we thought he had missed the remainder, and found them too late to bring them home. Next morning another man took the missing man's flock, having a double carbine with him. Our proprietor, with the black boy, started on the tracks of the lost sheep to see after the missing shepherd; they found his tracks, and ran them until they were destroyed by the flock. In looking to again find his tracks they came across a fire when the black boy sang out "here whitefellow." Judge Mr. -----'s surprise to see in the fire a body burning, and on turning it out, to discover that it was the man they had left a few hours before with the sheep, he could only be distinguished by a small piece of his face, and whiskers, the rest of the body completely burnt. Just as the boy called out, up jumped a black- fellow when he was shot, another escaping, the man's remains only just having been discovered. It appears by the track the man went to a lagoon within one hundred yards of his flock, while drinking was knocked on the head with a log of wood, they then burnt him, camping there, and threw his gun into the lagoon. Some days after the native police in company with a party of whites, started in pursuit, after tracking them for 5 days, they carne upon the natives, when a severe retaliation took place.

Young Meredith (I believe formerly managing for Swanston, Willis, and Co., on the Glenelg, Victoria), managing a station with a share, on the "Barior", for Matthew Hersey, with another young man, has been killed within a short distance of his station. From what news has come in it appears he was with his drays and was stuck up by blacks for some days, and had very little ammunition left, when he and the other started for the station for more help and more guns, &c, intending being back that day; but nothing was heard of them for fifteen days, when some travellers passing the drays sent a message to the station to know if they were coming back, when it was found that they had not reached the station. All hands turned out and found where they had camped in the middle of the day, as it is supposed, as their horses were found hobbled close by, but neither body could be found. The police are after the natives, I expect there will be a few less by this time, so you see by the above I have had a narrow escape and news has come in to-day that two more shepherds are killed by the niggers. I could name many more cases out here, and it is an everyday occurrence in this neighborhood. Only last Saturday I saw a large mob, I followed their tracks, but they escaped having no revolver, as we know the first chance they get at us there is no escape, they delight to smash us all to pieces, while we only give them an ounce of lead.

Since I last wrote to you I have been very bad with fever and ague, and still have it. To-morrow is my day, I dread it coming on, in fact I shall give the place a further trial and if not better must shift, as I can stand it no longer, it would kill me in 12 months, though to look at I appear all right.

Our sheep are in splendid condition, plenty of grass, in fact too much, as the sheep are unable to keep it down, and a stranger to go over the run would not believe there was 19,000 sheep on it, it is impossible to get them half-a-mile from the yard. I am by myself, the boss (as we call him) being down the country, and everything depending upon me.

A great deal of dissipation prevails, it is most difficult to keep from drinking, you know I never took spirits with you and never will for anyone.

MURDER OF MR. LLEWELLYN MEREDITH. (1865, February 20). The Mercury (Hobart, Tas.: 1860 - 1954), p. 2. Retrieved January 4, 2013, from http://nla.gov.au/nla.news-article8831223

Editor's Note – The Government Gazette in both 1863 and 1865 states that Tower Hill belonged to William Landsborough, yet other sources states the Llewellyn Meredith selected this block. Meredith's death is not registered in Birth Death and Marriages. Llewellyn Meredith was born about 1834, the son of John Meredith and Sarah Walker Jones who were married on the 9 August 1825 at St Martin's Birmingham. John Meredith was a 'varnish manufacturer'. Llewellyn had 8 siblings.

Robert McNeely was the Overseer at Tower Hill working for Meredith.

Mr. Meredith arrived in May of the same year [1864] on the Thomson, and took up and stocked Tower Hill station. During June of this year the Thomson and Aramac Creek were in high flood; Rule and Lacy were flooded out of their first camp, and removed to where Aramac station now is. Some stockmen looking after the company's cattle on an anabranch of Cornish Creek, were surrounded by water, and lived on jerked beef for a month.

Palmer, Edward (2012-01-24). Early Days in North Queensland (Kindle Locations 1232-1235). Kindle Edition.

In March of this year Mr. Meredith, of Tower Hill, formed a station on the east side of Landsborough Creek, naming it Eversleigh, and stocked it with cattle. In March also Bowen Downs sent cattle up the Landsborough for the purpose of stocking the west side of the creek. The men with the cattle had a very rough trip, as there was incessant rain, and the country became one vast quagmire; all their rations and ammunition were spoilt, and they had to live on young calf, "staggering bob," as they called it. Mr. E. H. Butler was in charge, ……..

Palmer, Edward (2012-01-24). Early Days in North Queensland (Kindle Locations 1249-1253). Kindle Edition.

Name of Run-Eversleigh No. 1.

Licensees-Charles Williamson and Co.

Estimated area-50 square miles.

Starting from the northern boundary of Landsborough River Company's Demeron Run, and running thence in a northerly direction on the **eastern** side of Landsborough Creek, which is its frontage, a distance of ten miles, and running five miles back.

Crown Lands Office, Brisbane, 4th August, 1864. Government Gazette

Editor's Note – In the 1864 Government Gazette Eversleigh No 1, 2 and 3 were selected by Charles Williamson & Co

SAIC Report – 23 March 1865

The directors of the Scottish Australian Investment Company have issued their report which is to be presented to the half-yearly meeting of shareholders called for the 27th January. They state that during the first half year of 1864 the rate of interest prevailing in the colony was high, yet, owing to the extreme and almost unprecedented wetness of the season, there was not that activity or prosperity in pastoral or agricultural operations which, would otherwise doubtless have existed; and this state of matters had, of course, not been without its influence upon the business of the company, the profits of the half-year now reported on not being quite equal to these of the preceding six months. The gross profits realised in the colony during the above period are £14,095 10s. 7d., to which must be added the sum of £1,547 12s. 2d., received in London for interest, commission, and transfers, &c, making a total gross profit for the six months of £15,662 0s. 3d. The colonial profits were entirely derived from the ordinary sources of the company's revenue by routs, interests and commissions. The directors proposed a dividend, payable on Wednesday, the 8th of February next, on the ordinary stock of the company, £200,000 at the rate of ten per cent, per annum, less income tax, which would require £10,000, and leave at the credit of the reserved fund £7,281 11s. 3d. The directors repeat the assurance that the intelligence which they continue to receive respecting the extensive property now so well known as "The Landsborough Runs", at Bowen Downs, in Queensland, in which the company has a large interest, is of a very interesting and promising character.

COMMERCIAL. (1865, March 23). The Brisbane Courier (Qld.: 1864 - 1933), p. 2. http:nla.gov.au/ nla.news-article1269973

Extract – W Landsborough Journal July 4, 1865

FROM BOWEN DOWNS TO PORT DENISON

	Miles
To crossing place of Cornish Creek	50

Thence to Fisheries	8
Duck Ponds	13
Place Called Public House Water-holes	25
Water-holes a mile to the right of the road	
South end of Lake Buchanan or Salt Lake	1
Whistling Duck Water-hole	6
Jump on the range	4
Natural Sandstone Tank	4
Pigeon Water-hole	8
Tomahawk Creek	6
Rocky Creek	6
Sandy Creek	9
Douthy's Camp	8
Douthy's Creek	5
Vine Creek Station near Belyando River	20
Cattle Station on Belyando River	31
St. Ann's on Belyando River	16
Mount Wyntt	18
Hidden Vale	12
Strathmore	25
Bogie Public House	25
Bowen (Port Denison)	40
	350

OVERLAND JOURNEY FROM ROCKHAMPTON TO PORT DENISON, VIA BOWEN DOWNS AND THE SALT LAKE. (1865, July 29). The Brisbane Courier (Qld.: 1864 - 1933), p. 5. Retrieved June 24, 2012, from http://nla.gov.au/nla.news-article1276003

Barney – September 1865

THE Port Denison Times reports another murder committed by the blacks. One of the late arrivals per "Maryborough," named Burney, had been engaged at Bowen to proceed to the Flinders with some drays, and on the morning of the murder, while the drays were camped at Bowen Downs, Barney's companions went out to look for the horses, leaving him in charge of the camp. On returning, they found Barney with his skull split, as if with a tomahawk, but it would appear the murderers were disturbed in their work, as nothing was missing from the drays. A search was at once instituted, and a mob of blacks, camped in the vicinity, dispersed in the usual approved manner."

TELEGRAPHIC MESSAGES. (1865, September 2). Rockhampton Bulletin and Central Queensland Advertiser (Qld.: 1861 - 1871), p. 2. Retrieved March 25, 2014, from http://nla.gov.au/nla.news-article51568304

We are happy to be in a position to contradict the report of the murder of the man Barney, said to have been committed on Bowen Downs. Mr. W. Castling, who left that place five weeks since, informs us that no such event had occurred, and that he saw Barney shepherding.

BOWEN. (1865, September 26). The Brisbane Courier (Qld.: 1864 - 1933), p. 3. Retrieved March 25, 2014, from http://nla.gov.au/nla.news-article1279242

Extract:—The following new Post Offices will be established during this *year* Bigge's Camp, Beaufort (on the Belyando River), Billi Creek (Bowen Downs) … Tamher (Barcoo River, Commissioner's Camp).

Pugh's QUEENSLAND Almanac DIRECTORY, Law Calendar 1866,

Charles Hugo Fredrick Vern – 12 May 1866
Murder Occurred On The Thomson River

The Empire

SATURDAY, JUNE 30, 1866.

[Extract] But while nil these grand designs are on the stocks, it must be noted with regret that the system of dealing with the aboriginal tribes in the North presents no features of improvement, and no advance towards mercy or humanity. We can well distinguish between acts of necessary self-protection and those reckless "dispersions" of the natives which now appear to form part of a settled policy. It must be premised, in fairness, that the papers report two murders by the natives; but it is also fair to state the particulars. One case is reported in, the Mackay Mercury, as having occurred at a place called Rockingham Creek, where several shepherds, well-armed, were attending to the lambing, and one of these men, it is said, "foolishly fired his revolver in bravado over the heads of some blacks who appeared". The blacks subsequently followed the men and, finding one alone, murdered him and buried the body in the sand – rather an unusual course with them. The last we hear of this affair is that the aborigines had taken to the scrubs, and that "a message had been sent requesting the assistance of the native police". The other murder occurred on the Thomson River, in the Mitchell district, the victim being a German who was travelling in search of employment and of permission to depasture a few sheep. His dead body was found, with several spear wounds, in a water-hole; and the correspondent of the Port Denison Times relates what followed. "The neighbours assembled, and immediately set off to chastise the murderers, and succeeded in doing so to a greater extent than, in the present haste, I dare mention. Of this, however, under any circumstances, perhaps the least said by me the better". Perhaps, so, indeed; but the writer goes on to express his disgust at the fact that the body of the murdered German was still suffered to remain in the bush unburied.

The Empire. (1866, June 30). Empire (Sydney, NSW: 1850 - 1875), p. 4. http://nla.gov.au/nla.news-article60598139

Editor's Note – This could be Charles Hugo Fredrick Vern who was killed by Blacks, on the 12 May 1866, at Aramac Creek and was buried where his body was found. – Police Gazette. There is not record of Charles Vern in Queensland's Birth, Deaths and Marriages.

Cozens alias Frenche – June 1866

BARCOO.

(From a Correspondent of the Rockhampton Bulletin.)

THE old proverb, "It never rains without it pours," is being exemplified here. On Monday last it commenced to rain, and is still falling (Tuesday evening.) The river is now bank and bank, and we shall have abundance of grass and water for the next twelve months. A report was circulated yesterday to the effect that a man named Cozens, alias Frenche, had been murdered by the blacks on Aramac Creek. On inquiries, it appears that he was acting as chainman to Dr. Boyd. Some horses being missing, the Dr. desired Cozens to remain at a waterhole till they came down to water. Cozens not re-appearing, a search was made, and his body discovered floating in the water, with marks on it which sufficiently attested the barbarous means employed to put him to death. This has been told me on good authority, and can be relied on in the main, but doubtless the incidents in connection with the tragic affair will be communicated to you by Dr. Boyd.

Everything is looking very dull here. Plenty of men are travelling about looking for employment, but the demand for labor is very limited.

There are a great number of loaded teams on the road up, and what with hawkers and others, I think our district is the best supplied of any in Queensland. What a change from two years ago, when the people were starving for want of flour!

BARCOO. (1866, July 2). The Brisbane Courier (Qld.: 1864 - 1933), p. 3. Retrieved June 1, 2014, from http://nla.gov.au/nla.news-article1270238

Frederick Williams – 12 August 1866

Frederick Williams[3] died of fever contracted while travelling in the north on the Flinders River. He was buried where he died on Aramac Creek.

[3] *Qld Ref: 1866/001223*

BOWEN

[Extract] – WE have received files from Port Denison to September 8, and take the following from the Times:

By the courtesy of Mr. Ellis Read we have some later information from the Albert River. The lambing has been excellent, about 92 per cent. Some of the stations are lambing, others shearing. Mr. E. B. Cornish is in Burke Town, and seems highly delighted with the place and its prospects, and is about to erect steam boiling-down machinery at Mr. Edkins' establishment. The cattle in the district are rolling fat. Messrs. Edkins Brothers shipped 40 tierces of beef and tallow in the Restless for Batavia. We are glad to hear that the sickness has entirely disappeared. The Burke Town people are in high spirits, and building is progressing rapidly.

[No heading]. (1866, September 22). The Brisbane Courier (Qld.: 1864 - 1933), p. 6. Retrieved June 25, 2012, from http://nla.gov.au/nla.news-page54554

Editor's Note – A Tierces is a former liquid measurement of capacity equal to 42 wine gallons. Batavia was the name at this time for Indonesia.

Edward Brooking Cornish – 27 October 1866

DEATHS – On the 27th instant, at Stoneleigh House, Darlinghurst, EDWARD BROOKING CORNISH, aged 44 years.

http://nla.gov.au/nla.news-article13146819 The Sydney Morning Herald (NSW: 1842 – 1954 Monday 29 October 1866

CORNISH – November 21st, at Stoneleigh House, Darlinghurst, Margaret, widow of E. B. Cornish, aged 35 years

Family Notices. (1866, November 23). The Sydney Morning Herald (NSW: 1842 - 1954), p. 7. Retrieved May 30, 2012, from http://nla.gov.au/nla.news-article13147212

[Extract] – On 19 January 1863 a partnership was drawn up between Morehead and Young (the Company's representative in Australia), who held a half share, William Landsborough (the explorer), holding a quarter share, and E. B. Cornish and N. Buchanan, each holding one eighth share. This was the partnership that was known in Queensland as the Landsborough River Company.

[Extract] – The environment also was unsuitable for European occupation and Gulf fever was a problem. It caused the death of Cornish, one of the original partners, as well as his wife's death, and it affected five of his children. Edkins, the manager of the Albert River Runs, was forced as a consequence of the climate to leave the Gulf country for a time.

THE SCOTTISH AUSTRALIAN COMPANY AND PASTORAL DEVELOPMENT IN QUEENSLAND 1860-1890; [By DAVID S. MACMILLAN, M.A.] (Read by C. G. Austin at a meeting of the Society on 23 June 1960.)

Editor's Note – Edward Brooking Cornish[4] was born on 15 January 1822 at South Pool, Devon, the son of Thomas Cornish and Sally Brooking. He married Margaret Raine in 1849.

They had nine children: Fanny Worsley (1850), Elizabeth Brooking (ca 1851), Thomas (1852-1928), Walter Raine (ca 1855-1927), Margaret Christine (1856-), Edward Arthur Brooking (Died as Infant), (1858-1859) Frances (1859), George William (1861), Charles Landsborough (1863-).

Both Edward and Margaret died of 'Gulf Fever' that he caught in his trip to the Albert River inspecting operations of the Scottish Australia Company.

LOSS OF SEVEN MEN AT PORT DENISON.

A GOOD deal of anxiety has been occasioned in Bowen during the past week (says the Port Denison Times, of the 18th January) as to the fate of a party of bushmen, who left the jetty on Monday morning avowedly for Stone Island, with the intention of having what they called a good spree; to assist them in carrying out their good intentions, they took with them some three dozen of beer and some brandy. They have not been seen or heard of since their departure, and there is but too much reason to fear that the boat may have capsized, and the whole party perished. A brother and a

[4] *NSW Ref: 1459/1866*

son of Mr. H D Sinclair were on board. The names of the other men we do not know, but believe that they came from Bowen Downs. There are three parties away in search of the missing – viz., C Heath, in the pilot boat; Sinclair, in a boat belonging to Heron; and Harry Wooster in his own craft. In a subsequent issue of the same paper we find the following – Harry Wooster gives the following account of his expedition in search of the missing boat – "He left the jetty on Thursday morning 16th instant, and commenced the search just on the other side of Adelaide Point, made Thomas Island, searching all the beaches connected with that island and the adjacent portion of the main land without finding any traces of the missing party. On Friday morning started again, and coasted along the Bluff (Cavanagh's); got information from Cavanagh's son and a black boy that the Martha had been seen on Monday afternoon heading towards Ben Lomond. In consequence of this information proceeded to Ben Lomond, searched all the creeks and Sinclair's Bay, and camped for the night, having seen no signs. On Saturday morning searched the mainland towards Gloucester Passage, still without success. Determined to return to port, taking Stone Island in the way. Arrived at Stone Island about sundown, landed on the south end of it, and on the beach discovered the body of one of the missing men. The man had evidently been drowned, and his body was in an advanced state of decomposition. It being by this time nearly dark, little further search could be made, and the boat returned to port, and immediately reported what they had discovered to the Police Magistrate. The man's name is believed to have been Jem Sayers. He was buried on Stone Island on Sunday morning, and a magisterial inquiry into the cause of his death was held by the Police Magistrate on Monday".

A long and patient inquiry has been held respecting the men who were lost in the Martha last week, but without much result as far as legally identifying the missing men goes. The names are supposed to be the two Sinclairs, son and brother respectively of Captain H D

Sinclair, the discoverer of Port Denison, James Sayers[5] (found drowned and buried on Stone Island), Thomas Donnelly, a blacksmith from Bowen Downs, Neal McGolrick, Henry Wilson, Roger Haynes, Charles Andrews and John Morrison.

http://nla.gov.au/nla.news-article1292325 The Brisbane Courier Qld. 1864 – 1933 Saturday 22 February 1868

Polling Place

Colonial Secretary's Office,
Brisbane, 20th May, 1868.
POLLING PLACE.

HIS Excellency the Acting Governor, with the advice of the Executive Council, has been pleased to appoint BOWEN DOWNS to be a Polling Place for taking the Poll at the Election of Members to serve in the Legislative Assembly of Queensland, for the Electoral District to Mitchell, in the event of an Election being contested in such District.

By His Excellency's Command,
A. H. PALMER.

Government Gazette May 1868

POSTAL MIS-MANAGEMENT IN THE NORTH.

SIR: I would respectfully beg leave, through the medium of your valuable journal, to draw public attention to the manner in which the postal arrangements for 1868 are carried out in this portion of Queensland. For the last three years residents in the South Kennedy have been favored with a bi-monthly, although somewhat irregular, mail. At beginning of the present year, tenders were called for contract to run a mail from Bowen township to Bowen Downs station — a distance of 320 miles — instead of the same line to

[5] *Qld Ref: 1868/C24*

Bully Creek only, as heretofore. This mail, although an increase in the distance of 140 miles, was also to be run in the fortnight. A few trips sufficed to show the contractor the impossibility of carrying out his agreement without employing another mail man to meet him half way, a fact which was patent to everyone acquainted with the road connecting the two localities before the attempt was made. He (the contractor and mailman) then applied for an extension of the period allowed by his contract, which has been acceded to. In consequence of this new arrangement, and the time lost while mails are lying at a road-side public house, awaiting the arrival of the Nebo mail, and vice versa, our communication with Bowen is only monthly, and Sydney three monthly should the down country mail not catch the monthly boat. Such a fact needs no comment. In this portion of Northern Queensland we receive but little indulgence from "the powers that be," with the exception of a few taxes, stamp duties, &c.; and it seems hard that, after payment of these, and a further compulsory gratuity of two guineas yearly for making up our mail bags, we should be staved off with "such a very inferior article" as the present postal arrangement. Really it is almost obtaining money under false pretenses!

SPINIFEX.

POSTAL MIS-MANAGEMENT IN THE NORTH. (1868, August 1). The Queenslander (Brisbane, Qld.: 1866 - 1939), p. 5. Retrieved May 16, 2014, from http://nla.gov.au/nla.news-article20319747

Sheep Washing Apparatus – 1869

(Extract) The Boomerang has brought up the plant for a patent sheep washing apparatus, intended for the Bowen Downs Station. We hope that Messrs. Morehead and Young will find their investment pay them to the utmost of their wishes. The invoice price of the plant in Sydney is nearly £1100, the freight over £150, and of course the expense of getting it conveyed over 300 miles up the country will be considerable. They have wisely engaged competent men from Sydney to erect the machinery. This, although adding to the cost, will materially diminish any risk of failure. If there were a few more with as much capital and as much energy in the expenditure of it, it would contribute greatly to the progress of the North. We are sorry to learn that in addition to the heavy unavoidable expenses the importers of this machinery have had to pay over £90 ad valorem duty. — Port Denison Times, January 9.

STATE OF THE INTERIOR. (1869, January 30). The Queenslander (Brisbane, Qld.: 1866 - 1939), p. 11. Retrieved April 27, 2012, from http://nla.gov.au/nla.news-article20322633

Martin Fitzgerald – 11 February 1869

Martin[6], a carter, was the son of Martin Fitzgerald [farmer] and Mary Malony, died on the 11 February 1869, from a liver disease and is buried at Bowen Downs on the 12 February, with John Campbell as witness. His wife Catherine Murphy, who was residing on the Darling River, notified the register in writing. He was about 48 years old and married Catherine Murphy in Melbourne. Martin was the father of Margaret – 14 years and Edward – 11 years.

Martin was born in Ireland but had spent about 17 years in Australia.

Qld BDM – Death Certificate

Aramac – 19 June 1869

PROCLAMATION.

By His Excellency SAMUEL WENSLEY BLACKALL, Esquire, Governor and Commander-in-Chief of the Colony of Queensland and its Dependencies.

WHEREAS by an Act passed in the thirty-first year of the Reign of Her Majesty, intituled *"An Act to consolidate and amend the Laws relating to the Alienation of Crown Lands,"* and numbered forty-six, in clause eighteen, power is given to the Governor, with the advice of the

[6] *Qld Ref: 1869/001164*

Executive Council, by proclamation in the *Government Gazette,* to declare what portions of Crown Lands shall be set apart, as the sites of new cities, towns, or villages, and also to declare what lands shall be reserved from sale for any public purpose: Now, therefore, I, SAMUEL WENSLEY BLACKALL, the Governor aforesaid, in pursuance of the power and authority vested in me, and with the advice of the Executive Council, do, by this my Proclamation, declare that the lands hereinunder described shall be reserved for township purposes, and be withheld from selection or sale by auction, otherwise than in town or suburban lots.

TOWN RESERVE, ARAMAC CREEK.

Mitchell District.

640 acres.

Commencing on the right bank of Aramac Creek at a tree marked broad-arrow over I, being also the south-eastern corner of the Boxdale Run; and bounded thence on the east by a line bearing north eighty chains; thence on the north by a line bearing west eighty chains; thence on the west by a line bearing south crossing Aramac Creek eighty chains; and thence on the south by a line bearing east crossing Aramac Creek eighty chains, to the point of commencement.

Given under my Hand and the Seal of the Colony, at Government House, Brisbane, this nineteenth day of June, in the year of our Lord one thousand eight hundred and sixty-nine, and in the thirty-second year of Her Majesty's reign.

[L. S.] SAM. W. BLACKALL.

By His Excellency's Command,

JAMES TAYLOR.

GOD SAVE THE QUEEN!

Editor's Note – The town developed in the 1860s, and was formally gazetted on 26 June 1869 – but not surveyed until 1875. Subdivided lots were offered for sale in 1879, which coincided with the creation of a Divisional Board for Aramac, the genesis of local government. The Board's area was 50,750 sq. km., with jurisdiction over an estimated 841 persons and 123 ratepayers.

http://www.sunzine.net/outback/aramac.html

Mail Run – 1869

83.—Blackall and Bowen Downs, via Home Creek, Cameron's, Aramac, and Ravenshead, — Once a fortnight, by horse, for one or two years.

92 – Bowen, Mount Douglas and Bowen Downs, via Strathmore, Hidden Vale, Mount Wyatt Gold-fields, Mount M^C^Connell, St Anne's Vine Creek, and Bully Creek, – Once a fortnight, by horse, for one or two years.

Classified Advertising. (1869, August 28). The Queenslander (Brisbane, Qld.: 1866 - 1939), p. 12. Retrieved May 2, 2012, from http://nla.gov.au/nla.news-article20325535

THE SCOTTISH AUSTRALIAN INVESTMENT COMPANY (LTD).

[Extract] "The date of the next half-yearly balance being the period when the returns of stock, and the accounts relative to the company's pastoral establishments at Bowen Downs in Queensland, and on the Albert River at the Gulf of Carpentaria in the same colony, are to be made up and submitted, in accordance with the intimation given in the last report, the directors have on the present occasion only to make a general reference to their progress. They have to intimate, however, that they have taken over the interest of the late resident manager of these establishments, and that they have in view the acquisition of the shares of the company's other co-partners therein. This proceeding will of course materially increase the sums standing directly against the investment, but the great proportion of this increase will consist only of a transfer of debit balances duo by two of these co-partners. It is needless to observe that the directors would have preferred effecting, at the least, a partial sale of these properties era this time; the state of the market, however, for pastoral properties in the Australian colonies has, as already stated, for some time been quite unfavorable for such a procedure. In the meantime the directors continue to refrain from carrying anything to the credit of profit and loss account in respect of the company's pastoral property.

"The latest communications from Bowen Downs report the stock there as in a thriving condition, and the country in a very luxuriant state, and very favorable for the lambing which had shortly before commenced. Wages were still high, but tending downwards; and not-withstanding the low price of wool, the relation between the cost of management and the returns of this establishment are gradually becoming much more satisfactory, and a steady future progress in this direction may be looked for as the numbers of stock increase.

"Although it is contemplated to look to breeding as substantially the source from which such increase is to be obtained, the directors have learned with satisfaction, by a recent mail, that advantage had been taken of exceptional circumstances to effect a purchase of a very superior and. lot of sheep, mostly females, at a very low price. These sheep were depasturing in the immediate neighborhood of Bowen Downs, and were sold under the pressure that had existed for some time in the Australian colonies. This purchase will about replace (as respects numbers) a lot of wethers which were to be sold as having become ready for the market, and will provide as the same time enlarged means for future increase.

"At the end of February last, the date of the last received sheep return from Bowen Downs, there were on those runs, after sending away 11,852 for sale -as mentioned above, 58,263 sheep, exclusive of unweaned lambs and the 13,900 sheep above reported as having boon purchased.

"The clip of wool for 1867 would make about 220 bales. The clip of 1868 is estimated to make about 335 bales. The bales contain on an average 450 pounds of wool each.

"At the 31st of December last the cattle on the Bowen Downs Runs were about 15,000, and on the Albert River Runs about 5,000, exclusive of a number of young cattle unbranded, and calves.

"A satisfactory sale of a considerable number of Bowen Downs cattle had just been concluded in Sydney, delivery to be taken at the station.

"Favorable anticipations are confidently expressed by Mr. Young, the sub-manager, and by Mr. B. D, Morehead, the resident manager at Bowen Downs, as to the results of the arrangements recently made for the local management of the establishment at the Gulf of Carpentaria, but no very recant communication had been received from Mr. Edkins, the resident manager there, who by latest accounts was on his way to that station, after visits to Sydney and to Bowen Downs, where a lot of cattle had been arranged to be moved to the Gulf runs.

"The great and pressing want of the Australian colonies, there can be no doubt, is at present the discovery of a remunerative market for the immense quantity of surplus sheep and cattle which they are capable of producing; and it is very satisfactory to observe that to the attainment of this very important object the attention and efforts of many persons are persistently and intently directed, and it seems likely that one or other of the processes of preserving meat for exportation now in course of trial, will ere long prove successful.

"Of the £200,000 of the 6 per cont. guaranteed preference stock of the company, £188,328 has been taken up, leaving only £11,672 more to ho allotted. The amount of debentures issued by the company outstanding at the 30th of June last was £105,290 as against £100,390 at the 31st of December last."

THE SCOTTISH AUSTRALIAN INVESTMENT COMPANY (LIMITED). (1868, October 24). The Brisbane Courier (Qld.: 1864 - 1933), p. 7. Retrieved March 24, 2014, from http://nla.gov.au/nla.news-article1310970

Editor's Note — The two partners' 'shares of the company's other co-partners' are Nat Buchanan and William Landsborough. It is also interesting to note that the average bale of wool was 450 pounds. The wool would have been scoured wool but to press this in to a bale is fascinating, as today's press only press about this weight.

Sherwin Crisp – 25 November 1869

Sherwin Crisp[7] a labourer on Bowen Downs, died on 25 November 1869 at Bowen Downs from heart disease. Fred Bennett also a worker from Bowen Downs was the informant. Sherwin was buried at Bowen Downs on the 27 November by Tom White. The death was registered in the Tambo Death Register, on the 20th January 1870 by Fred Bernett.

Qld BDM – Death Certificate

[7] *Qld Ref: 1870/C1029*

1870s

Manager's Residence On Mount Cornish Station, Ca. 1872

John Oxley Library, State Library of Queensland Negative number: 35064

Manager's House At Bowen Downs Station, 1875

John Oxley Library, State Library of Queensland Negative number: 35056

Charles Barkley – 3 May 1870

Born in England, Charles Barkley[8], died of fever on the 3 May 1870 on the Eastern side of the Thomson River on the Mount Cornish run. Mr T. A. McKenzie of Bandour reported the death of this 41 year old man. Charles was a Hut-keeper for Mount Cornish and as such would shepherd the sheep daily and maintain any improvement in his area.

Magistrate 1 July 1870

[Extract] Colonial Secretary's Office, Brisbane, 1st July, 1870.

HIS Excellency the Governor, with the advice of the Executive Council, has been pleased to appoint the under-mentioned Gentlemen to be Magistrates of the Territory.--

KILNER, FREDERICK, Sub-Collector of Customs, Bowen;
PATERSON, THOMAS MACDONALD, Rockhampton;
THOMAS, ALFRED CAYLEY, Bowen Downs.

By His Excellency's Command,
A H. PALMER.

Government Gazette 1870

Mary Guild – 9 November 1870

Mary[9] the daughter of Edward Guild and Elizabeth Smith died on the 9 November 1870 due to accidental poisoning at Bowen Downs. It is presumed she was buried there but the actual grave site may be at the Homestead. She was only 2 years 9 months old, and the sister of David born about five months later on 14 March 1871.

Police Gazette

8 *Qld Ref: 1870/001038*
9 *Qld Ref: 1870/001040*

Regina v Mackenzie and Others – 15 February 1871
Before His Honor Judge Blakeney

Regina v Mackenzie and Others – John Mackenzie, Michael Magrath, and William Cornish were indicted that they, on the 21th of September last, at Bowen Downs, did steal twenty oxen, twenty cows, twenty steers, twenty heifers, and twenty calves, of the goods and chattels of Robert Archibald Allison Moorehead and Matthew Young. A second count charged them with having said stock in their possession knowing them to have been stolon Mr. Blake, Q C, prosecuted, assisted by Mr. Hely, and Mr. Paul, instructed by Mr. Harris, defended the prisoners The case was a very peculiar one, the evidence against the prisoners being for the most part circumstantial, and a large number of witnesses were produced by the Crown to support of the charge. The main facts as shown by the evidence were as follows: – The prisoner Mackenzie some time since had taken up country adjoining Bowen Downs station, the property of Messers. Morehead and Young, but Mackenzie's yards and huts were on the Thompson River, about 110 miles from the head station of Bowen Downs. Mr. Thompson, the manager at Bowen Downs, when out on that run in September last, remarked in several places on the Thompson River the tracks of large mobs of cattle going in the direction of Mackenzie's station. Mr. Butler, one of the stockmen on Bowen Downs, had also remarked the cattle tracks, and one night when out on the run had seen a mob of about 100 head of cattle rounded up at a camp fire some distance from him, but having that evening lost his horses he was unable to follow them up. He then returned to Bowen Downs head station, and made a report of the circumstance. The manager of the station then sent for Mr. Wheeler, of the Native police, and that officer and his men followed the tracks of the cattle seen by Butler until they came to the yards belonging to Mackenzie; further search was then made, and some few miles up a creek the party came upon 88 head of cattle the property of Messrs. Morehead and Young, the mob of cattle consisted mostly of cows, without their calves; two of the cows in the mob were identified as belonging to Bowen Downs, irrespective of the brands upon them. In another place not far off, close to Mackenzie's milking yards, the search party discovered one hundred clean skinned calves, many of whom were subsequently mothered by the cows found in the first yard. The prisoner Mackenzie, on being questioned, admitted that the yards were his but said that he made no claim to the cattle. The principal evidence to connect Mackenzie with the custody of the cattle was given by a man named Birch, who deposed that about ten days before Mr. Wheeler's party came to the prisoner's place he met a man connected with the Bowens station, who told him to tell Mackenzie that the coast was clear, and would be so for a fortnight, Birch was at that time living with the prisoners, and duly delivered the message to Mackenzie, next day the prisoners Mackenzie, Magrath, and Cornish, started away from their station on horseback, and about five days afterwards they returned with a large mob of cattle, it being late when they arrived; he did not see the cattle, but he heard them lowing in the stockyards all through the night, Mackenzie and the other prisoners started with the cattle early next morning, and were away all day; when Mackenzie returned in the evening, he said that he had driven the cattle so far up the creek that they would not be easily found; the prisoners also said that they got a fright when going up the creek with the cattle, from seeing a man, whom they believed to be from Bowen Downs, riding towards them – how they had separated, and one rode up one creek and another in a different direction – but it turned out to be a false alarm after all, as the man they met was from "Forrester", and not from "Bowen Downs". The jury remained in consultation until after 11 o'clock, at which hour the Judge returned to court to receive the verdict, which was "not guilty".

ROMA DISTRICT COURT. (1871, February 15). The Brisbane Courier (Qld.: 1864 - 1933), p. 3. Retrieved May 31, 2012, from http://nla.gov.au/nla.news-article1295174

OUTRAGES BY THE QUEENSLAND BLACKS.

THE blackfellows of the Bowen Downs country have lately murdered a Chinaman at or near, an out station of the Scottish Australian Investment Company. Mr. Pierce, the overseer of that station having reported the same to Mr. Kerr, acting superintendent in the absence of Mr. A. C. Thomas, sending to Blackall for the troopers. The troopers came and got on the tracks of the murderers. From the appearance of the body, having its throat cut, it was at first doubted whether the murder had not been committed by a white man. On inspection, however, the troopers soon came to the conclusion that it had been done by blackfellows. The chief indication that led to that conclusion was, we believe, the appearance of a wound on the skull, which there could be no doubt had been inflicted by a blackfellow's tomahawk. The black troopers started in pursuit of the murderers and got to the foot of the range, but between the time they had been sent for and the time they arrived at Jericho the floods had risen, and they could not go any further on account of the waters, having to swim and wade nine miles at a stretch from Scrubby Creek to Reedy Creek. The Mitchell district blacks have lately committed another outrage besides the one mentioned above. In this case the victims were white men, who were camped at a place known as Forester's Creek in a hut made of grass, as is the fashion in that part of the country. One of them was killed outright, and the other was we fear mortally wounded. The one who was killed was at the outside of the hut putting the billy on the fire, when the blackfellows came up and pushed a spear through each of his kidneys, cross fashion, thus fairly pinning him to the ground. These blackfellows we are informed do not use their spears as missiles, but push with them. One of them then drove a spear through the wall of the hut, wounding the other man severely in the side, and sending the weapon right through his groin. This man immediately broke off the spear, and reached down his revolver, which was hanging above his head, loaded and fired at the black scoundrels, who ran away. He has been carefully treated, and the remainder of the spear extracted, and when our informant left he was alive, but it was much feared that he could not last long. The name of the man who was speared in the hut was Andrew Mackenzie, brother of John Mackenzie, and in charge of the run during the absence of his brother in Rockhampton, where he was undergoing his trial on a charge of cattle-steeling preferred against him by Mr. A. C. Thomas, of Bowen Downs. The name of the unfortunate man who was killed outright was, we believe, Boulton, but our informants are not confident on that point.

Darling Downs Times.

OUTRAGES BY THE QUEENSLAND BLACKS. (1871, April 12). Empire (Sydney, NSW: 1850 - 1875), p. 3. http://nla.gov.au/nla.news-article60870988

Thomas Burns – 30th April 1871

Thomas Burns[10], a man aged about 50 years, died at Bowen Downs of fever and other causes on 30 April 1871. His actual burial site is unknown.

Three Missing: Supposed killed by Aboriginals – 1871

[Bowen – Extract] Friday afternoon.

Advices from Bowen Downs state that three men are missing from the district. They are supposed to have been murdered by the blacks.

The Belyando blacks are reported to be becoming very saucy. They threaten to drive the white men from the country! The blacks are of late very troublesome in all the inland districts hereabouts.

BOWEN. (1871, July 8). Rockhampton Bulletin and Central Queensland Advertiser (Qld.: 1861 - 1871), p. 2. Retrieved May 2, 2014, from http://nla.gov.au/nla.news-article51582586

[10] *Qld Ref: 1871/C1107*

We (Port Denison Times) hear report, of more outrages by the blacks, this time in the Bowen Downs district. The account, are not very clear, but as far as we can ascertain there are three men missing and supposed to have been killed by the aboriginals. One was a shepherd who was engaged with Mr. McGlashan, jun., at a camp not more than two mile, from the head station shepherding a flock of sheep that had got boxed. Sometime during the middle of the day, when the sheep were camped, Mr. McGlashan told the man to go to the station, got some food, and come back again. The man went, but has not since been seen. The second case is that of a man who was overtaken by the Bowen Downs mailman, and brought by him to nine miles this side of Pigeon Holes, but he being behind time could not wait to accompany the man further, but directed him to Mr. McGlashan's station, warning him not to camp on account of the blacks, but to proceed right onward. It is further reported that some gins have said that the man was killed and his body hidden under a log. The third case was a man who is known to have started on his road to Bowen, is supposed to have been seen by Mr. Rule, and his tracks to have been seen by the Bowen Down, mailman. He has not since been heard of. We also hear that the Belyando blacks have become very saucy, and announce their intention of driving the white men out of the country. However ridiculous this threat may be, it is still indicative of the frame of mind of our black neighbors, and shows that in mercy to both races a lesson should be taught them to convince them of the absurdity of their ideas, and to inculcate the wisdom of submission. Nearer home Mr. John Clark, of Euri Creek, has been very much annoyed by the black-fellows lately, and when obliged to come into Bowen yesterday would not have ventured to leave his house but that a man was stopping there whom he could trust with firearm, to protect the place during his absence.

The Courier. (1871, August 8). The Brisbane Courier (Qld.: 1864 - 1933), p. 2. Retrieved June 9, 2012, from http://nla.gov.au/nla.news-article1329760

Sydney Flood – July 1871

TARDY JUSTICE. – In 1868, two men (George Hughes and James Elliott) were tried at Capeville for the serious crime of highway robbery under arms, and at the District Court held at Bowen shortly afterwards sentenced to twelve years' penal servitude. At the time public opinion ran strongly in favour of the condemned men, strengthened by their previous good character and the fact that the principal witness for the prosecution was a Mongolian, unable to speak English, but who was a little too certain in swearing to the identity of the prisoners. For two weary years the convicted were incarcerated, their punishment rendered even more severe by the knowledge of their own innocence; and it is probable that, notwithstanding the numerous memorials forwarded to the Colonial Secretary, setting forth the extenuating circumstances of the case, the unfortunate men would have completed their sentence had not Nemesis in the form of a fatal fall from a horse overtaken the true culprit, at Messrs. Rule and Lacy's station, on Aramac Creek. A man named Sydney Flood lay dying from a severe fracture. When finding that all hope of recovery was passed, he sent for the station owners, and confessed that he and his comrade (Sam the Grasshopper) were the perpetrators of the crime, and in confirmation of his statement, narrated circumstances, which could only be known to a person actually on the spot. The depositions are forwarded to Brisbane, and after mature considerably the authorities, the men brought before the Bench and discharged. No reparation, however, is made or offered for the gross indignity that has been done them – the slight that has been put on their name, they are simply discharged, and no doubt they thought no price too high to pay for their liberty. Since that time they have resided principally on Ravenswood, holding prominent positions amongst us, and certainly it gives no unqualified satisfaction to us to be in a position to state from our own observation, that their conduct whilst here has always been exemplary. The only redress left the injured men is to take legal proceedings against the Chinaman who so willingly and positively; swore away their liberty. This course they have at last been able to do, having discovered the whereabouts of their old accuser. Our police reports give the evidence taken in the case of George Hughes v Ah Wung Gung Woo for perjury; the case was adjourned for other witnesses, but judging from the evidence taken, it is probable that no conviction will be obtained. However, the opportunity still remains to bring an action for false imprisonment, and this was the course that should have been taken at first. – Ravenswood Miner.

THE LATE HON. GILBERT ELIOTT. (1871, July 29). Rockhampton Bulletin and Central Queensland Advertiser (Qld.: 1861 - 1871), p. 4. Retrieved May 19, 2014, from http://nla.gov.au/nla.news-article51582745

Sammy Sammy – 21 September 1871

Sammy[11] a 30 year old Chinese shepherd, who was born in China, was murdered by the Blacks while working on one of Bowen Downs' Outstations. Sammy's informant was Alfred C Thomas an employee of Bowen Downs who also registered the death on the 20 October in writing at Tambo. With James Pearce as a witness, Robert Kerr buried him on the 23 September at Bowen Downs.

Qld BDM – Death Certificate

Quick Dispatch – 23 September 1871

QUICK DESPATCH. – On June 5 forty-one bales of wool was received at Bowen Downs Station by one of our carriers, who delivered them here on July 17, and on the 22nd of the same month they were landed in Sydney. At the time when strong effort are being made to divert this traffic from its legitimate port it is as well that this fact should be known. – *P. D. Times*

LOCAL ITEMS. (1871, September 23). Rockhampton Bulletin and Central Queensland Advertiser (Qld.: 1861 - 1871), p. 5. http://nla.gov.au/nla.news-article51583187

[11] *Qld Ref: 1871/001111*

Chiverton alias Redstone – 29 September 1871

Chiverton[12] the son of James Redstone and Jane Galley, a carpenter like his father, died from 'congestion of the lungs'. He died in Aramac after only being ill for 14 days, and was buried there by John Smith with David Thompson as a witness. He was born on the Isle of Wight, England. Chiverton had married Margaret Dickson in Springsure in the year he died. He was only 23 years old.

Qld BDM – Death Certificate

Herbert Cecil Davis – September 1871

A Variety of reports have been current as to the fate of Mr. Herbert C Davis, brother of Mr. Sydney Beavan Davis, of Rockhampton, who left Bowen Downs station about April last. The *Bulletin* says that "Mr. Murray, Chief Inspector of Police, has sent his brother, who was in charge of a detachment of Native Troopers on the Belyando, out to Bowen Downs and the stations on the Thomson River, to make inquiries respecting the missing gentleman, in order if possible to ascertain his whereabouts. Mr. S B Davis is in possession of information that his brother deposited money in the bank at Fort Bourke, in December last, and judges from that circumstance that he at that time contemplated travelling South, and is now probably somewhere in the back districts of New South Wales or South Australia. Another circumstance favourable to this supposition is that lately letters from Sydney, addressed to Mr. Herbert Davis, have been forwarded to Rockhampton to the care of Mr. S B Davis. It is to be hoped, therefore, that no calamity has befallen the absent one. The following paragraph on this subject, in the Ravenswood Miner, has since received confirmation: – "Sub-inspector Fitzgerald brings word of the murder of Mr. Sidney Davis' brother and a stockman on Bowen Downs station. The murderers were led by a boy well known in the neighborhood by

[12] *Qld Ref: 1871/C1112*

the name of 'Alligator'. A stockman, stationed some distance from the scene of the butchery, was also 'stuck up' by the same party, but he succeeded in making a gallant and successful resistance, leaving the dreaded 'Alligator' fortunately amongst the slain". On inquiry at the office of the Commissioner of Police, we learn that there is every reason to believe that the report of Mr. Davis having been murdered is correct. Mr. Armstrong the Police Magistrate at Blackall, wrote on September 21 to Clermont that Mr. Moorehead, M. L. A, had reported to him that Mr. Davis and his black boy had been murdered by the aborigines. No authentic account of the details of the tragedy, however, have as yet come to hand.

http://nla.gov.au/nla.news-article1333436 The Brisbane Courier (Qld.: 1864 - 1933) Wednesday 18 October 1871 Page 2 of 4

The inland mail has brought further intelligence in confirmation of the reported death of Mr. Herbert Davis. Writing from Bowen Downs, Thompson River, under date 29th September, Mr. Alfred C. Thomas, communicates the following to Mr. S. B. Davis, of this town: – "Your brother, Mr. H. C. Davis, who used to be here, left this station three or four months ago with two black-boys, to go across the desert to the Belyando. Some lately caught black-boys give some painful rumour about him, and the enclosed letter found in a blacks' camp rushed lately by Mr. Kerr, would appear to give some consistency to the reports. The letter is known to have been written by your brother, to his mother, and he is supposed to have had it with him when he went away. The Native Police are coming up, and when we have more time a search will be made at the spot indicated by the black-boy some distance from here. The blacks have been very troublesome here lately, and a Chinese shepherd was killed last week at Jericho". We may add that Mr. Sydney Davis identifies the letter as being in his brother's handwriting. Saturday week's Peak Downs Telegram contributes the following towards clearing up the mystery. We may premise that the Mr. Armstrong spoken of is the Sub-inspector of Police stationed at Blackall: – "A report reached us a few weeks ago, that Mr. Herbert Davis, a brother of Mr. Sydney B. Davis, who for some time represented this constituency in Parliament, had been killed by the blacks. As it was only a report, which we were unable to substantiate, we called no attention to it at the time, but information has now come to hand that leaves no reasonable doubt as to its truth. Authentic intelligence has been received from Mr. Armstrong, of Blackall, to the effect that Mr. Davis was for some time missing, and that it has now been discovered by the Native Police that he and his black-boy have been murdered by the blacks between that township and Bowen Downs, everyone who knew Mr. Davis will regret to hear of his melancholy death". The Ravenswood Miner contribute the following additional information: – "Sub-inspector Fitzgerald brings word of the murder of Mr. Sydney Davis' brother and a stockman on Bowen Downs Station. The murders were by a boy well-known in the neighbourhood by the name of the 'Alligator'. A stockman stationed some distance from the scene of the butchery was also 'stuck up' by the same party, but he succeeded in making a gallant and successful resistance, leaving the dreaded "Alligator" amongst the slain."

http://nla.gov.au/nla.news-article51583430 Rockhampton Bulletin and Central Queensland Advertiser (Qld.: 1861 - 1871) Saturday 21 October 1871 page 4 of 6

Charles Douglas Mackay – 17 October 1871

THE MURDER BY THE BLACKS. – The blacks are very bad on the Thompson country. The gentleman referred to last week is a Mr. Mackay, who, we now hear, is missing, so that he may possibly turn up again. Two Chinamen and one or two others are also missing, and it is feared that they have fallen victims to our coloured brethren! – Since the above was in type we have seen a letter from Mr. Armstrong, acting Police Magistrate at Blackall, from which we make the following extract: – "Mr. Fred Murray is now at Bowen Downs, 150 miles distant from here, where another murder has been committed by the blacks. This time a young man named Mackay has fallen a victim. His horse having been discovered with the saddle on running at large in the bush first excited uneasiness for his safety. A search was instituted, which resulted in his body being found frightfully mutilated. Nicholson (acting sub-inspector) has been constantly during the last month at Bowen Downs. He has recovered Herbert Davis' horses in the range between Aramac (Rule and Lacy's) and Surbiton station. Three horses have been recognised at Bowen Downs as those Mr. Davis had with him when he left Jericho, early in May last, for Clermont. The finding of the horses leaves no doubt of his melancholy fate. I fear Mr. Murray can effect little towards throwing further light on this painful subject, as lapse of time and the account the blacks give of having burnt the body will prevent his doing so".

PEAK DOWNS. (1871, December 16). Rockhampton Bulletin and Central Queensland Advertiser (Qld.: 1861 - 1871), p. 6. Retrieved April 30, 2012, from http://nla.gov.au/nla.news-article51583884

Editor's Note – Charles Douglas Mackay[13] the overseer from Bowen Downs was the stockman mentioned in the above article. He was killed by the blacks on about 17 October 1871 on Cornish Creek. He was only 29 years old, he was buried on the 27 October by Robert Kerr at Bowen Downs, with Joseph Romsden as a witness.

There is no record of a Herbert Charles Davis dying in Queensland in 1871. Herbert Davis age 18 years, born in England, died in 1879 (Qld. Ref: 1879/C316). Sydney Beven Davis, son of John Davis and Harriot Dowrick, died in 1884.

Mr. Alfred C. Thomas was manager of Bowen Downs at this time and maybe the 'Chinese shepherd was killed last week at Jericho' was Sammy Sammy murdered on the 21 September 1871.

RESERVE FOR NATIVE POLICE STATION.

Aramac Creek, Mitchell District.

640 acres.

Commencing on the right bank of the Aramac Creek at a point opposite to a tree marked broadarrow over D, being the south-east

13 Qld Ref: 1871/001114

corner of the Gemini run and the south-west corner of the Boxdale run ; bounded thence on the west by a north line one hundred and two chains fifty links, said line being formed by a part of the east boundary of Gemini and by a part of the west boundary of the Boxdale run; thence on the north by an east line one mile ; thence on the east by a south line fifty-seven chains fifty links to the right bank of the Aramac Creek; and thence on the south by that creek downwards to the point of commencement.

Government Gazette 10 July 1872

Frederick Maier – 13 August 1872

A CORRESPONDENT kindly sends us authentic particulars of a murder recently committed at Messrs. Rule and Lacy's Aramac Station, Thompson River. A shepherd named Myers, a black boy, named Sambo, and his gin, were employed together in lambing a flock of ewes. It is presumed they quarrelled, but, at any rate, the black "nullahed" Myers, and then all but chopped his head off with an axe. The Native Police were on the spot next day, and were running the boy's tracks when the mail left a few days since.

LOCAL ITEMS. (1872, September 21). Rockhampton Bulletin (Qld.: 1871 - 1878), p. 5. Retrieved May 19, 2014, from http://nla.gov.au/nla.news-article51790155

We, *Brisbane Courier*, have been favoured by the Commissioner of Police with the particulars, so far as yet ascertained, of the murder of a shepherd named Frederick Maier[14], on the Aramac Creek Station, which has been referred to in a telegram. On August 13, Mr. Alexander Gordon brought intelligence to the police station at Marathon that a man had been found murdered at the Sixteen-mile Sheep Station. On the police arriving at the spot, they found the body of deceased lying in front of his hut. There was a frightful wound, about an inch and a-half wide, on the back and partly on the right side of the head, apparently inflicted by an axe, when the

[14] *Qld Ref: 1872/C781*

deceased was lying on the ground. Another wound was discovered behind the right oar, apparently inflicted by some blunt instrument. An aboriginal native named Tambo, who was looking after lambs at the station, and is well known, having been for some years employed by different squatters on the Thomson River, is supposed to have been the perpetrator of the deed, us he left the place on the same day, taking with him his gin and piccaninies. A double-barreled gun and some ammunition was taken from the hut, but nothing else. Sub-inspector Dunne, Sergeant Hill, and some native troopers were on the track of the blackfellow, who can scarcely escape capture.

A Question of Identity. (1872, September 21). Australian Town and Country Journal (Sydney, NSW: 1870 - 1907), p. 24. Retrieved May 19, 2014, from http://nla.gov.au/nla.news-article70497210

Editor's Note – Frederick was born in Germany was only 28 years old when he murdered. Even though the surname is different – Myers – Maier – it would be presumed to be the same man.

WHOLESALE CATTLE-STEALING.

A remarkable cattle-stealing case was tried at Roma, Queensland, about three weeks ago. Henry Redford was charged with having stolen 400 head of cattle from Bowen Downs in March, 1870. The number missed from the station at the time was 1,000. One animal was a valuable bull. The witness who threw most light on the case was James McPherson. He was in company with Redford and three other men, named McKenzie, Doudney and Brooke, on Bowen Downs station in the year 1870 in charge of drays and horses belonging to a man named Forrester. They all went 25 miles up the Thomson River, and there built cattle-yards. When the yards were completed, he, with the others, mustered a large number of the Bowen Downs cattle, and filled the yards with them. The cattle were afterwards drafted off in mobs of 200 and 300 at a time to Forrester's camp. The white bull outside the court was amongst the cattle taken at that time, the object being that he would keep the cows and heifers quiet, of which there were a large number in the mob. Ultimately the whole of the cattle were driven off by Redford, McKenzie, and Brooke towards the southern colonies. The witness was not a very satisfactory one, it must be admitted. He had escaped from punishment himself because the jury thought him insane. He was sent to Brisbane, but broke out of the reception-house. The authorities re-arrested him in New South Wales, and gave him a free pardon to induce him to furnish fair evidence at the present trial. But there was proof, independently of McPherson's statement, that, in the month of June, Redford sold the bull and two cows to a man named Allan Walke, in South Australia, at a place 1,000 miles from Bowen Downs. The bull was identified with readiness by the owners. The jury acquitted the prisoner. Much surprise was evinced at the verdict, in which the judge joined; and after having requested the foreman to repeat it, he said, "Thank God, gentlemen, that verdict is yours, not mine". The costs of the witnesses in this case were over £600.

WHOLESALE CATTLE-STEALING. (1873, March 5). The Argus (Melbourne, Vic.: 1848 - 1956), p. 6. Retrieved April 28, 2012, from http://nla.gov.au/nla.news-article5849359

William Robins – 27 March 1873

William[15], a shepherd for Bowen Downs died after suffering dysentry for 7 days. William Richards buried William at Bowen Downs on the 27th March 1873 the day he died with R Kerr and James Kelly as witnesses. His death was registered in Tambo on the 15th April 1873.

Qld BDM – Death Certificate

[15] *Qld Ref: 1873/C920*

Charles Lidder – 24 May 1873

Charles Lidder[16] was 20 years old, [general servant] when he was killed due to a fall from his horse at Mount Cornish on the 24th May 1873. He was buried at Mount Cornish.

Louis Kohn [Hahn] – 4 June 1873

Louis Kohn[17] was a working man who became lost in the bush three miles west of Marathon, an out-station of Mt Cornish, sometime in 1873 – exact date unknown. The 'deceased had lost two front teeth and a purse containing a cheque in favour of Louis Hann for £3 14s 7d., a Miner's Right, Cape River 1871, October 14th and a portion of an old agreement was found close by' was included in the police report on the body. He died of starvation. It is surmised that he was buried where he was found.

Police Gazette

Fraser – Turner – 16 August 1873

MARRIAGES.

FRASER-TURNER. – On the 16th August, at Helidon, by the Rev. William Nelson, Sydney Pechey Fraser, of Kilmorey, Maranoa, son of Thomas Hiram Fraser, banker, London, to Jane Margaret Turner, second eldest daughter of William Turner, Helidon.

Family Notices. (1873, August 30). The Brisbane Courier (Qld.: 1864 - 1933), p. 4. Retrieved May 30, 2012, from http://nla.gov.au/nla.news-article1325937

Editor's Note – Sydney and Jane had the following children: Mary Francis [1874], Thomas Graham [1876-1876] Sydney Edward [1877], Sydney Harold [1878], Katherine Phylis [1880], Jessie Muriel [1883], Alice Vere [1885]

[16] *Qld Ref: 1873/C926*

[17] *Qld Ref: 1873/C932*

Edward Albert Trouson [Tronson] – 1 March 1874

Edward[18], an Ex-Constable of Police, aged of 28 years, died of thirst on the 1 March 1874 on the Beaconsfield Run an out-station of Bowen Downs. Edward was of fair complexion and was fully identified by the 'hat, shirt, trousers, belt and tan-coloured boots'. Joseph Harris was the last to see him alive.

[Police Gazette]

Constable Tronson has been found dead on the Thomson River, Bowen Downs.

BRISBANE. (1874, March 18). Evening News (Sydney, NSW: 1869 - 1931), p. 2. Retrieved March 25, 2014, from http://nla.gov.au/nla.news-article107146453

£10 REWARD.

STOLEN or Strayed, from Bowen Downs Station, one Chestnut Horse, branded W **near** shoulder, ∞ over EW over ∞ off neck, white stripe **on near face.** If stolen, the above reward will be paid on conviction; £3 for information that will lead to the recovery of the horse; or £5 if delivered to

H. E. BAILEY,

Bowen Downs, Mitchell District.

Government Gazette January – June –1874 – Page 259

James Merry Gilmour – 10 June 1874

Department of Public Works, and Mines,
Gold Fields Branch, Brisbane, 14th October, 1874.

THE following Donations have been received by the Curator of the Brisbane Museum, during the month of September, viz.:-

Dr. Bancroft...an ornament made of the hairs of the bandicoote, worn by the natives of Cooper's Creek, and brought by Sub-Inspector Gilmour.

---

[18] *Qld Ref: 1874/001125*

Government Gazette

THE NEW COMMISSION OF THE PEACE.

A Government Gazette Extraordinary has been issued, containing the annual amended list of Justices of the Peace for the colony of Queensland. The greater number of omissions have been caused by absence or death. Some of the omissions will be an improvement to the list:—

Gilmour, James Merry, Maranoa District.

THE NEW COMMISSION OF THE PEACE. (1867, January 19). The Brisbane Courier (Qld.: 1864 - 1933), p. 6. Retrieved March 2, 2014, from http://nla.gov.au/nla.news-article1279400

Colonial Secretary's Office,

Brisbane, 19th March, 1868.

HIS Excellency the Acting Governor, with the advice of the Executive Council, has been pleased to promote Mr. JAMES M. GILMOUR, Acting Sub-Inspector of Police, to the rank of Sub-Inspector.

By His Excellency's Command, A. H. PALMER.

Government Gazette

The Peak Downs Telegram, of June 24, says:— "We are informed by Mr. P. McWhannell, who lately arrived in town from Rodney Downs, on the Aramac, that Mr. Inspector Gilmour[19],, of the native police force, died very suddenly about a fortnight ago at Bowen Downs. Mr. Gilmour was for many years in the native police, and was considered to be a very efficient officer. No doubt many of our readers will regret to hear of his sudden death."

Mackay. (1874, July 11). The Queenslander (Brisbane, Qld.: 1866 - 1939), p. 10. Retrieved April 23, 2014, from http://nla.gov.au/nla.news-article18331712

DEATHS.

On the 10th June, at Bowen Downs, Queensland, suddenly, James Merry Gilmour sub-inspector native mounted police, second son of John Gilmour, Esq., Eling, London, late of Glasgow.

[19] *Qld Ref: 1864/C1122*

Family Notices. (1874, August 1). Australian Town and Country Journal (NSW: 1870 - 1907), p. 36. Retrieved February 18, 2014, from http://nla.gov.au/nla.news-article70483805

Many Toowoomba friends will remember J. Merry Gilmour, Esq., of the native police. That gentle man died a short time since at Bowen Downs Station, after a few days of severe illness, which terminated in a fatal fit of apoplexy.

DALBY. (1874, October 10). The Darling Downs Gazette and General Advertiser (Toowoomba, Qld.: 1858 - 1880), p. 4. Retrieved February 18, 2014, from http://nla.gov.au/nla.news-article75470320

RETURN in Intestacy, showing gross amount received, gross amount paid, and the balance in hand in each Estate from the 1st day of January to the 30th day of June, A.D. 1875, inclusive.

Name of Intestate.	Received.	Paid.	Balance in hand.
	£ s. d.	£ s. d.	£ s. d.
James Merry Gilmour ...	118 18 8	163 14 2	25 7 0

Gov Gazette 1875

JOHN COSTELLO.

Pastoralist and Explorer.

THE historic robbery of cattle from Bowen Downs station, Central Queensland, is told in the "Life of John Costello", written by his son, Michael M. J. Costello, and published in Sydney this year by Dymock's Book Arcade. John Costello, pioneer, pastoralist, and explorer, in one of the many excursions from his own station, Kyabra, came on the tracks of a large mob of cattle which had been travelled down the valley of Cooper's Creek. On his return to Kyabra he told Inspector Gilmour of this discovery and expressed his astonishment at finding these evidences of a travelling mob so far away from any road or stock route. The inspector was not a little surprised, as he knew of no squatter who had sent away any stock, or had any intention of doing so. The graders, having been informed, made a thorough reconnaissance, and it was found that a large draft of cattle had been removed from the back portion of Bowen Downs property. The cattle thieves had taken the route that John Costello, years before, had followed when taking horses to

Adelaide. "It was a bold and sensational scheme," says the writer of the book, "and the wonderful part of it is that it would have been successfully accomplished but for Costello's chance discovery. The mob actually reached Adelaide, but were only just disposed of when overtaken by the pursuing owners. In due course there took place one of the most memorable criminal cases in the history of early pastoral events in Queensland. There proved to be 1200 mixed cattle in the stolen mob, and the case for a conviction appeared evident beyond all doubt. The court was held at Roma, and a remarkable white bull was brought all the way back as an exhibit and evidence in connection with the famous trial. But the most amazing result followed the Jury's deliberation—the accused were acquitted. The verdict was such as to cause the higher legal authorities to remove the assizes from Roma for a period."

JOHN COSTELLO. (1930, October 2). The Queenslander (Brisbane, Qld.: 1866 - 1939), p. 7. Retrieved February 23, 2014, from http://nla.gov.au/nla.news-article23129536

Editor's Note – In 1862 James had selected Bindebango, Bandemarengo, Homebain East and Homebain in the Maranoa district and it seems he was a resident in the Maranoa District. James a Sub-Inspector of the Native Mounted Police, died from jaundice [Jaundice is often seen in liver disease such as hepatitis or liver cancer. It may also indicate leptospirosis or obstruction of the biliary tract, for example by gallstones or pancreatic cancer, or less commonly be congenital in origin] and he suffered for 5 days at Bowen Downs. John Gilmour, James' father was a Merchant. James, born in Glasgow Scotland, and was only 42 years old when buried at Bowen Downs on the 10 June 1874 by Chas Foster.

Shearing is now finished on Bowen Downs, and the old washing plant has been taken up to make room for the very extensive new plant. This is one of the largest and finest in the colonies, being supplied with all the latest improvements, and got up in first-rate style. The first three loads, which came up by Clermont and Aramac, are now delivered. The carriers speak well of the road, the so called desert being abundantly supplied with grass and water.

Some more teams by the same road are expected in a week or two; some other teams, that loaded at the same time with the balance of the machinery, and are coming by way of Springsure and Blackall, have not yet been heard of, and are known not to be on this side of the fatter town, whilst the drays that came by Clermont delivered their loading a fortnight ago. This fact speaks for itself as to which is the best and shortest road.

Aramac, Thompson District. (1875, February 23). Rockhampton Bulletin (Qld.: 1871 - 1878), p. 3. Retrieved May 2, 2014, from http://nla.gov.au/nla.news-article51784555

Bimbah outstation at Mount Cornish, ca. 1874

John Oxley Library, State Library of Queensland Negative number: 35065

Leichhardt's Party

Brisbane Thursday

The police authorities at Aramac have sent a telegram stating that two graves have been discovered at Saltern Creek by men engaged in dam-making. The skeletons were disinterred, and pronounced to be aboriginals on the first presumption; but afterwards they were thought to be the remains of Leichhardt's party.

BRISBANE. (1875, August 6). The Sydney Morning Herald (NSW: 1842 - 1954), p. 7. Retrieved June 10, 2014, from http://nla.gov.au/nla.news-article13358525

James Carr – 22 September 1875

James[20], a stockman died from a heart disease after only suffered for about 10 minutes. He was only about 30 years old. Robert Kerr held an inquest at Bowen Downs in relation to this death. James was buried on Cornish Creek where he died by William Waghorn.

It was supposed that James was born at Greenock Scotland.

Qld BDM – Death Certificate

Ambo, an outstation of Mt Cornish Station, Queensland, 1876

John Oxley Library, State Library of Queensland Negative number: 35063

Isabella Bennett – 6th January 1876

Isabella Bennett[21] was the fifth child of William Hamilton Bennett, a stockman, and Isabella Bowman. Isabella was born on 26th December 1875 at Mount Cornish and died of thrush just 11 days later, also at Mt Cornish where she is buried. Isabella's death was certified in writing by her father W H Bennett who also buried her.

William and Isabella had the following children: William George [1856], Sahra Rebecca [1858], Daniel James [1860], Charles H [1862], Emily Isabella [1864], Mary Elizabeth [1864-1899], Walter Thomas [1866-1869], Henry Fleetwood [1868-1955], Annie [1870], Matilda [1874-1874], Louise [1877] and Alice Maud [1880-1888].

[20] *Qld Ref: 1875/C2278*

[21] *Qld Ref: 1887/004570 & 1876/002279*

49	Ditto ...	Foxhall No. 1 ...	56	0	0
50	Ditto ...	ditto No. 2 ...	40	0	0
51	Ditto ...	Barcaldine Downs No. 1	40	0	0
52	Ditto ...	ditto No. 2 ...	48	15	0
173	Ditto ...	Cedar Creek ...	18	15	0
174	Ditto ...	Glen Patrick ...	18	15	0
2	The Scottish-Australian Investment Company	Rutilus ...	9	0	0
10	Ditto ...	Bowen Downs ...	94	12	0
11	Ditto ...	Betawong ...	83	12	0
12	Ditto ...	Crossmoor ...	72	12	0
13	Ditto ...	Balang ...	99	0	0
14	Ditto ...	Pickwick Goshen ...	83	12	0
15	Ditto ...	Bamvil ...	55	0	0
16	Ditto ...	Buggeraga ...	83	12	0
17	Ditto ...	Horsehalt ...	105	12	0
18	Ditto ...	Bangull ...	110	0	0
70	Ditto ...	Corindah ...	39	12	0
71	Ditto ...	Coreenah	35	4	0
72	Ditto ...	Duntulla ...	79	4	0
73	Ditto ...	Cornwall ...	92	8	0
74	Ditto ...	Gemini ...	83	12	0
75	Ditto ...	Oatway ...	52	16	0
76	Ditto ...	Rayban ...	79	4	0
77	Ditto ...	Emu Plains ...	35	4	0
78	Ditto ...	Rainesby ...	52	16	0
79	Ditto ...	Tablederry ...	82	10	0
81	Ditto ...	Kateroy ...	105	12	0
82	Ditto ...	Acacia Downs ...	55	0	0
83	Ditto ...	Rio Downs ...	105	12	0
85	Ditto ...	Goodberry ...	94	12	0
86	Ditto ...	Longway ...	83	12	0
91	Ditto ...	Sardinia ...	53	18	0
133	Ditto ...	Forrester ...	60	18	0
	Ditto ...	ditto (arrears)	21	0	0
128	Ditto ...	Taberna ...	6	5	0
142	Ditto ...	Christians' Land ...	8	15	0
130	Ditto ...	The Huffer ...	12	10	0
133	Ditto ...	Jabiru ...	7	10	0
143	Ditto ...	Gelebele ...	12	10	0
175	Ditto ...	Jericho ...	21	0	0
178	Ditto ...	Thistlebank ...	34	10	0
179	Ditto ...	Spring Downs ...	12	10	0
154	Ditto ...	Lochandhu ...	19	10	0
824	Ditto ...	Boydam ...	7	10	0
	Ditto ...	ditto‡ (license fee)	2	5	0
870	Ditto ...	Ambo§			
902	Ditto ...	Alma‡ ...	3	2	6
131	Thomson, Jas. ...	Terrick Terrick ...	55	0	0
132	Ditto ...	Beriedale ...	60	0	0
136	Thomson, Thomson, Russell, and Govett...	Portland Downs ...	37	10	0
137	Ditto	Hessington	[illegible]	0	0

List of Runs owned by The Scottish-Australian Investment Company – 1875

Government Gazette

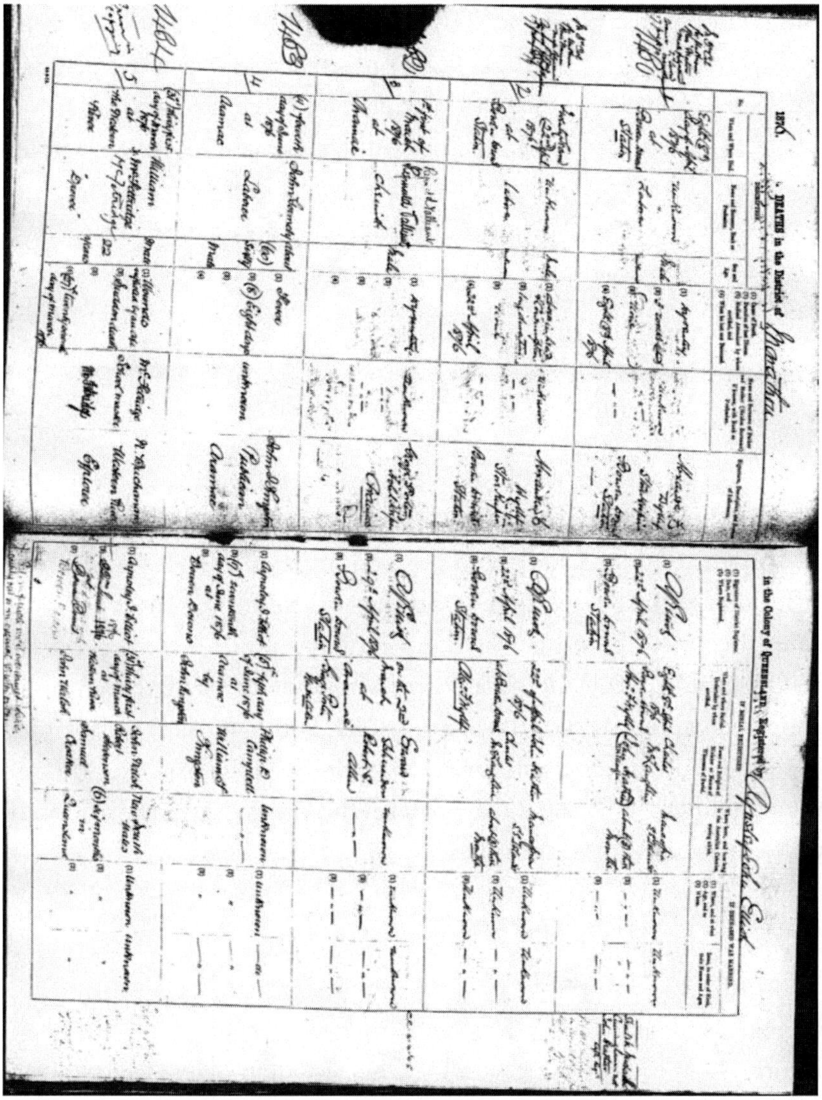

Extract from Queensland Death Register 1876

Thomas Nicholson – 14 January 1876

Thomas Nicholson[22] the son of Phoebe a 'Dam Sinker,' was born at Roscommon, Ireland. He had only been in Australia about 8 years ago. However, on the 14th January 1876 he died at the Twenty Mile Creek on the road from Mount Cornish to Aramac from excessive drinking. His death was certified in writing by Edward Perry Overseer at Mount Cornish. His occupation was. It is presumed he was buried where he died at Twenty Mile Creek by Isaac Page.

Qld BDM – Death Certificate

Reginald Vaillant/Valliant – 1 March 1876

Mr. Vaillant[23], a chemist, who has been residing at Bowen Downs for some months past, arrived here about a week ago: he was then suffering from a severe attack of dysentry and he was in a very weak state; the unfortunate gentleman gradually sank, and died on the first instant. During the short time Mr. Vaillant has been amongst us he has gained the good opinion of all, and his loss is to be much regretted, both as a neighbour and as a professional man, as, though not a qualified M.D., he did away with the pressing want of a doctor in the district. – Correspondence Copperfield Miner.

Aramac. (1876, March 15). Rockhampton Bulletin (Qld.: 1871 - 1878), p. 2. Retrieved April 10, 2014, from http://nla.gov.au/nla.news-article51903096

IT is with much regret we (P. D. Times) announce the death of Mr. Reginald Vaillant, formerly a resident of this town. The sad event occurred last month at Bowen Downs, at which place deceased had established himself in business as a chemist and druggist, and we believe his intention was to have returned to Bowen in a few months, and re-open business here. The cause of death was dysentery.

[22] *Qld Ref: 1876/002281*
[23] *Qld Ref: 1876/C1482*

BRISBANE. (1876, March 27). Rockhampton Bulletin (Qld.: 1871 - 1878), p. 2. Retrieved April 10, 2014, from http://nla.gov.au/nla.news-article51903300

Editor's Note – Reginald married Maria Marsland on the 19 July 1874. He died in a hotel at Aramac and George Porter, the Hotel Keeper, was the informant. He came in from Bowen Downs on 29 April 1876. George Porter, the Undertaker, buried Reginald in Aramac Cemetery on the 2 March.

Scarrbury – 1876

RESERVE FOR A TOWNSHIP, UNDER THE NAME OF SCARRBURY, ON ARAMAC CREEK.

On the road from Aramac to Bowen Downs, Mitchell District.

4 square miles.

Commencing on the right bank of the Aramac Creek at a point where that creek is intersected by a wire fence, and being about five miles thirty-two chains below the junction of Rodney Creek, where there is a tree marked broad-arrow over J; and bounded thence on the east by a north line along the wire fence one mile twenty-four chains; thence on the north by a west line two miles; thence on the west by a south line two miles, crossing Aramac Creek; thence on the south by an east line two miles to the before-mentioned wire fence; and thence again on the east by a north line fifty-six chains to and across Aramac Creek to the point of commencement.

Given under my Hand and Seal, at Government House, Brisbane, this nineteenth day of November, in the year of our Lord one thousand eight hundred and seventy-six, and in the fortieth year of Her Majesty's reign.

By Command, JOHN DOUGLAS.

Government Gazette 1876

William McFetridge – 31 March 1876

The following account of an atrocious murder committed by.an aboriginal on the Western River is taken from the Copperfield's

Minor: – On March 27, a dray was dispatched from Mr Crasthwaite's cattle camp on the Western River, to either meet a dray from Mount Cornish with rations or to proceed to that station with supplies, which is a distant from the camp some 180 miles. The dray, was in charge of Stevenson a man in the Crasthwaite's employ and a young man called McFetterage[24], about nineteen years of age, who was travelling down the country on his return to New South Wales. Stevenson had also with him a Diamantina aboriginal. On the 28th the dray had crossed the branches of the Western River, and was stuck up by some boggy country about five miles from Mr. Crasthwaite's cattle camp. Stevenson left McFetterage and the black boy with the dray and returned to camp to report the state of the road, but the river rose so high towards evening that he had to remain at the cattle camp, until the morning of the 31st, when two other men returned with him to get the dray out. On their arrival at the dray they could see no signs, of anyone about. On looking under the dray they saw McFetterage lying on the ground with his face to the near wheel. On lifting the tarpaulin they saw that the back of the head was smashed in, with the brains protruding. Examination showed that the black boy was not about, and that the axe was gone. The murder must have been committed only two hours before Stevenson arrived, as the fire was alight and signs as if breakfast had been partaken of shortly before. There was nothing missing but the axe. The murder was reported to sub-inspector Carroll at Mount Cornish on April 8, and he immediately started out to arrest the black-boy. There is growing complaints in the western district of the inefficient police protection afforded.

Queanbeyan Post Office. (1876, May 10). Queanbeyan Age (NSW: 1867 - 1904), p. 2. Retrieved May 31, 2012, from http://nla.gov.au/nla.news-article30600834

Editor's Note – William, the son of a schoolmaster was born in New South Wales and was only 22 years old when he died.

N Buchanan, Western River Explorer, reported his death but A J Elliot of Bowen Downs informed the register in Aramac. John Walsh buried William on the

[24] *Qld Ref: 1876/C1484*

31 March at Western River where he had been attacked. He had only been in Queensland for 6 months.

Matow – 8 April 1876

Matow[25], a Polynesian labourer at Bowen Downs died from dysentery. The informant was Alex Wyllie the storekeeper of Bowen Downs, and he buried him at Bowen Downs, the day he died. Michael Cunningham was the witness at the grave side. Matow had only been in Queensland about 3 months.

Qld BDM – Death Certificate

Navoren – 22 April 1876

Navoren[26] a Polynesian labourer on Bowen Downs died also from dysentery like his friend. Navoren had only been in Queensland for about 3 months. He was buried on 22 April at Bowen Downs Station by the storekeeper Alex F Willie.

Qld BDM – Death Certificate

Aramac.

[FROM A CORRESPONDENT.] April 12.

IN perusing your valuable columns through, and not finding you represented by a reporter for the Aramac township and Marathon district, you may be thankful for a few jottings of such a ruing and prosperous district. The Aramac township is, comparatively speaking, but a new place, but nevertheless likely to make one of the many futures of Queensland, being the centre of one of the finest pastoral districts in the north of the colony, and the main road for the Palmer, Western River, Darr, Lower Thomson, and all the

[25] *Qld Ref: 1876/C1480*
[26] *Qld Ref: 1876/C1481*

Upper Barooo. The town comprises three stores, chemist's shop, butcher, blacksmith, and wheelwright; Government Sayings Bank, Court house, and saddler of the first type; two vendors of James Hennessy, and not of the first-class style; and the National, to be opened in a short time, which I feel sure will do a good exchange trade. Of course the buildings are not of the finest architectural designs, but with time may improve, and much wanted, especially the hotel accommodation, which is wretched. But annual licensing day, to be held shortly, will if I am not informed wrong, put the applicants to the test; for several crooked deaths have happened lately, mostly caused by the bad liquor sold, and from the want of proper accommodation supplied.

A Government land sale was held at the Aramac on the 20th of March, and all the lots put up were competed for in a most spirited manner, fetching fabulous prices in most instances. What I mean by fabulous prices is, that they greatly exceeded the expectations of the most sanguine. A great many buyers were from the south, business men, who contemplate starting here.

Mr. Alexander Gordon, a gentleman who has been among us as manager of Travers and Gibson's Aramac Station for so many years, has left the old employ to manage Mr. Beard's station, on the Darr. Although lost to the town, he still resides in the district, and very glad we all feel, for Mr. Gordon was looked upon as the friend of all. Mr. Robinson, the inspector of the Scottish Investment Company, is on a business tour to Bowen Downs and Mount Cornish stations, and I feel sure he will feel well pleased with the present grassy appearance of both.

The usefulness of the black trooper was brought before our notice the other day. A German shepherd was dispatched from Bowen Downs head station to take up his abode at an out station, some thirty miles distant. 'He was put on the right track by Mr. McKean, and followed it successfully for nearly all the road; he camped for refreshments, but in starting again lost the track and got lost in the desert. The overseer, not receiving the new man, went in search of him to the head station, when Mr. McKean, on finding out that the shepherd had not arrived at his destination, at once thought that he was bushed. Sergeant Toby was sent for, undone tracked the poor fellow for several days, ultimately finding the old man after six days starving. I am told that the clever tracking of Toby was something excellent. The party came one the shepherd while taking a rest, and he seemed quite hearty, considering the long time he had fasted, and said he was steering west, but goodness knows where west would have brought him to. I am sure he must have been thankful for the cleverness of noble Toby.

The 24th of May will be a day well kept to do honor to our most gracious Queen by all the swells and notable of stations far and near by a grand day's racing, styled the "Belltopper Meeting," to take place at Bowen Downs. Some six events are to come off, which are likely to produce some true sport, as the district of Marathon contains some good horses. I will send you a good report of the events. The Aramac races will follow in June, so we may expect to be kept alive.

Aramac. (1876, May 6). The Queenslander (Brisbane, Qld.: 1866 - 1939), p. 7. Retrieved May 26, 2014, from http://nla.gov.au/nla.news-article18342268

Department of Public Lands,
Brisbane, 12th May, 1876.

RESERVE FOR A CEMETERY AT ARAMAC.

Mitchell District.

2 acres 2 roods.

Commencing at the most northern corner of suburban portion No. 4, township of Aramac, county Rodney, district of Mitchell, and bounded thence on the north-east by a north-west line five chains; thence on the north-west by a south-west line five chains ; thence on the south-west by a south-east line five chains; thence on the south-east by a north-east line, being part of the north-west boundary of the said suburban portion No. 4 five chains to the point of commencement.

Government Gazette May 1876

Editor's Note – I have included these individuals who have been buried in Aramac Cemetery as they worked at Bowen Downs and then were taken to Aramac where they died and were buried. Another reason is that the first burial on record until these came to light was Muriel Edith Forsyth a one year old child buried on 2 December 1878. Reginald Vaillant/Valliant – 1 January 1876; John Gormely – 4 June 1876; Harriet Nicholls – 14 August 1876; William Innes – 24 September 1876; Thomas Scott Willamson [Welsby/ Wilkie] – 1 February 1878.

John Gormely – 4 June 1876

John[27] a labourer from Bowen Downs was taken ill with fever for about 8 days he went into Aramac. The publican John J Kingston reported his death. He was buried in the Aramac Cemetery on 5 June by John Kingston, with Phillip D Campbell and William Kingston as witnesses.

Qld BDM – Death Certificate

Unknown – June 1876

From a private letter received from the Aramac, we learn that another alleged case of flogging to death, at the Mount Cornish Police Barracks, has been reported to the Aramac police. In this case the blackfellow was tied to a tree and flogged to death with fencing wire. This report should be sifted thoroughly and immediately, or the central and western districts of Queensland will get a rather unenviable notoriety in that respect.

Peak Downs. (1876, June 7). Rockhampton Bulletin (Qld.: 1871 - 1878), p. 2. http://nla.gov.au/nla.news-artivle51904361

[27] *Qld Ref: 1876/C1483*

Harriet Nicholls – 14 August 1876

Harriet[28], just 32 years old, died from supposed heart disease. She was buried on the day she died in the Aramac Cemetery. She had come from England where she was born and was in Queensland for 2 years and 10 months.

Qld BDM – Death Certificate

Neil McLean – 29 August 1876

Neil McLean[29] was the husband of Karen Johnson whom he married on the 4 September 1873 and the father of Christine Mary, born on the 9 February 1875 and Matilda born on the 29 June 1877. Neil, a horse driver, died from internal rupture when a horse rolled on him. He was buried on Mount Cornish near Marathon. After his death, Caroline Johnson became partners with Queey Sang Ah Quee in Muttaburra and they had five children. Caroline lived on to be 92 years of age and is buried in the Muttaburra Cemetery.

William O'Hea – 12 September 1876

William O'Hea[30], a 28 year old reporter, died after having consumption for three years. He became ill and actually died at Aramac Station where he is buried. He had been in Queensland for about 20 years.

Qld BDM – Death Certificate

From our Peak Downs exchanges we learn with much regret of the death, at Aramac, of a young Victorian journalist on a visit to this colony, Mr Wm O'Hea. The deceased gentleman was for many years a member of the reporting staff of the Melbourne Argus, and his health recently failing, he obtained leave of absence, and accepted an invitation from Mr. R. Travers to visit his station on

[28] *Qld Ref: 1876/C1491*
[29] *Qld Ref: 1876/C1488*
[30] *Qld Ref: 1876/C1489*

the Aramac. He came to Queensland a few months ago, and during his short stay in Brisbane, on his way to the west, made a very favorable impression by his modest, unpretending, and gentlemanly manner. He had been staying at Mr. Travers' station for some months past, and seemingly benefited much from the mildness of the climate. Recently he has contributed some very interesting papers to this journal on the great western country, the last to hand of which we publish to-day in our third page under the title of "Out on the Aramac, by a rambler from the South," and we had reason to hope that we should receive many more from his pen, but the disease from which he suffered, consumption, must have suddenly and unexpectedly, taken an unfavorable turn, for we now learn that he died on the 12th instant. The Copperfield Miner, in noticing his death, says: - "During his residence at the Aramac he had gained the respect and esteem of all for his many amiable qualities. His remains were followed to the grave by nearly the whole population of Aramac and the burial service of the Church of England was read by Mr. E. K. Ogg, of the Queensland National.

Telegraphic. (1876, September 30). The Brisbane Courier (Qld.: 1864 - 1933), p. 5. Retrieved May 19, 2014, from http://nla.gov.au/nla.news-article1390870

William Innes – 24 September 1976

William Innes[31] a shepherd who was 65 years old died in Aramac after 'chronic affection of the throat'. George Porter was the informant who reported his death. William was buried in the Aramac Cemetery on the day he died.

Qld BDM – Death Certificate

[31] *Qld Ref: 1876/C1490*

Ah Young – 13 October 1876

Ah Young[32] a Bowen Downs shepherd died in the bush, from injuries received in a 'quarrel' on the 13 October 1876. The informant was David Tully the overseer of Bowen Downs, who alone with Carl Olsen buried him on the 16 October 1876. Ah Poon was the last to be seen in his company and also accused of his murder.

Police Gazette — Qld BDM – Death Certificate

Editor's Note – His death certificate states he was buried in the bush at Bowen Downs on the 16 October by David Tully the overseer at Bowen Downs.

George Maggs – 26 October 1876

George Maggs[33] was a 54 year old shepherd at Bowen Downs whose death was notified by E K Russell the accountant at Bowen Downs. He died from dropsy and was buried on the 26 October 1876 by E K Russell at Bowen Downs. It was not known where he was born but he had been in Queensland for 33 years.

In the Supreme Court of Queensland.
IN ITS ECCLESIASTICAL JURISDICTION.
In the Will of George Maggs, late of Bowen Downs Station, in the District of Mitchell and Colony of Queensland, shepherd, deceased. NOTICE is here by given, that after the expiration of fourteen days from the publication hereof, application will be made to the said Honourable Court, that Letters of Administration, with the will annexed, of all the goods, chattels, credits, and effects of the abovenamed George Maggs, deceased , may be granted to Edward Kerra Russell, of Bowen Downs Station, near Aramac , in the said colony, the sole devisee and legatee named in the said Will.

[32] *Qld Ref: 1876/001492*
[33] *Qld Ref: 1876/C1493*

Dated this fifth day of January, A.D. 1878.
FRANCIS PRATT WINTER,
Drummond Street, Clermont,
Proctor for the said E. K. Russell.

TRANSMISSION BY DEATH.

"REAL PROPERTY ACTS OF 1861 AND 1877."

NOTICE is hereby given, that application has been made for Registration of transmission by Death of Land, and according to particulars as follow. Any person desiring to oppose must do so by Caveat, on or before day specified below.

Name of Deceased Proprietor.	Date of Death.	Name of Claimant.	Description and Situation of Land.	Estate claimed to be transmitted.	Particulars of Will or otherwise.	Date within which Caveat may be lodged.
George Maggs, otherwise George Miggs, late of Bowen Downs Station	1876. 26 Oct.	Edward Kevin Russell, of Bowen Downs Station	Allotment 6 of section 6, town of Campbell's Camp, portion 178, Nundah	Fee-simple	Will dated 30th August, 1876	1878. 28 Oct.

Kanaka – 13 November 1876

There was a Kanaka killed by a fall from a horse, on the 13th instant, at Budgeragar, an out-station belonging to Mount Cornish. He only lived a few hours after his fall. Kanakas are in great favor in this part of the world. At Bowen Downs the sheep-washing is nearly all done by them. I am informed that there used to be sixty white men employed at that washpool, and now that there are only five. There's a squad of Kanakas at Mount Cornish too; in fact, there are very few stations about here without them.

The Thomson. (1876, November 18). The Brisbane Courier (Qld.: 1864 - 1933), p. 7. Retrieved May 4, 2012, from http://nla.gov.au/nla.news-article1393017

William Henry Durdon [Dooban] – 6 December 1876

And

Harry [Kanaka] – 8 December 1876

Both William Doodan[34], who was identified by the ring on his finger and Harry[35] both died on the Bowen Downs Road at Belltopper

[34] *Qld Ref: 1876/001499*

[35] *Qld Ref: 1876/001504*

Creek, from burns. Harry was a Labourer, while William was a General Servant, who was fully identified and was last seen with W. H. Doohan in his company.

Police Gazette

Benjamin Ambrose – 1 April 1877

Benjamin Ambrose[36] an American Negro was a labourer who drowned on the 4 April 1877 at Marathon the out-station of Mt Cornish.

Police Gazette

We hear that a man named Charles Campbell, employed at Mount Cornish, Aramac, had his leg broken the other day while mustering, and it was feared that amputation would be necessary. It appears that Campbell, who is said to be the best stockman on the station, was trying to stop a mob of cattle which had broken away, but the excited animals, regardless of the stock-whip, ran down both the horse and its rider in their headlong career. It is surprising that the accident was not more serious.

The Bulletin; WITH WHICH IS INCORPORATED THE GLADSTONE OBSERVER. (1877, May 4). Rockhampton Bulletin (Qld.: 1871 - 1878), p. 2. Retrieved May 27, 2012, from http://nla.gov.au/nla.news-article51909460

Blackall [Our Correspondent – Extract] Eight hundred heifers from Watna, Victoria, passed here yesterday, for Wilson's station, on the Gregory; also three hundred head fat cattle for Dalby, from Mount Cornish station.

Telegraphic. (1877, May 14). The Brisbane Courier (Qld.: 1864 - 1933), p. 2. Retrieved September 22, 2014, from http://nla.gov.au/nla.news-article1363598

[36] *Qld Ref: 1877/001507*

Scouring Sheds, Bowen Downs Station, Ca. 1877

John Oxley Library, State Library of Queensland Negative number: 33244

What Is Left Of The Washing Apparatus – 2012

Photo: Peter Ahern

Editor's Note – There are four deaths in the vicinity of the Bowen Downs Washpool – Gideon Pryor [31 March 1880], John Barry [26 January 1887], James Hammond [5 December 1896], John Murphy [23 July 1897]

Unknown Grave at Wash Pool

Photo: Louise Moloney

Landsborough River – 1 August 1877

(FROM OUR OWN CORRESPONDENT)

June 1

I am a constant reader of your excellent paper, the *Queenslander*, but it is very seldom, if ever, I notice anything in connection with this district, or, I should say, this part of the Mitchell district, which in my opinion is the finest pastoral district in Queensland; that is saying, a good deal, but I have travelled over most of the colony. To give you some idea, I must start from Aramac township, or station, two miles distant from the town. This station, is the property of Messrs Travers and Gibson, it is stocked with sheep and cattle, and is a very fine run most of which is high undulating downs, with patches of gedia and other timber, affording good shelter for the cattle, and is well watered by Aramac Creek running through its centre, also many smaller creeks too numerous to mention. The township of Aramac is now becoming a place of some importance. Three years ago, when I last paid this part of the country a visit, it was looked upon as, a halting place for travellers , but this time I noticed a very great change – new hotels, a bank, butcher's shop, a blacksmith, three stores, in fact, business places of all kinds, and everyone seemed to be doing a good business. After leaving the township to go west, the first station is the celebrated Bowen Downs. The country between here and Aramac is of the finest description. The first fifteen miles from the township is beautiful rolling downs, then there are twelve miles of gedia and myall country, thickly studded with saltbush, then eighteen miles over, the most beautiful downs I have ever seen. When, this has been travelled you arrive at Bowen Downs head station, which to a stranger seems more like a township than a station, there being so many buildings. I believe at the present time there are over 100,000 sheep on this station, and its capabilities are about five times that number. The run being very extensive, the improvements here are of the first order. Three miles from the head station is the new woolshed, it is not quite finished, but will be in August, when shearing commences. The shearing floors hold sixty shearers. It is one of the largest sheds I have ever seen, and should think its cost would be nothing under £3,000. Four miles from this is the washpool, which is very complete, with all the latest improvements. The buildings are of brick, including engine house and shearing shed. The number of sheep washed per day, I believe, is 3,000. This station is the property of the Scottish and Australian Investment Company, also the adjoining station, Mount Cornish, which is stocked with cattle, and I think I can safely say that it is the largest cattle station in Queensland, if not the largest in the colonies. I believe the book muster is about 36,000 head. From here the cattle go north and south to market, and no sooner is one mob started than another is being got ready.

At this point there are different roads down the Thomson River south, the Darr River west, and the Landsborough River north-west. The direction I now take for, the first station, thirty miles from Mount Cornish, is Culloden, the property of Mr. J C Boch. This run is similar to Mount Cornish in country – all fine rolling downs, with plenty of shelter, and is well watered, having twenty four miles frontage to the Landsborough River, on both sides also about fifteen miles frontage to Tower Hill Creek. The head station is four miles from the river on Butler's Creek, a pretty site for a head station. The adjoining station to this is Culloden West, so called from being west of the former station. This station, to use a vulgar yet somewhat common term, is the pick of the Landsborough country. The head station is situated on Culloden Creek, a tributary of the Landsborough River, eighteen miles from its junction. The only way I can describe this run is to take you on to the top of one of the watersheds from where you can see to the top of the next, distant about twelve to fourteen miles. The country between is rich downs studded with different kinds of timber, and intersected with small creeks. The head station is yet in its infancy, the station having only been formed little more than a year, but I hear of stone houses and other improvements of the first water. I may here add that the greatest drawback of the Landsborough – in fact, nearly all of the Western country – is the want of timber for building purpose; in some places it has to be carted from sixty to seventy miles. At the last, mentioned station the property of Mr. S Lord of Essdale Station, Brisbane River they are carting timber from Mount Connell, a distance of fifty miles. The next station, to this in a north easterly direction, is Rockwood, the property of Mr. Rourke, of Dotswood, near Townsville, and under the superintendence of, Mr. C. C. Williams. To a visitor it is very remarkable for its beautiful view from the head station, looking west over the top of the trees which grow along the banks of the Landsborough, the high downs can be seen. With Lubra Creek running through their centre. Twenty miles up this creek there is another cattle station being formed; its name I do not know. It is the property of Mr. E. R Edkins, of Mount Cornish, and will make an excellent run, the country being all that could be desired. Ten miles north of the head camp on Lubra Creek, is Rockwood Creek. On this creek there are 10,000 sheep, the only sheep between here and Bowen Downs, the distance about 100 miles. They are the property of Mr. W. S. Paul, of Glendarriwill Station, near

Springsure; they are a fine lot of sheep and in splendid condition, fit for market. A draft of these sheep, I believe, start for Rockhampton in July, they have been shepherded since February by three Kanaka boys in thirty-three hundred flocks, which says wonders for the fattening qualities of the country, as on most country sheep must be run in eighteen hundred to two thousand flocks to fatten. There is only one more station I have to mention, Cameron Downs I have not been there, but I believe the country is similar to the rest of the Landsborough country, which is second to none in the colonies.

Landsborough River. (1877, August 1). The Brisbane Courier (Qld.: 1864 - 1933), p. 6. Retrieved February 11, 2014, from http://nla.gov.au/nla.news-article1365432

Alexander Jeffray (Jeffery) – 9 November 1877

ARAMAC. November 16.

At the magisterial enquiry at Scarbury concerning the death of Jefferies[37], an employee at Mount Cornish, a warrant has been issued for the arrest of Martin, who stabbed him.

ARAMAC. (1877, November 24). The Queenslander (Brisbane, Qld.: 1866 - 1939), p. 1. http://nla.gov.au/nla.news-article19762954

Tuesday, April 9.
CRIMINAL JURISDICTION
Before His Honor Sir James Cockle, C. J.
MANSLAUGHTER

Samuel Ainsley Norman, *alias* Doctor, *alias* Martin, alias Hunter, was charged that he did, on October 14, 1877, at Scarbury, feloniously kill and slay one Alexander Jaffrey. The prisoner, who was undefended, pleaded not guilty. A jury having been empanelled, the Crown Prosecutor stated the case, and called Thomas Gilbert, who deposed that he was a bushman, and on the 14th October last was stopping at the Scarbury Hotel; he knew prisoner by the name of Martin, and heard him called 'Doctor'; on October 14 he left the

[37] *Qld Ref: 1877/C1525*

hotel between one and two o'clock in the afternoon in company with the prisoner and a man called Clancy; they travelled along the Thomson road, and after going a few hundred yards Clancy returned to the hotel; witness and prisoner proceeded two miles further to camp; prisoner went back to look for Clancy, and returned by himself about two hours afterwards, bringing a bottle of schnapps with him; a man named Jeffrey joined them at the camp, and on being asked to have a drink acceded, and had a drink from the bottle brought by prisoner; the prisoner had a drink, and remarked that the grog would be no good because witness and Jaffrey had not put the cork in the bottle, and that they did not care a d — n for anyone else so long as they (witness and Jaffrey) had their liquor; Jaffrey said, "D – n you and the grog"; prisoner replied in similar words, and Jaffrey pushed prisoner down, who said words to the effect that he would take a tussle out of him (Jeffrey); prisoner and Jaffrey got up and went on to the road to fight and then knocked prisoner down; directly after, the former said witness and said prisoner had stabbed him in the upper part of the left arm, near the joint; it appeared to the witness to be a cut with a knife or other sharp instrument; it was about one inch long and a quarter of an inch in depth; witness tied the wound up, and at the time saw a knife in prisoner's hand; it was a clasp knife, and when opened was about a foot long; the knife produced was similar to that referred to, but he would not swear to its being the knife he saw in prisoner's hand; he accompanied Jaffrey to Scarbury, and reached the hotel there about eight in the evening; prisoner did not accompany them; next morning Jaffrey showed him a mark on his breast; prisoner was standing on the road about three or five yards from Jaffrey when the latter said he was stabbed.

By prisoner: Jaffrey returned to Scarbury on horseback; he was not previously acquainted with prisoner before meeting him at Scarbury; prisoner had said his name was Martin; prisoner may have gone back twice for Clancy; witness and Jaffrey had a drink out of the bottle after the latter was stabbed; he would not swear prisoner did not say, "I will not allow myself to be struck by any one"; he did not see any blows struck by either prisoner or Jaffrey; the quarrel occurred between seven and eight o'clock at night; he did not see Jaffrey knock prisoner down, but heard the latter fall; it was a dark night; he did not remember prisoner tearing his coat up to bind Jaffrey's wound; when they returned to the hotel he spoke to prisoner who was lying on the ground; prisoner was not then insensible; witness saw prisoner and Jaffrey in the hotel together on the following morning, and he saw prisoner wash and dress the wound; they appeared to be on friendly terms; he heard Jaffrey say he was sorry for what had happened the previous night; he saw no other wounds to bind up excepting that on the arm; the mark on Jaffrey's breast did not appear to be from a stab and witness told him so; Jaffrey said that was where prisoner stabbed him; the breast mark might have been done by the man's nail; he saw Jaffrey drinking on the morning after he received the wound; he saw him have four drinks, although he might have had more; Jaffrey complained of his arm. and said it was very sore, on the 15th; they were all at Butler's camp on the 15th: there was rum in the camp, of which Jaffrey partook; prisoner advised him not to drink it; on the 16th he did not hear prisoner ask Jaffrey if his arm was all right; witness left the camp on that day in company with prisoner and Clancy, leaving Jaffrey behind; he left prisoner at Camoola, on the Thomson River, as the latter wished to give his horse a day's spell; he again saw prisoner at Evesham, on the Darr River, about three weeks after the stabbing affray, but did not speak to him; witness had been drinking on the 15th, but was not affected by the liquor he drank.

By Mr. Beor: Prisoner and Jaffrey left the hotel on the 15th, about noon, and witness and Clancy overtook them on the road to Butler's camp.

John Clancy deposed that he was a bushman, and on October 15 he was travelling on the road; he left the Scarbury Hotel on that day in company with Gilbert; he knew prisoner by the name of the Doctor; he joined the prisoner and Jaffrey on the road from Scarbury at their camp; he noticed a scab on Jaffrey's arm; he returned to the place where they were camped on November 9, and found a knife on the ground; the knife produced was exactly like that found by witness excepting that the latter was broken across the centre; the knife produced was broken differently; at Scarbury Hotel he gave the knife to a man connected with the Ashton's circus.

By the prisoner: The knife produced he would swear positively was not the one he found; he and Gilbert were concerned together in breaking-in horses; he saw Gilbert the worse for liquor at the Scarbury Hotel on the 15th; he was nearly having a fight with him; he saw prisoner had a swelled lip when he returned to the hotel on the night of the 14th, and on the morning of the 15th he noticed it was very much swollen, and that there was a good deal of blood about it and also on prisoner's shirt; he heard Gilbert say that he had struck prisoner on the lip; prisoner washed Jaffrey's arm and placed some sticking plaster on it; on the 16th Jaffrey said the wound would be well in a couple of days and that prisoner could go on, meaning, be believed, that prisoner need not stay any longer with him; Jaffrey did not appear to suffer severe pain; Jaffrey was a big, powerful man, weighing between thirteen and fourteen stone; he was drinking at the Scarbury Hotel on the 14th and 15th, but not to any extent; on the 14th Gilbert was drinking, and may have had ten glasses of grog.

John Clifton deposed he was a licensed publican and kept the Scarbury Hotel on October 14, 1877; he knew the prisoner by the name of Martin; the prisoner and Jaffrey were at the hotel on the date mentioned and left in the afternoon; they returned in the evening, when Jaffrey showed him a stab in the fore part of the arm; the cook at the hotel washed and bandaged the wound; Jaffrey left on the following day and returned again nine or ten days afterwards in a spring cart which witness had sent for him; Jaffrey had to be lifted out of the cart and put to bed, being unable to walk; Jaffrey died in the hotel about November 9; he saw Jaffrey frequently during the time he was ill; he was in a bad condition, weak wine and water was given him, no other liquor: when Jaffrey returned there was a quantity of blood on his clothes.

By the prisoner: It was a clean cut that he saw; it did not appear a serous one; when Jaffrey returned he said the cut had healed up, and he complained of a pain in the left leg which witness saw was in a swollen condition; Jaffrey told witness that he struck prisoner first and knocked him down; no medical man attended Jaffrey during his illness; he heard Jaffrey had a fall and hurt his leg; on the night of the 14th he noted prisoner on his return to the hotel had a cut lip, and the next morning he saw prisoner's face was generally swollen and one eye blackened; he saw the man who was camped with Jaffrey; he saw him on the 17th, but did not recollect his taking any grog away; he was not aware of Jaffrey having been drinking before he returned to the hotel.

Dr. Benjamin Poulton deposed he resided at Aramac, and was a bachelor of medicine at the University of Melbourne; he made a post mortem examination of a body at Scarbury on November 11; it was the body of an adult male, and he found upon examination that death resulted from blood poisoning, due to the absorption of matter from the wound in the forearm; the wound was a clean cut, and could have been inflicted by the knife produced or any sharp cutting instrument; the abscess in the arm and leg was caused, he believed, by the absorption of matter from the wound referred to; there were a few slight scars on the breast, which might have been inflicted any time during the month previous to the death.

By Prisoner: The abscesses were the elect of blood poisoning: he did not attend Jaffrey when alive; the wound in the first instance was not serious; if the man had proper medical attendance he believed he would not have died; did not think the abscesses could be caused by a fall on the leg, though their formation might have been accelerated in such a manner; he had not heard previously that Jaffrey had hurt his leg; some men suffered from impurities of the blood in the Barcoo district, but he did not think more than anywhere else; he knew men suffered from what was vulgarly termed the 'Barcoo Rot;' the wound aught have been inflicted by Jaffrey staking at another person holding a knife in his hand; he was a surgeon but not a member of the Royal College of Surgeons; he held a diploma from the Melbourne University as a bachelor of medicine, which includes a surgical as well as a medical qualification; he received his diploma in November 1874.

Constable Bernard Connor deposed he was stationed at Mount Cornish; he was present at Scarbury on November 11, when a body was exhumed; he identified it as that of Alexander Jaffrey; he apprehended the prisoner at Beechall Creek, a distance of 520 miles from Scarbury on November 21; in reply to witness, prisoner said his name was Hunter; witness told prisoner the charge and hand cuffed him; prisoner said, "Are you sure it is not for manslaughter you arrest me? Had I seen an account of the man's death in the papers I would have returned to Aramac and given myself up to the police".

By Prisoner: Had never spoken to Jaffrey; had only seen him once when alive; he used a dozen horses in pursuit of prisoner; heard of his being at Tocal Station at the end of October.

Herbert Swayne deposed he was a store keeper at Mount Cornish, about 27 miles from Scarbury; he received a letter and afterwards went to Scarbury on November 2; he there saw Jaffrey in a bed in the hotel; Jaffrey showed witness his left arm, on which be noticed a scab; he remained nine days, and was present at Jaffrey's death; Jaffrey was in a raving state of mind; he was not present at the burial; Jaffrey declined to have medical attendance.

By the Prisoner: He had given men in the Mount Cornish district medicine, for which be received no payment; he had been prosecuted in the Aramac Police Court for practicing as a medical practitioner without a diploma.

William Francis Burton deposed that he was a bushman residing at Scarbury.

By prisoner: He was owner of the Scarbury Hotel, and knew a man named Alexander Jaffrey; he saw him brought in a spring-cart to the hotel on November first; heard him say he had fallen in his tent on a log and hurt his leg; he complained of pain in his leg after his arrival.

Thomas Gilbert recalled, deposed that he struck prisoner on the 14th October, as Jaffrey wanted to get on to him again; that occurred after Jaffrey showed witness the wound; at the time prisoner had the knife in his hand, and said if Jaffrey did not leave him alone he would stick him again; prisoner said that he had a revolver in his saddle bag; he struck prisoner on the hip because he refused to put the knife down. This closed the case for the Crown, and the prisoner called a witness who did not appear. The Crown prosecutor addressed the jury, and the prisoner followed with an ingenious and well-delivered defence. The Court then adjourned; the hearing of the case will be resumed this morning.

Wednesday April 10th
Before His Honor Sir James Cockle, C. J.
MANSLAUGHTER

Samuel Ainsley Norman, *alias* Doctor, *alias* Martin, alias Hunter, charges with the manslaughter of one Alexandra Jaffrey, appeared before the court. The case had been heard the previous day, and his Honor summered up the evidence, after which the jury having retired for ten minutes returned a verdict of not guilty.

CRIMINAL JURISDICTION. (1878, April 13). The Capricornian (Rockhampton, Qld: 1875 - 1929), p. 14 - 15. http://nla.gov.au/nla.news-article65765000

Editor's Note – as can be seen Alexandra's surname has taken to being spelt in many ways – Jaffrey, Jefferies but in Queensland BDM, it is Jeffray.
He was born in born Scotland and was aged 36 years when he died.

Bush Fires on the Thompson River.

During the put month (writes the correspondent of the Copperfield Miner) several disastrous bush fires have taken place; nearly all the stations from this river to the Western River—with the exception of Darr Water—having suffered to some extent. I am glad to report, however, that no lives have been lost, although a number of persons travelling from Camoola to Maneroo had a very narrow escape from being burnt to death. The parties in question was Mr. Moran, of the Mount Cornish Police Barracks, a number of native troopers, Mr. Josephson, the travelling jeweller, and his coach driver, who had charge of the buggy containing the valuables. From a conversation that I had with Mr Moran, it appears that they were all travelling, together in the direction of Maneroo when the fire broke out, and the driver ,of -Mr. Josephson's buggy, fearing for the safety of his master's goods, as the wind was blowing with hurricane violence and carrying the fire towards them at a great pace, turned the horses heads back in the direction of Camoola and galloped them along the road for six or eight miles before any of the others, who hardly recovered from their astonishment at seeing him travel, could stop him; and there, is no doubt that he would have proceeded: on for some considerable distance farther had the horses not knocked up. By the time Mr. Moran and Mr. Josephson palled him up the fire, which had been gaining ground rapidly, had nearly reached them, and the former gentleman had only efficient time to burn a patch of ground in front and press all the horses on to it when the fire rushed past, and closed them in on all sides. Mr. Moran escaped with only a few burns on his neck and hands, but Mr. Josephson and his man wore not so fortunate, both of them being very badly burnt, the latter especially, as in urging his tired horses on to the burnt ground in front his clothes caught fire, and endeavuoring to tear off his "crimean" severely scorched the whole of the upper part of his body; he is now under Dr. Poulton's care at Aramac, and I have no doubt doing well. At Maneroo, Mr. Fraser and his employees were out for two nights beating out the tire to save the head station; and at Eversham the whole of the grass in the horse paddock was swept away. During a heavy thunderstorm on the Darr Water station, the vivid flashes of lightning set fire to the horse paddock which is being formed there, but fortunately no damage was done, the heavy rain falling immediately after putting out the fires.

Bush Fires on the Thompson River. (1877, December 18). Rockhampton Bulletin (Qld.: 1871 - 1878), p. 3. Retrieved May 2, 2014, from http://nla.gov.au/nla.news-article51913509

John Casey – 22 January 1878

John[38], a male in his 50s, died on the road between Bowen Downs and Mount Cornish just 9 miles from the Mount Cornish homestead. Aynslie John Elliott, manager of Bowen Downs, was the informant who notified the Register, John W Chandler, in Aramac on the 14 February 1878. He was buried where he died from '*supposed want of water*' by the road by Charles Ellison with Bernard Connor and Patrick Laing as witnesses.

Qld BDM – Death Certificate

Apii – 30 January 1878

Apii[39] a Polynesian labourer, born in the South Seas, died at the Bowen Downs head station on 30th January 1878 from leg wound that became poisoned. The wound festered for about 3 months. E R Russell from Bowen Downs was the informant and with the help of Aynslie John Elliott, he was buried at the homestead on 31st January.

Qld BDM – Death Certificate

[38] *Qld Ref: 1878/C2020*

[39] *Qld Ref: 1878/C2019*

'Wilkie' – Thomas Scott Williamson Weleby – 1 February 1878

Wilkie[40], a pianist, was found dead by William F Jones a stockman from Aramac Station. It is supposed he died from 'want of water'. J Moss and Patrick Lang as witness buried Wiklie, in the Aramac Cemetery on the 14 February. Wilkie was born in England and was about 43 years old when he died.

Qld BDM – Death Certificate

Muttaburra – 2 February 1878

PROCLAMATION.

By His Excellency Sir ARTHUR EDWARD KENNEDY, Knight Commander of the Most Distinguished Order of St. Michael and St. George, Companion of the Most Honourable

A. E. KENNEDY, Order of the Bath, Governor and Commander-in-Chief of the Colony of Queensland and its Dependencies.

IN pursuance of the authority in me vested, and in accordance with the provisions of *"The Crown Lands Alienation Act of* 1876," I, Sir ARTHUR EDWARD KENNEDY, the Governor aforesaid, with the advice of the Executive Council, do hereby notify and proclaim that the lands hereunder described shall be reserved for a Township, under the name of Muttaburra.

RESERVE FOR A TOWNSHIP, UNDER THE NAME OF MUTTABURRA, ON THE THOMSON RIVER, MITCHELL DISTRICT.

Resumed from the Betawong and Betawong Upper Runs.

Area-2,560 acres.

Commencing on the most western branch of the Thomson River about forty chains above the site of the proposed bridge, at a tree near the junction of a small creek marked broad-arrow over TR ; and bounded thence on the north by a west line one mile fifty-one

[40] *Qld Ref: 1878/C2022*

chains ; thence on the west by a south line two miles ; thence on the south by an east line about two miles to the western branch of the Thomson River above-mentioned at a point forty-five chains below a tree marked broad-arrow over SE over III ; and thence on the east by the right bank of the said western branch upwards to the point of commencement.

Given under my Hand and Seal, at Toowoomba, this second day of February, in the year of our Lord one thousand eight hundred and seventy-eight, and in the forty-first year of Her Majesty's reign.

By Command,

GEORGE THORN. GOD SAVE THE QUEEN I

Government Gazette – February 1878

Baba – 14 February 1878

Baba[41] a Polynesian labourer died at the Bowen Downs head station from dysentery which he had for about 4 weeks. William Kennedy with A Capper as a witness buried him at Bowen Downs. Baba had only been in the 'colonies' for two years and six months.

Bowen Downs

Bowen Downs – 1 sub-inspector, 1 constable, and 6 troopers.
Bowen Downs, E. K. Russell – Post Office
Elliot, Aynsley John, Bowen Downs – JP
Ranken, J. T. C., Bowen Downs – JP

Gov Gazette January – June 1878

[41] *Qld Ref: 1878/C2023*

George Horseman McLean – 17 February 1878

George[42], the son of George McLean, an engineer and Maria O'Brien, was born in Aramac and died from '*supposed to be croup*' when only six weeks and one day old. His father was working at the Bowen Downs Wash Pool, which is where baby George died and was buried by his father on the 18 February.

Qld BDM – Death Certificate

Editor's Note – George and Maria had another child Thomas Manalra born on the 22 March 1883 and died just 2 months later on the 11 May 1883.

Lolbassie – 4 May 1878

Lolbassie[43], a Polynesian labourer working at Bowen Downs station, died on the 4 May 1887 from a '*disease of the liver*' which he had suffered for about four weeks. Donald Beaton, with A J Elliott and R E McDonald as witnesses, buried him at the Bowen Downs Station on the 6 May. Lolbassie was born in the Solomon Islands and had only been in Australia for two years and four months.

Qld BDM – Death Certificate

Police Gazette – 26 October 1878

Henry Hart has been recently seen at Bowen Downs Station. He was then in charge of a mob of horses, which are supposed to have been stolen by him, and was making for the new township of Muttaburra, and travelling in company of Jack Atheridge, bookkeeper at Mount Cornish Station, and a man named Cann, who was going with Atheridge to Mount Cornish. Offender will probably assume the name of John Harvey, under which name his wife had lately addressed letters to him. It is believed that he is

[42] *Qld Ref: 1878/C2028*
[43] *Qld Ref: 1878/C2027*

identical with Michael Harte (see Police Gazette, 1870, page 45), he is much taller now. 26th October 1878

Page 116 – Police Gazette

BOWEN and BOWEN DOWNS – 1878

Mail once a fortnight.

Bowen (post-office) to Strathmore (De Salis & Macdonald)	67
Thence to Hidden Vale	33
Mount Wyatt	15
Old St Anne's station	32
The Bridge	16
Bowman's	2
Mount Douglas	32
Bully Creek	24
Bowen Downs	135
Total	356

BOWEN DOWNS and HUGHENDEN.

Mail once a fortnight.

Bowen Downs (post-office) to Tower Hill head station	43
Thence to Buchanan's	18
Rookwood	22
Christison's sheep station and Hughenden (Grey's) (receiving office)	80
Total	163

Pugh's Almanac 1878

Mount Cornish – 1 sub-inspector, 1 constable, and 6 troopers

Pugh's Queensland Almanac Directory, Law Calendar 1879,

Thomas Erhardt — 23 March 1879

Muttaburra

[Extract]: A Swede[44], who had been staying some weeks in town, and who was well known and liked in the district, committed suicide by hanging him-self to a tree in the billabongs of the Landsborough on Sunday evening. An enquiry was held to-day by Mr. E. R. Edkins, at which it was elicited that deceased had left the town to camp with some mates on the creek, and having heard that his brother (Charles Ehrardt) had committed suicide at Millchester, he appeared to have let it prey upon his mind to such an extent that he was watched by his friends, but managed to get away after dark and hang himself with a saddle strap, and though immediate search was made on his being missed, he was not discovered till daylight.

Work is, I am sorry to say, not as good as it might be, and we are all getting a touch of tightness in the money market; but we hope for the best Blight in the eyes is the fashion, almost everyone having one if not more eyes in a sling.

Muttaburra. (1879, April 26). The Brisbane Courier (Qld.: 1864 - 1933), p. 7. Retrieved January 20, 2014, from http://nla.gov.au/nla.news-article895229

Editor's Note – The actual grave site of Thomas Erhardt is unknown.

Bowen Downs – 13 September 1879

BOWEN DOWNS.

August 18.

Bowen Downs is once again the scene of activity, the washing and shearing is in full swing, and everything presents a lively appearance. The sheep are in fine condition, and are cutting on an average ½ lb. of wool more per head than last year. The season has been exceptionally good, and I don't think I am far wrong in saying that the clip will exceed the anticipation of the company. The first consignment of wool, comprising two waggon-loads, left here for

[44] *Qld Ref: 1879/C1543*

the Comet rail way on the 4th of this month; three other waggon loads left on the 12th, and several other teams are now being loaded. There are about forty shearers at the shed and thirteen knock about hands; about forty hands are also employed at the washpools. The following are the prices of labor and of provisions:— Labor: Shed hands, 25s. per week and rations; washers, 5s. per day and rations; shearers, 4s. per score without rations. Rations: Flour, £4 10. per bag; sugar, 7d. per lb.; tea, 3s. 6d. per lb.; preserved potatoes, 1s. 6d. per lb.; beef, fresh, 2d.; salt, 3d; ewes, 5s.; wethers, 7s. each.

On the 11th a subscription was raised for a man who was stricken with fever, and within half-an-hour the handsome sum of £15 10s. was raised. The next morning the manager (Mr. Elliott) with his usual kindness had the man conveyed to Aramac in his own buggy, to obtain medical assistance. One could not possibly wish for pleasanter weather, either day or night, than what we are now experiencing.

RAMBLER.

BOWEN DOWNS. (1879, September 13). The Queenslander (Brisbane, Qld.: 1866 - 1939), p. 345. Retrieved June 3, 2012, from http://nla.gov.au/nla.news-article20328495

1880s

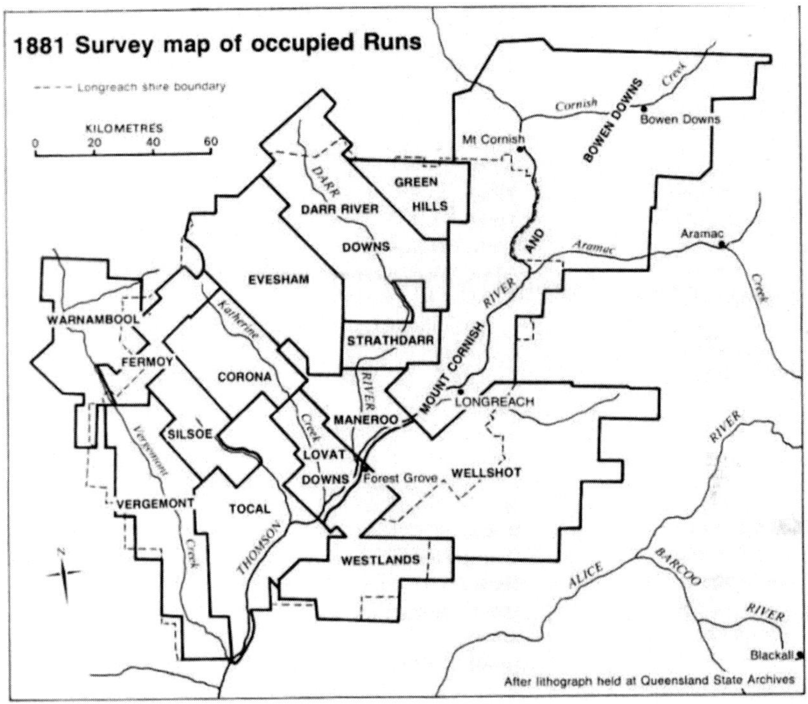

1881 Survey Map of Occupied Runs

Source: The Longreach Story: Angela G I Moffat

James Shield – 18 March 1880

James Shield[45] the son of David Shield and Mary Purvis was born on 12 March 1880 and died just 6 days later at Mount Cornish where he was born. His death was due to croup which he suffered for 24 hours. His father was the overseer at Mount Cornish and buried this infant at Mount Cornish on the 19 March 1880. John McPherson was the witness at the burial. T S Sword registered James' death on the 9 April in Aramac.

[45] *Qld Ref: 1880/C1374*

David and Mary had the following children: George James: 1874 – 1948, Robert Andrew: 1876 – 1876, David Robert: 1878 – 1926, James: 1880 – 1880, Francis Ivory: 1881 – 1915, Mary Purvis: 1883 – ?, Archibald Septimus: 1894 – 1948

Gideon Pryor – 31 March 1880

Gideon[46] was a 37 year old English bushman, who drown at the Bowen Downs Wash Pool Lagoon a long way from his birth country. John Rule identified as the manager of Bowen Downs was the informant for this death. On the 1 April 1880, James Bra….. buried Gideon, at Bowen Downs, with John Mahon and Thomas Tonkin as witnesses.

Qld BDM – Death Certificate

Country News.

[FROM OUR OWN CORRESPONDENTS.]

SCARBURY.

July 16.

WE have a petition on foot for the opening of more roads vid Scarrbury to Muttaburra, which would prove a great convenience to travelling stock from the South, bound for the West. I will give you more particulars. Our energetic townsman, Mr. J. Kennedy, storekeeper, is starting an express coach to run from Muttaburra vid Scarrbury and Aramac to Emerald, the railway terminus, which will run once a month, so that business people wanting goods quickly will have a good opportunity of getting same at a small charge. The town having been surveyed, I expect we shall soon have a land sale, which will be an inducement to others to settle down. Mr. Kennedy is adding improvements to his premises, which is a proof that the place is going ahead.

46 *Qld Ref: 1880/C1376*

Country News. (1880, August 7). The Queenslander (Brisbane, Qld.: 1866 - 1939), p. 166. Retrieved September 21, 2014, from http://nla.gov.au/nla.news-article20334628

LOST IN THE BUSH – 9 August 1880

LOST IN THE BUSH. — The *Aramac Mail* of the 31st July says:— A very narrow escape from death in the bush is reported from Scarrbury. A little boy only seven years old, son of Mr. J. Kennedy, of that place, had been sent out by his father on the morning of Friday week last with a blackfellow, to tail some horses in the Mount Cornish bullock paddock. They missed a mare from the mob, and the little fellow, feeling quite confident in his bushmanship, left the horses in charge of the blackboy and went off to find her. This, however, he failed to do, and got lost himself. After wandering about in the paddock all day he found a gate after sundown and went through it. He rode on for a good part of the night, crossing a portion of Beaconsfield run, and pulled upon a flat under Mount Rodney. Here he dismounted, tied, his horse up, and endeavoured to get some rest. But he must have had an uncomfortable time of it, as he had neither food or matches with him, and the night was bitterly cold. In the morning he mounted again, and, being now weak, was obliged to let tile horse take his own course. The animal, finding his head free, turned for home, and brought the boy to the fence of the bullock paddock. There are gates along the fence at intervals of five miles, and the little fellow ran the fence till he found one. After proceeding for some little distance the horse brought him out on the Aramac and Scarrbury road, about twenty miles from town. He came out close to a tree which he recognised. He now knew where he was, and made straight for home, where he arrived on Saturday evening, having been out two days and a night without food, fire, or covering. He was very much exhausted when he reached home, but soon got round, and is none the worse for his adventure. Mr. Kennedy desires particularly to thank Mr. Hall of Camoola, and the young gentlemen at Ambo for the promptness with which they came to his assistance. They were out with the blacks looking for the tracks, and traced the boy to where he had been searching for the mare, but they never hit upon the point where he struck away from the country where the horses wore running. They did not make a wide cast, as it never occurred to them that he had gone out of the paddock. The period during which the boy was absent was one of great anxiety, and Mr. Kennedy's friends will be glad to know that all ended happily at last.

The Morning Bulletin, ROCKHAMPTON. (1880, August 9). Morning Bulletin (Rockhampton, Qld.: 1878 - 1954), p. 2. Retrieved September 20, 2014, from http://nla.gov.au/nla.news-article52020894

Editor's Note – This would have been Alexander George Kennedy [born 21 December 1872] son of John Kennedy and Frances Mary Hall Wilson.

John Kennedy also opened the Scarbury Hotel in late 1881, as well as running the store there for a number of years.

Hugh Murray – 12 August 1880

Hugh Murray[47], a shearer, died at the Bowen Downs Shearing shed of heart disease under no suspicion circumstances. William Davison, J Moss and others were the last to be seen with him. Hugh was the son of Alexander Murray.

Police Gazette

Editor's Note – Hugh aged about 35 years old, was the son of Alexander Murray a gardener. Hugh was born in Sutherland, Scotland, although he had been in Queensland for twenty one years.

A J Elliot JP, the manager of Bowen Downs held an inquest in relation to cause of death was Hugh Murray's cousin. Thomas Tonkin was the undertaker who buried him at the Bowen Downs Shearing Shed on the same day he died. R Williams and H A Stoll were witness to the burial

[47] *Qld Ref: 1880/001396*

John Henry Raynor – 7 October 1880
Aramac

(FROM OUR OWN CORRESPONDENT.)

October 20,

The body of a man, stabbed to the heart, has been found in the dam near Muttaburra. It is evident that a murder has been committed. The clothes of the deceased had been burned in the camp fire, and there is as yet no clue to his identity.

COLONIAL TELEGRAMS. (FROM OUR OWN CORRESPONDENTS.) QUEENSLAND. (1880, October 21). Morning Bulletin (Rockhampton, Qld.: 1878 - 1954), p. 3. Retrieved April 30, 2012, from http://nla.gov.au/nla.news-article52022294

Aramac.

(FROM OUR OWN CORRESPONDENT)

November 2

John Raynor, who was arrested last week for the murder of the man whose body was found in the Acacia dam, near Muttaburra, committed suicide last evening by cutting his throat with a knife which the constable had lent him to eat his meals with.

The question whether the next pastoral show shall be held at Muttaburra or Aramac has been decided by the votes of the members, of whom, sixteen were in favor of the proposed alterations, whilst forty-six voted for holding it at Aramac, as usual.

Aramac. (1880, November 3). The Brisbane Courier (Qld.: 1864 - 1933), p. 2. Retrieved April 30, 2012, from http://nla.gov.au/nla.news-article898818

The Acacia Dam Murder.

In the Courier of October 21 there appeared the following telegram from Aramac: "The body of a man, stabbed to the heart, has been found in the Acacia Dam, near Muttaburra. It is evident that a murder has been committed. The clothes of the deceased had been burned in the camp fire, and there is as yet no clue to his identity."

On Tuesday last a telegram announced the arrest of a man named John Raynor, at Bowen Downs, on suspicion of having committed the murder, and on the day following came the intelligence that Raynor had committed suicide by cutting his throat. Below we publish some details respecting the finding of the body of the murdered man, and the discovery of certain clues to the murderer, supplied by our Aramac correspondent, which will be read with interest. We are as yet unable to say whether Raynor's description tallies with that of the man described by our correspondent as having been in the company of the man whose body was found in the dam, or on what grounds suspicion fell upon Raynor. All this will doubtless appear at the investigation into the latest phase of this horrible tragedy. Our correspondent writes, under date 21st ultimo:– "There is every reason to believe that a most foul and cold-blooded murder has been perpetrated at a dam on the Muttaburra road, distant about seven miles from that place. A benighted horseman being thirsty, took occasion to dismount for a drink. He had stretched himself out on a projecting root, and was about to imbibe, when he observed something in the water. He put his hand to it, and, to his horror, discovered a corpse within a few inches of his face. He was quickly in the saddle, and pushed on for Muttaburra, and reported the matter to the police. Early next morning Mr. Edkins, accompanied by Dr. Harris and the senior constable, proceeded without delay to the spot in order to hold the enquiry prescribed by law. No foul play was suspected, the belief being that the poor follow had drowned himself in a fit of delirium tremens. The body was drawn to land and Dr. Harris proceeded to examine it. It was almost nude, being only clothed in a cotton singlet. Round the neck was a broad leather strap; this the doctor removed. He then discovered a stab in the side that had apparently been made by an ordinary sheath knife. Opening the body he found the knife had penetrated to the heart, and must have caused immediate death. In his opinion, the wound could not possibly have been self-inflicted. The party buried the body and made a search round about, but could discover nothing. The corpse, I should mention, was considerably decomposed; the face was completely gone; there was, however, a little hair at the back of the head. In the doctor's opinion death must have occurred at least a week previously. Deceased seemed to be about 50 years of age, and 5 ft. 6 in. in height.

The next day the senior-constable returned with some black trackers to make a further search. They found the remains of a camp fire, in which articles of clothing had evidently been burned. Among the ashes were several buttons. Leading from the camp fire to the water was a smooth track, along which the body had apparently been dragged by the strap found round the neck. On searching the water they found a new pair of remarkably heavy blucher boots, with plain (not furrowed) iron tips round the heels; a piece of white blanket, and a pair of grey blankets sown with black thread to a pair of red, both pairs very old; also a new canvas water-bag slit on one side, so as to make it sink; also a piece of soap, and a new tin pannikin marked on the side with a triangle about half an inch high and the eighth of an inch at the base. The triangle was shaded with small lines.

Returning to Muttaburra it was ascertained that two men had been noticed to pass through that township about a week previous. One of them was of the supposed age and stature of the deceased, and wearing boots similar to those found in the water. The other was a younger and taller man, with a broad strap round his swag of the same kind as that found about the neck of the corpse. The elder man had money, and said he was going down to Sydney for a spell. They only stayed about an hour in the town; the older man paid for everything, the younger one appearing to have no money whatever. The young man seemed to be impatient, and was constantly urging his companion to come on. The boots, water-bag, and pannikin were not purchased in the township, but must have been procured further west, most probably at some station. The old man's swag was rolled in calico, and it is not known whether the blankets belonged to him or to the murderer. It is not known whether the old man had his money in notes or cheques. He paid silver for the small purchases made at Muttaburra. These are all the circumstances I have been able to procure as yet. The most rational supposition is that the unfortunate man was stabbed to the heart while asleep by his travelling companion for the sake of the money he was known to have about him.

With all his cunning, the murderer has left several clues, which, if properly followed up, may lead to his detection. His great safe-guard lies in the fact that any person who may give information exposes himself to the risk of a heavy pecuniary loss. The allowance for the expenses of witnesses is altogether inadequate. Indeed it does not cover the coach and railway fares to Rockhampton and back. Is it too much to ask that the Government should offer free passes to Rockhampton and back, and reasonable compensation for loss of time, to any individual who may come forward with evidence? It would be an evil precedent to permit the miscreant who perpetrated this most foul and cowardly murder to escape the penalty that his crime merits."

The Acacia Dam Murder. (1880, November 4). The Brisbane Courier (Qld.: 1864 - 1933), p. 3. Retrieved May 16, 2012, from http://nla.gov.au/nla.news-article896415

THE MOUNT CORNISH: MURDER. The mate of the man who was found murdered in the Acacia dam, was apprehended on Thursday. He had taken the name of the old man, and the other evidence against him was so conclusive that he was committed for trial without delay. On Saturday, however, the guilty wretch managed to possess himself of a knife, and put an end to his existence. An inquiry was held in the usual course, and thus quickly terminates what is known as the Mount Cornish tragedy. – Champion.

The Morning Bulletin. ROCKHAMPTON. (1880, November 15). Morning Bulletin (Rockhampton, Qld.: 1878 - 1954), p. 2. http://nla.gov.au/nla.news-article52022811

Thomas Cleg – 29 October 1880
The Acacia Dam Murder
Suicide of the Murderer

(From the Aramac Mail)

On Monday last we received the startling intelligence that the man who had been arrested at Bowen Downs had lodged in the

Muttaburra lockup for the murder of a man, name unknown, at the Acacia Dam, had anticipated the course of the law by cutting his throat. So far as we can learn, it is not usual to take special precautions against such suicides except in the case of convicted murderers, but one would think that where the presumptive evidence of guilt was so strong as in this case, the necessity for preventative care would be equally great. It appears that the prisoner's handcuffs were removed for a time to enable him to cool and eat his food. He was engaged on the evening of Thursday week in cooking some steak for his supper, and whilst the constable in charge (Constable Ryan) turned away for a moment he took the opportunity of ending his miserable existence. The evidence taken at the enquiry with regard to the suicide is, we must say, incomplete, inasmuch as it does not show how prisoner came to have the knife in his possession; but the presumption is that he was allowed to use it in the process of cooking the meat. We certainly consider it far from prudent to allow a man charged with an atrocious murder access to anything that could be used as a weapon, especially when there is only one constable to watch him. Instead of cutting his own throat he might have plunged the knife into the constable, removed his irons and escaped. We are assured, however, that Constable Ryan was not to blame, as the handcuffs were removed by the order of Sub-Inspector Ahearn. It is, of course, almost impossible to prevent a really determined man for committing suicide. Only recently we heard of a man making away with himself by stuffing a handkerchief in his throat. At the same time a murderer in the position of the one at Muttaburra would have been as likely to commit another murder as suicide, and for this reason more the than ordinary caution, should have been observed. Senior Constable Chandler is doubtless a good deal disappointed at losing his prisoner in this fashion. The capture reflects great credit on him, especially when it is remembered how he was hampered by his duties as land agent and C. P. S.; but the good effect of the prompt discovery of the man who beyond all possibility of doubt the murderer will remain as a deterrent to others who may be tempted to commit a similar crime.

The inquiry into the case was resumed on Saturday before E. R. Edkins J. P., and included the magisterial enquiry into the death of the prisoner. The first witness called was:

Senior-Constable Chandler, who deposed to proceeding to the Acacia Dam on the 17th and there finding the articles noted in our report of the 24th ult – viz, a pair of boots, billy, water-bag, pannikin, and some blankets, the latter wrapped around a large stone; also to finding a track made by some body being dragged along from where a camp fire had been lit to the water's edge. From information he received shortly afterwards he proceeded to the Bowen Downs wash-pool, where he saw a man calling himself Raynor cooking. Raynor was pointed out to him by a man named John Ledgwood as a man the latter had seen at the Ten-mile dam on the 8th in company with another man. Witness got into conversation with Raynor, who in answer to questions said he had come from the west, and had been working for a month at Manuka. Witness asked him if he knew a man named Herbert Phitzner, and he replied in the negative. He told witness he had come into Muttaburra on a Thursday, and had camped near the Chinaman's garden. Witness then asked him what he had done with the mate, the man he had come into Muttaburra with. He said he and his mate came twenty miles that day, from the Dam on the Darr road and had dinner at Phillip's hotel. After dinner they went and camped at the Chinaman's garden – about 12 o'clock, and about half an hour afterwards his mate told him he had an opportunity of having his swag carried into Aramac by a man on horseback. About two hours after this he missed one of his dogs and then followed his mate and the one on horseback to the dam on the Aramac road. Just as he got to the dam two men started away from it on foot. The man he had travelled from Evesham with and another man were camped at the dam, and he got his dog from them. Witness then asked Raynor if the man who was travelling with his mate had any horses; he replied that he had, but that they were turned out. He had noticed no one else camped at the dam. Raynor then went down to the creek for water. Witness asked him if he was certain there was no one else at the dam, and he replied, "I was never at the dam; I know nothing of the road between Aramac and Muttaburra". Prisoner then got into a punt and went a little way down the creek for water. Witness followed him along the bank, and when he returned asked him if he was certain he had never been at the dam. This time he replied that he had, having followed a dog of his. When asked why he denied having been there at first, he said, "You took me so much by surprise. I didn't know what to say". Witness then asked him the time, and he said he had got no watch on him; asked him what he had done with the watch he had the night before, and he replied that he had sold it to a man on the station, pulling out a purse and showing witness a cheque £4 drawn by Mr. Elliot, which he said he had got for the watch, and then said he did not get it – he got an order. Witness asked to see the order but Raynor said he had not got it; he had given the watch to a man the day before on trial, and it was to be returned if it did not suit. After this conservation witness arrested him on a charge of murder. He said "All right, sergeant, I will go with you". On being searched nothing was found on him but the purse before mentioned. After his arrest he picked out his clothes and blankets (produced in court), and picked out his knife from amongst others. He was then taken into Muttaburra and handed over to Constable Ryan. On the 29th Senior-Constable Chandler returned to the wash-pool to make further search, and among the ashes in the fireplace which Raynor had been sitting he found a watch-pouch with a watch enclosed bearing the name of Flavelle Brothers and Roberts, No 24971. The watch was then going. After a further search amongst the ashes he found a tin box containing a Saving Bank book, No 55261, endorsed John H Raynor, in the pocket of which were two cheques – one in favour of James Raynor for £19 17s. and the other in favour of one Blakely for £5, both drawn on the Brisbane branch of the bank of New

South Wales and signed J. S. F. Schollick. They were numbered 325 and 328 respectively, and both dated September 27 1880. The ashes were then screened and the remains of a chain found. Witness produced two knives, both newly ground, both of which had been found in prisoner's swag. There was also some five penny worth of coarse gold in the swag.

Constable Patrick Ryan, being sworn, deposed that, prisoner, John Raynor, shoemaker, native of England, about 40 years of age, was handed over to his charge on the evening of the 28th by Senior Constable Chandler; prisoner was charged with murder; prisoner was in witness' charge during the evening of the 28th; he did not speak except to ask for a drink of water and a pillow; witness gave him a drink and blankets; conversed with the prisoner during the 29th; about half-past six on the evening of that day witness removed the handcuff from prisoner's right hand to allow him to cool his supper; prisoner lit the fire, made some tea and was cooking some steak on a grid-iron; witness turned away to light a lamp, but on turning around again could not see the prisoner; on going towards the fire place saw the prisoner draw his hand across his throat, and blood flow from him; witness spoke but he did not reply; the prisoner was falling and witness caught him in his arms; he never spoke afterwards; the knife produced was found by witness covered with blood' prisoner had never done or said anything that would lead him to believe he intended to commit suicide; witness had given him a book and newspaper to read during the 28th.

Henry Lewis Harris, medical practitioner being sworn, deposed that about half-past seven o'clock in the evening he went to the lockup and saw a man lying in the fireplace; pulling him out to examine him, and found two incised wounds – one transversely across the wind-pipe, but not severing it, about two inches in length, and only superficial; the other so the kayak severing the deeper st.....3; the latter was about four inches longer and about two inches in depth; this was the cause of death; the knife produced would be sufficient to cause such a wound; had seen deceased before whilst in the lockup; but saw nothing in his manner to cause one to suppose he would commit suicide.

James Elliott, hotel keeper Muttaburra, deposed to having seen the body of deceased that morning; he had seen the man before, alive, about the 7th or 8th instant; thought it was on a Thursday at his hotel; he was then accompanied by another man; they had dinner and some drinks; witness had some conversation with them during dinner, and they led him to believe they came from Kensington Downs; the other man paid for what he had, in silver; he was bout 5ft 7in in height, and appeared older than the deceased; the deceased hurried the other man (who appeared to wish to stop in town longer) away, wishing to camp at the ten-mile dam; deceased's cloths were very dirty, and his swag also was dirty; the blankets produced were like those deceased was carrying; the other man had a clean swag covered with calico, and was very clean in his apparel and person; he had on a clean pair of white trousers and striped shirt; and complained that his boots, which were new, with rivets at the side, were hurting him; the boots produced are like the one he noticed; witness had never seen him since; the deceased left a little in advance of the other man; the swag carried by the elder of the two appeared to be the largest; witness had heard of a dead body being found in the ten-mile dam, and the description of the elder man; the younger man did not remove his hat during dinner, and appeared to be anxious to get away – the other was not.

Abraham Shepherd, labourer, Muttaburra, deposed to seeing the dead body now lying in the lockup; had seen the same man living about three weeks ago, a little way the other side of the first bridge, and in company with another man who appeared younger; deceased called witness as he was passing with his dray, and witness had some conservation with him; he said they had come from the Western, and were going to Aramac to have a week's spell; after which they intended to proceed to Brisbane; the two started on, saying they had plenty of time to be to the ten-mile; before they started witness saw both swags open; the blankets produced are those which were carried by the younger man of the two, whom witness had not seen since; witness recognised the billy produced; deceased was carrying the billy, also a small water-bag similar to the one produced; before they started they rolled both swags into one and the mate of the deceased carried the swag; the rations were rolled in a calico fly; they had two dogs with them; one black and the other a well-bred blue-coloured sheep dog, which witness could recognise again

Constable Ryan, re-sworn, stated that the blankets and billy produced were the ones sworn to be Senior-Constable Chandler as having been found in the Acacia Dam, near where the dead body of a man was found; witness was present when they were found.

The verdict of the court was that the deceased met his death from a self-inflected wound, and that from the evidence taken, and other evidence that might have been taken if necessary for trial now existed, deceased was the person seen in company with some other person, name unknown, whose body was found in the Acacia Dam, and strong presumptive evidence existed as to deceased being the murderer.

It is now thought that the name of the murdered man was John or James Raynor, the murderer, having assumed the name in order to be identified with the bank book and cheques found in his possession.

The [?]. (1880, November 25). The Northern Miner (Charters Towers, Qld.: 1874 - 1954), p. 2. Retrieved June 3, 2012, from http://nla.gov.au/nla.news-article76718425

Editor's Note – As stated in this last article the actual murdered person was John Henry Raynor[48] who was murdered on or about the 7 October 1880, and was a 45 to 50 year old labourer.

The murderer was Thomas Cleg[49], a 60 year old, shoe maker, who committed suicide, on the 29 October 1880, in the Muttaburra Lock-up.

[48] Qld Ref: 1880/001405

[49] Qld Ref 1880/001406

Murdering Dam – 2014

Photo: Louise Moloney

Twelve Months later 28 October 1881

We have to record a singular apparition which scared a party of men a few nights ago out of all the senses they had derived from a liberal nature. It was evening, and they were camped at Acacia Dam, the scene not long ago of a most foul and dastardly murder. The crime will be too fresh in the minds of our readers to require recapitulation. The party were seated on the ground, not far from the grave of the murdered man. The sun had disappeared, and the shades of night had closed in. Suddenly to their horror a huge head with staring eyes was seen to arise from the grave of the murdered man. The outline of the head was indistinct in the darkness, but the eyes glared with a light that was terribly real. Heels was the word, and all, whites, blacks, and Chinamen rushed in frantic vehemence from the haunted spot. One man was said to have been so terrified that he could not pull up till he reached Mount Cornish station, distant about twenty miles from the scene of alarm. And there was not so much in it after all. A wag of a blackfellow had filled the skull of a bullock with some fire-sticks, fastened it to a pole, and quietly elevated it. No doubt he enjoyed immensely the sight of the skedaddle he had produced.

Aramac Items. (1881, October 28). The Western Champion (Blackall/Barcaldine, Qld.: 1879 - 1891), p. 2. Retrieved May 27, 2012, from http://nla.gov.au/nla.news-article77211828

Ernest T Drury – 27 October 1880

An Aramac telegram states that a young man named Drury shot himself in the fore-head at Coreena station yesterday, and there are no hopes of his recovery.

TELEGRAPHIC INTELLIGENCE. (1880, October 28). The Maitland Mercury & Hunter River General Advertiser (NSW: 1843 - 1893), p. 3. Retrieved April 1, 2014, from http://nla.gov.au/nla.news-article813030

A young man on Coreena station named Drury[50] deprived himself of life by putting a revolver to his forehead and sending a bullet right through his head. It appears that he had put his name to a bill, and the fact of not being able to honor it preyed upon his mind, and he eventually freed himself from earthly cares in the way mentioned. When I call it a case of suicide I write advisedly, as although the man is not dead there is no hope of his recovery.

Country News. (1880, November 6). The Queenslander (Brisbane, Qld.: 1866 - 1939), p. 603. Retrieved February 11, 2014, from http://nla.gov.au/nla.news-article20336457

Editor's Note – Ernest, 24 years old, was born in the East Indies.

STUCK UP BY A BLACKFELLOW – 29 November 1880

STUCK UP BY A BLACKFELLOW. – We (Aramac Mail) are informed that a blackfellow endeavoured to stick up a hut at Ambo, an out-station on the Mount Cornish run, one day last week. Full details are not to hand, but the particulars seem to have been as follow:– The hut, or rather tent, was occupied by a married couple, the husband had gone out into the bush, and the only person within

[50] *Qld Ref: 1880/B13810*

hearing was the cook. A blackfellow, armed with a knife, came up and importuned for "patter" or tobacco, which was refused, and the cook coming over, the two went into the hut and barricaded the door. The marauder then climbed up the wall and slit the gable, which was of calico, with his knife. There was a firearm in the hut, and upon the black-fellow endeavouring to enter by the hole he had made, the cook fired at him, but missed. Several shots were fired at the intruder, all without effect; but thinking the reception rather warm he at last decamped. It is greatly to be hoped the miscreant may be caught and punished in an exemplary manner. The native police have been removed from Mount Cornish, and if the perpetrator of this outrage should not be chastised it is probable others will be emboldened to break out and commit depredations.

The Morning Bulletin. ROCKHAMPTON. (1880, November 29). Morning Bulletin (Rockhampton, Qld.: 1878 - 1954), p. 2. Retrieved May 23, 2012, from http://nla.gov.au/nla.news-article52023084

Donald Cameron – 16 January 1881

Donald[51], a 55 year old baker, died from 'want of food and water' on Marathon an out-station of Bowen Downs. He was 5 foot 4 inches tall and identified with the following: 'Bedford cord trousers, cotton shirt, with Crimean shirt over it'. Donald was said to be well known in Brisbane as a pie-man.

Police Gazette

STATION AND STOCK – We are informed on good authority that the management of the Scottish Australian Investment Company have decided to sub-divide the Mount Cornish bullock paddock, stock it with sheep, and transfer it to the Bowen Downs station. It is calculated that the paddock, which consists of about four hundred square miles, will carry 70,000 sheep. From 30,000 to

[51] *Qld Ref: 1881/C1600*

40,000 breeding ewes will start from the Nive immediately after the shearing for Bowen Downs. 15,000 fat wethers have been sold from Bowen Downs to Mr. Pattison, of Rockhampton, to be delivered in the wool. They will start immediately. We also learn that Messrs. Rouse have disposed of their station, Culloden, to Mr. J. Govett. The price has not transpired. Mr. Govett, we regret to say, met with an unpleasant accident a few days ago. He was riding by night in the neighbourhood of Muttaburra, and came in contact with a fence, the existence of which he was not aware. He was thrown heavily to the ground and received some rather nasty cuts on the face. Fortunately no bones were broken, and he sustained no serious injury. His friends therefore need feel no uneasiness should they hear any exaggerated accounts of the occurrence.-Aramac Mail.

THE MINISTERIAL CRISIS IN VICTORIA. (1881, July 4). Morning Bulletin (Rockhampton, Qld.: 1878 - 1954), p. 2. http://nla.gov.au/nla.news-article52052963

James Quinn – 14 August 1881

SUDDEN DEATH – A man named Quinn[52], Christian name unknown, died suddenly on Sunday 14th instant, at Mr. Turnbull's camp, near Stainburn. Mr. Turnbull was taking a mob of cattle to the north of Bowen Downs. Requiring a hand he engaged Quinn on Thursday evening. On Friday Quinn spelled in the camp. On Saturday, he went to work, and seemed perfectly well. On Sunday morning Mr. Turnbull roused him to get the horses. He sat up on his blankets, and put his boots on. He fell back in an almost unconscious state, and died in about an hour. Previous to his death he asked for chlorodyne, but there was none in the camp. He also asked for a pannikin of tea, but could not drink it when it was given to him. Mr. Turnbull rode in and reported the matter to the Police Magistrate, who held the customary inquiry. *Aramac Mail.*

WESTERN MAIL NEWS. (1881, August 29). Morning Bulletin (Rockhampton, Qld.: 1878 - 1954), p. 2. http://nla.gov.au/nla.news-article52054089

---

[52] *Qld Ref: 1881/000013*

Editor's Note – James Quinn was born in Blackwater Northern Ireland. He died on the 14th August 1881 aged about 50.

Aynslie John Elliott – 9 November 1881

MARRIAGE

ELLIOT-KEANE:– On the 9th June, at St Joseph's, Rockhampton, by the Rev. Dean Murlay, Aynsley John Elliot, J. P., Langton Downs Clermont, second son of John Elliot, Esq , Benwell Lodge, Northumberland, England, to Jeannie, third daughter of Mr. John Keane, Brisbane.

Family Notices. (1873, June 25). The Brisbane Courier (Qld.: 1864 - 1933), p. 2. Retrieved June 13, 2012, from http://nla.gov.au/nla.news-article1320443

DEATH.

ELLIOT.— On the 9th November, at the Railway Hotel, Rockhampton, Aynsley John Elliot[53], late manager of Bowen Downs Station. Aged 33 years.

Family Notices. (1881, November 17). Morning Bulletin (Rockhampton, Qld.: 1878 - 1954), p. 1. Retrieved May 30, 2012, from http://nla.gov.au/nla.news-article52055757

In the Supreme Court of Queensland.
ECCLESIASTICAL JURISDICTION.

In the WILL of AYNSLEY JOHN ELLIOT, of Bowen Downs, in the Colony of Queensland, Station Manager, Deceased.

NOTICE is hereby given that, after the expiration of fourteen days from the date of publication hereof, application will be made to the said Honourable Court that PROBATE of the WILL of the above-named Aynsley John Elliot, deceased, may be granted to EDWARD ROWLAND EDKINS, of Mount Cornish, Queensland, and JOHN CAMERON, of Kensington Downs, Queensland, the Executors named in the said Will.

Dated this Fourth day of January, 1882.

J. R. BAXTER BRUCE, Proctor for the said Executors.

[53] *Qld Ref: 1881/002334*

Classified Advertising. (1882, January 7). The Brisbane Courier (Qld.: 1864 - 1933), p. 6. Retrieved June 13, 2012, from http://nla.gov.au/nla.news-article3410848

Editor's Note – Aynsley, who was born in Scotland, was the son of John Elliott and Mary Scott. He was manager for Bowen Downs from 1870 until he died in 1881. Aynsley married Jane in Rockhampton in 1873 and was the father of: Reginald Aynsley [1876], Arthur Bowen [1878-1951] and Aynsley John [1879 – 1880].

He was buried in the Rockhampton Cemetery after dying from phthisis – which is a disease characterized by the wasting away or atrophy of the body or a part of the body, or Tuberculosis of the lungs – from which he suffered for about 2 years.

Annie Augusta Butler – 19 January 1882

BUTLER.—January 19, at Bimbah Station, Aramac, Annie[54] A., dearly beloved wife of E. H. Butler, and fourth daughter, of the late Moore Neil Campbell, of Dubbo, and deeply regretted daughter-in-law of Mrs. Butler, Glebe Point.

Family Notices. (1882, February 11). The Sydney Morning Herald (NSW: 1842 - 1954), p. 1. Retrieved March 31, 2014, from http://nla.gov.au/nla.news-article13504950

Editor's Note – Annie Augusta Butler the wife of Edmund Henry Butler died just a few months after giving birth to her daughter Fanny Marion. Annie was the daughter of Moore Neil Campbell and Fanny Deliste. It is not known where she is buried but it is likely to be Bimbah.

Edmund and Annie had two children: Edmund Campbell born 25 July 1880 and Fanny Marion[55] who was born on 4th November 1881 and died on 29 March 1882. Edmund was at one stage an overseer at Bowen Downs and helped track down the cattle that were stolen by Harry Readford.

Edmund remarried Catherine Esther Crorin and they had four children: Thomas John born 29 December 1886, Henry Edmund born 8 April 1887, twins Norman Patrick Pierce and Frances Catherine born 8 March 1889

[54] *Qld Ref: 1882/C5*
[55] *Qld Ref: 1882/C9*

Unknown Grave at Tuaburra

Photo: Judith McClymont

Infant [Female] Cain – 24 February 1882

Female Cain[56], born on the 24th February 1882 and died the same day after only living for 7 hours, was the daughter of John Cain and Rebecca Bailey. The Cains were at Ambo an out-station of Mt Cornish and at the time, John Cain was a horse driver. John and Rebecca also had three other children: John – 30th December 1879, Elsia – 29th September 1883 and Ellen Maud – 31 August 1885.

Police Gazette

[56] *Qld Ref: 1882/C2119*

Margaret Alice Harrison – 11 April 1882

Margaret Alice Harrison[57] the daughter of Thomas Bentley Harrison and Annie Frances Pearce was born on the 23 January 1882 and died of convulsions on the 11 April 1882. She was the sister of William Edward – 10 April 1880 – 14 January 1906, Thomas John Leslie – 7 October 1885, Lindsay – 1 July 1889. Margaret died at Ambo.

Police Gazette

Billy The Cook – 25 July 1882

[Extract: Aramac] A man whose name we (Mail) have not been able to ascertain, but who for some time was engaged as cook at Mr. W. Clapton's Albion Hotel, Aramac, has been found dead on Bangall Creek, between Muttaburra and Kensington Downs. The only name be was known by here was 'Billy[58] the Cook.'

WESTERN MAIL NEWS. (1882, July 15). The Capricornian (Rockhampton, Qld.: 1875 - 1929), p. 6. Retrieved June 25, 2014, from http://nla.gov.au/nla.news-article71986408

Editor's Note – Billy was born in the Solomon Islands, and was aged about 25 years. In Qld BDM, he is registered a Bill Billy. He was buried where he died on Bangall Creek west of Muttaburra.

Martin Schaumbach – September 1882

FOUND DEAD.-The body of a roan was found last week by some of the station black boys near Bimbah, on Mount Cornish run. When discovered it was hanging by a bridle rein to the limb of a tree, showing beyond doubt that deceased had put an end to his own existence. The body was in an advanced stage of decay, both the arms having dropped off. It has, however been identified as that of one Martin Schaumbach[59], who had formerly been cooking on

---

[57] *Qld Ref: 1882/C2127*
[58] *Qld Ref: 1882/C1838*
[59] *Qld Ref: 1882/C22*

Mount Cornish. In February last he was in Aramac and drinking heavily. He then went to Muttaburra and continued in the same course. After leaving the latter place he does not seem to have been seen alive by any person. His saddle, however, and horse had been found at no very great distance from the spot where his body has just been discovered. The suicide was a particularly determined one. The bough from which the body was found suspended was so low that both the feet were resting on the ground. Schaumhnch must therefore have deliberately refrained from allowing his weight to bear on them until insensibility had supervened. A magisterial inquiry was held on Monday in Muttaburra, and the proceedings forwarded to the Attorney-General. - Aramac Mail.

Local and General News. (1882, September 15). The Western Champion (Blackall/Barcaldine, Qld.: 1879 - 1891), p. 2. Retrieved March 31, 2014, from http://nla.gov.au/nla.news-article77212785

Editor's Note – Martin Schaumhnch was a bushman. E H Butler the manager of Bimbah reported finding his body at Brutus Lagoon, Bimbah and registered his death on the 25 September 1882 in Aramac. He was buried where he was found.

John Cann – 12 April 1883

John Cann[60], an old and respected resident of Tablederry, near Muttaburra, was drowned on Thursday. The deceased was getting water at the dam when he overbalanced himself and fell in the water. The funeral yesterday was largely attended.

COLONIAL AND INTERCOLONIAL. FROM OUR SPECIAL CORRESPONDENTS. (1883, April 20). The Western Champion (Blackall/Barcaldine, Qld.: 1879 - 1891), p. 2. Retrieved May 7, 2012, from http://nla.gov.au/nla.news-article77213341

Editor's Note – Tablederry was an out-station of Mt Cornish.
John married Anne Agnes Holman at St Pancras Church London 28th July 1842. They lived in Blackwood Victoria until about 1864. Children:

John Kennedy Cann born 14 August 1843, christened St Pancras Church London. Hotelier and Cobb & Co Stage Coach operator in Blackwood Victoria. Married Rebecca Olivia May Perry 26 March 1869 in Richmond Vic. Died 11

[60] *Qld Ref: 1883/002467*

February 1894; William Henry Walter Cann born 31 August 1845, christened St Pancras Church London. Butcher in Muttaburra. Married Janet Mather 13 March 1879 Qld. Children: Jessie Agnes Mary born 12 Oct 1882 Qld. He died in 1920 in Queensland; Jane Mary Cann born 22 Nov 1847, christened St Pancras Church London. Married George Smith on the 14 April 1869 at Goulburn NSW.

Anne Adelaide Cann born North Adelaide 3 Sept 1850, registered City of Adelaide. Married Thomas Connors in September at Goulburn NSW.

Mary Charlotte Cann born Richmond North Melbourne 11 March 1854, registered City of Melbourne. Married Oswin James Hall 3 May 1876 in Muttaburra Qld. [Source: Frances Dillon].

Their second son William Henry Walter Cann is buried in Queensland. He was a butcher in Muttaburra and married in to Janet Mather. They were the reason that Ann and John senior travelled north after retirement in Vic.

[Source: Robert Holman]

John Cann's Headstone– 12 April 1883

Old Muttaburra Cemetery

Photo: Betty Wakley-Bunkell Domain Name Trust

Archibald Drummond Graham – 2 June 1883

DEATHS.

Graham – On the 2nd June, at Bowen Downs (in consequence of injuries sustained through a fall from his horse), Archibald Drummond, eldest and beloved son of the Hon. William Graham M.L.C, Highlands, Brisbane, aged 18

The Brisbane Courier (Qld.: 1864 - 1933) 7 Jun 1883: http://nla.gov.au/nla.news-article3418824>.

Editor's Note – Archibald Drummond Graham [61] was the 18 year old son of William Graham and Louisa Elizabeth Turner born on 7 September 1864. He was the eldest child having 5 siblings: Annie Hope born on the 9 February 1866 – died within twelve months on the 21 December 1866; William Edward, born on the 13 May 1867, his second brother Charles on 26 August 1868 and other brother Austen Douglas on the 15 September 1869; Mary his second sister was born on the 23 January 1872, his youngest brother John on the 1 May 1874 youngest sister Katherine on 1 March 1876. Archibald is buried at Tuaburra an out-station of Bowen Downs, where a headstone marks his grave.

Archibald Drummond Graham – Tuaburra Cemetery

Photo Judith McClymont

61 *Qld Ref: 1864/000106 & Qld Ref: 1883/00013*

[Extract] As we approach the outstation of Tuaburra, I perceive a tomb enclosed with a neat iron railing. Mr. Fraser states that a young friend named Archibald Graham came up to the station to gain experience. About eighteen months after, he was galloping after a mob of horses when he came into a violent collision with a horse that was on the outside of the mob. Poor Graham fell with the horse and fractured the base of his skull. The tomb was sent up by his parents and erected under the supervision of Mr. Fraser. The overseers attend to the grave, exercising much care in keeping it free from weeds and in painting the railings.

THE CENTRAL WEST. (1898, November 14). Morning Bulletin (Rockhampton, Qld.: 1878 - 1954), p. 6. Retrieved June 2, 2012, from http://nla.gov.au/nla.news-article52542099

Robert Rattray – 17 September 1883

Robert Rattray[62] the 23 year old son of Henry Rattray and Euphemia Giffin died from internal injuries, on the 17 September 1883 at Ambo the Mt Cornish Out-station.

Police Gazette

Jeremiah Faleny – 14 October 1883

Jeremiah[63] was born in County Cork, Ireland and was about 47 years old when he died on the 14 October 1883, from inflammation at Mount Cornish. As he died at Mount Cornish, he was also buried there the same day.

Frederick John Clarence Kennedy – 4 December 1883

KENNEDY. -On the 4th December, at Scarrbury after a few hours illness, Fredric John Clarence, third dearly-loved son of John and

[62] *Qld Ref: 1883/002468*

[63] *Qld Ref: 1883/000019*

Frances Kennedy, aged 7 years and 11 months. Nipped in the bud of promise to bloom in realms of bliss.

Family Notices. (1883, December 21). The Brisbane Courier (Qld.: 1864 - 1933), p. 1. Retrieved September 21, 2014, from http://nla.gov.au/nla.news-article3425238

Frederick[64], the son of John Kennedy and Frances Mary Hall Wilson was born on the 2 January 1876 at Kensington Downs and died on the 7 March 1883 just 7 years later from a 'brain fever' or as we know today as 'heat exhaustion'. Frederick died at Scarrbury where his father was a store keeper, mail contractor as well as a grazier. Frederick was buried at Scarrbury.

Editor's Note – John and Frances had nine other children: Charles Edward William – 15 October 1870; Alexander George – 21 December 1872; Frederick John Wildash – 18 June 1874 – 7 March 1875; Maria Frances Maude – 14 November 1878; Ada Jessie May – 13 May 1881; Jessie Violet Marion – 8 May 1883; Frank Gilbert Wilson – 19 April 1885; Neville Claude Mervyn – 10 December 1887; John Rupert Wilford – 17 April 1891.

Lankey Daley – December 1883

We regret to learn that a man named Daley is supposed to have been lost on Bowen Downs run. The dog poisoner at Bowen Downs discovered a swag near Sandy Creek, between Reedy Creek and Aramac. On examination, this was found to contain a pocket book, with memos of sheep tallies for washing, and the name Lankey Daley, also a memo about some shearers' names. The swag appeared to have been lying for some time in the bush. From these indications it seems probable that the lost man is one Daley, who had been employed at Reedy Creek, the Bowen Downs overseer's station, and also at the Bowen Downs washpool. It would appear that Daley had been endeavouring to make his way through the bush to Reedy Creek, and perished for want of water. When he began to succumb to heat, thirst, and fatigue, he would naturally

[64] *Qld Ref: 1875/000002*

leave his swag, in the hopes of getting through with his life. The absence of the body is easily accounted for. A constable came from Aramac on Wednesday to assist in the search, but it is almost certain that the unfortunate man has been added to the long list of those who have perished in the bush. – Mitchell Mail

Reuter's Cablegrams. (1883, December 19). The Northern Miner (Charters Towers, Qld.: 1874 - 1954), p. 2. Retrieved May 4, 2012, from http://nla.gov.au/nla.news-article77189116

Captain Brown – Early 1884

An elderly man, well-known in this district as Captain Brown (says the Mail), and who had not been heard of for some time, has met with his death in the bush. The body was found by some blacks in one of the Bowen Downs paddocks, and was reported by them to the manager, Mr. S. P. Fraser. He immediately went out with a party to do what might be necessary. On examining the corpse Mr. Fraser couldn't discover no signs of foul play. The pockets contained a silver watch, some papers, and 3s. 6d. in silver. There being no suspicious circumstances; Mr. Fraser had the body interred at once. He considers that death must have occurred at least two months ago. There have been no sheep in the paddock for a longer period, and no boundary rider, which accounts for the corpse not having been discovered previously. Deceased was carrying his swag, and appears to have endeavoured to make his way from Stainburn to Bowen Downs. How he came to leave the road can only be a matter for conjecture. Probably he did as so many others have done; finding himself thirsty, he left the road to look for water and perished. Deceased was about sixty-five years old at the time of his death.

WESTERN MAIL NEWS. (1884, March 19). Morning Bulletin (Rockhampton, Qld.: 1878 - 1954), p. 2. Retrieved May 31, 2012, from http://nla.gov.au/nla.news-article52030351

Editors Notes – Maybe Captain Brown is George Brown – 14 January 1884. George Brown[65], was a 60 year old Salomon Islander who stood 6 foot 1 inch tall and died

---

[65] *Qld Ref: 1884/00009*

on Bowen Downs during January 1884, due to thirst. There is a question of the exact date but it may be the 14th January 1884.

John Harting – 12 May 1884

It is reported to the Mail that a man named John Halting[66], a German, died at Bowen Downs last Sunday, the cause being assigned as heart disease, aggravated by over exertion, deceased being a hard-working man. The man owned a dray, five draught horses, a saddle horse, and had money in the Q. N. Bank at Muttaburra. Deceased left no will, and after an examination the body was ordered to be interred.

Another case of sudden death occurred on Monday last, at Lenehan's dairy, on the road to Muttaburra. Deceased, whose name was Duncan Warren[67], had lately been in the Aramac hospital for a fortnight suffering from fever, and after leaving that institution he left Aramac with the intention of getting work in connection with some sheep from Saltern Creek, which were camped on the road to Muttaburra. Drink was stated to be the chief cause of the man's death, his age was about 32 years, and he was believed to have hailed from Ipswich.

"Aramac Jottings." The Western Champion (Blackall/Barcaldine, Qld.: 1879 - 1891) 30 May 1884: 2. <http://nla.gov.au/nla.news-article79726991>.

Editor's Note – Duncan Warren was the son of William Warren and Euphemia Mackenzie and died on the 12 May 1884

Michael Keating – 20 December 1884

Queensland Death Certificate — Registration Number 1886/2127.
Died about 20 December 1884. Near Stainburn Downs

---

66 *Qld Ref: 1884/000017*

67 *Qld Ref: 1884/000014*

Michael Keating[68], Shearer, male

Cause: Supposed delirium tremens. Lost in bush, left swag at water, body found about 1 mile from there.

Parents: Michael Keating, farmer, Bridget Keating

Informant: James Looker, Grazier, Stainburn Downs

Registration of Death: Edmund F. Craven, January 11 1886, Aramac.

Burial: 9 January 1886, Stainburn, certified by John Connor

Witnesses to burial: J. Looker, P. Gleeson

Where born: Kilbaha, County Clare, Ireland. 20 years in Queensland.

Married: Toowoomba, Queensland, aged 23, to Sophy Sara Elizabeth Wilks.

Issue: William George, 6 years; Catherine Eleanor, 5 years.

Other information: 1886 Deaths in the District of Aramac in the Colony of Queensland. Registered by Edmund F. Craven.

Description: Height about 5 ft 11 in; Frame large; Stout build; Hair, Beard, Moustache – light sandy colour; Good set teeth; No marks violence; Body not decomposed but dried like a mummy. Eyes and ears eaten away. E F. Craven

Since identified as Michael Keating. EFC

Editor's Note – The above is as taken form his death certificate. Michael's wife was Sophia Sarah Elizabeth Wilkes.

Source: Dotti Kemp, Taringa – dottikemp@bigppond.com

Robert Roberts – 28 December 1884

Robert Roberts[69] a South Sea Islander died on Bowen Downs on the 28 December 1884 and was buricd were he died. His grave site is unknown.

68 *Qld Ref: 1886/C2*

69 *Qld Ref: 1885/C3*

Patrick Dowling – 23 February 1885

Patrick Dowling[70] the son of John Dowling and Bridget Walsh, died on the 23 February 1885 from a fever and dysentry from which he had suffered for a month on Bradley's Creek. He was 26 years old labourer. He was buried at Bradleys Creek the same day he died by J Smith.

Patrick was born in Dublin, Ireland and had been in Australia for about 11 years. Patrick was married to Angus Boyle in Rockhampton in 1884. Angus lived in Muttaburra.

Qld BDM – Death Certificate

Ann Gilbert Coaton – 2 April 1885

Ann Coaton,[71] the daughter of Nathaniel Gilbert and Emma Gilbert King, was born in Leicestershire England. She came to Australia when she was about 3 years old and had been in Queensland only 19 months. She was 33 years old when she died from Typhoid fever at Mount Cornish where she is buried. She was married to James Edwin Coaton and the mother of Annie, born on the 30 December 1884 and died less than twelve months later on the 15 October 1885.

Arthur Healy – 15 April 1885

Arthur Healy[72], the son of Michael Joseph Healy and Mary Theresa Boyle, died from croup, on the 15 April 1885. He was the brother of Mary Ann – [1881]. It was just three months later that his mother, aged 24 years, Theresa Boyle, born in Ireland, daughter of Michael Boyle and Ann died from Enteric fever, on 6 July 1885. Theresa is buried in the Muttaburra Cemetery in an unknown grave

[70] *Qld Ref: 1885/003253*
[71] *Qld Ref: 1885/000014*
[72] *Qld Ref: 1885/003266*

site. The address where Arthur died, was Bangall Creek an out-station of Mt Cornish.

Henry Joseph Bender – 1 June 1885

Henry Joseph Bender[73], the son of Henry Bender and Mary Kehone [Keohane, Keone, Kehoane], was born on the 12 August 1884 and died 9 months later on the 1 June 1885. He was the middle child between Mary Clare – 2 February 1883 and Ellen – 19 June 1886. Henry died at Scarrbury and it seems he is buried there.

Unknown – July 1885
Died from Want of Water.

Brisbane, Tuesday.

THE following telegram was received from the police at Blackall by the Commissioner for Police:- Senior-constable Sinnott, Aramac, reports that Hugh Lomond, a dog poisoner, found the dead body of a white man about nine miles from Eastmore Station, on the Clermont and Bowen Downs road. The body which was much dried up, and without clothing, appeared to have been dead for eight months. No clothing, except his boots, was found near the body. Nothing is known of him, and he is supposed to be a traveller who had died through want of water. The body was buried by order of Mr. C. A. Bowles, J.P.

MAIL NEWS. (1885, July 28). The Brisbane Courier (Qld.: 1864 - 1933), p. 5. Retrieved March 25, 2014, from http://nla.gov.au/nla.news-article3445260

[73] *Qld Ref: 1885/C18*

Jessie Mary Lloyd – 20 September 1885

Jessie Mary Lloyd[74] was the second child of Richard Carre Lloyd and Isabella Smith who married on the 11 July 1871. Jessie was born on the 20 March 1874, and died on the 20 September 1885. Jessie was the sister of Harriet, Nina – 1880, Marjory – 1883, Llewellyn – 1886 – 1886, Owen – 1888, Ada – 1888-1913, Brian – 1891, Russell – 1896. Her parents ran "Blue Gate Dairy" just north of the Muttaburra Township, but would contract to Mt Cornish for such jobs as fencing.

At the time of the tragedy, Jessie was only 11 years of age and her father was working as a teamster between Bowen and Muttaburra. During the off season (wet season), Mr Roland Edkins on the Mount Cornish Run employed the Lloyds.

Jessie Mary Lloyd – 20 September 1885

Photo: Betty Wakley-Bunkell Domain Name Trust

An extract from the Journal of Mrs Edwina Edkins who lived at Mt Cornish from 1872 until 1905 tells of – 'the very sad incident' –

"*Mr Richard Lloyd one of Mr. Edkins' contractors for fencing was camped out with his family on the Ambo out-station, west of the Thomson River. One of his little girls was badly burned by their campfire and the poor mother knowing that she was in great danger, sent to Mr Edkins for help. Harriet, her eldest*

[74] *Qld Ref: 1885/C3293*

daughter, then 13 years of age and quite a girl, jumped onto a horse with a man's saddle and rode at a great pace reaching Mount Cornish homestead on Sunday afternoon. After hearing her sad story Mr Edkins made all haste with buggy and horses but alas! When he reached the camp, little Jessie was already dead." "Harriet Lloyd was known in the district as a brave girl – she on one occasion swam the river with the mail in a heavy flood when men were afraid to face it".

This lonely gravesite at 'No Name Creek' at Ambo, out on the western downs country, miles from any habitation personifies the courage and fortitude shown by the early pioneers of the outback – forging a new life in a daunting land.

Mary White – 26 November 1885

Mary White[75], born on 21 November 1885 and died at the age of just 6 days old, on the 26 November 1885, was the daughter of Thomas White and Catherine Redmond. Thomas was the care-taker at Bradley's Creek, an out-station of Mount Cornish, where she died. Mary was the youngest sister of Thomas – [died 1874], James – [1874], Thomas – [1874] [triplets], Emily – [1878], William – [1880], Anne Catherine – [1883].

Yee Ung – 17 December 1885

Ung[76], born in Canton China, had lived 10 years in Queensland before he died in Muttaburra. He was the gardener at Mt Cornish and died from Laryngeal. He was buried in the Muttaburra Cemetery but the actual grave site is unknown.

[75] *Qld Ref: 1885/003303*
[76] *Qld Ref: 1885/000027*

William Landsborough – 16 March 1886

DEATH OF MR. W. LANDSBOROUGH.

A brief telegram sent us from Caloundra yesterday evening announces the death of Mr. William Landsborough[77], one of our oldest pioneer squatters, and an explorer whose name will always be connected with the story of the opening up of this great continent. Mr Landsborough was a son of the Rev Dr Landsborough, of Saltcoats, Scotland, a naturalist of some renown. His two elder brothers preceded him to Australia, and they having engaged in squatting pursuits in the New England district. He also, on arrival in New South Wales at an early age, took up country in the same district. The run proved unsuitable for sheep, and he was obliged to abandon it, taking employment on sheep and cattle stations until the discovery of gold, when for a time he turned digger. In this pursuit he had sufficient success to enable him in 1853 to take up Country on the Kolan, which was then a frontier station. In 1856 his explorations northward resulted in the discovery of Glen Prairie, Fort Cooper, and Oxford Downs; he subsequently found some of the finest pastoral country on the heads of the Thompson, and traced the Gregory and Lower Herbert (now the Georgina) Rivers to their sources, but owing to bad times in 1860 he lost the whole of his interest in several now well-known stations. Early in 1862 he started on his expedition in search of Burke and Wills, and from the Albert River on the Gulf of Carpentaria succeeded in reaching Melbourne. This journey occupied nine months, and it was quite thought he had been lost. On his arrival he received a public welcome from the Victorian colonists, and the Governor of the colony presented him with a service of plate worth £500, and a most flattering address. He was honoured with a public dinner in Sydney, and a congratulatory address was presented to him by Sir George Bowen in Brisbane. He married in Sydney the sixth daughter of Captain Rennie, and

77 *Qld Ref: 1886/000532*

afterwards visited India, the Continent, and England. The Royal Geographical Society presented him with a gold watch "for finding a practicable route in Australia from north to south". After two years absence he returned to Queensland, and sat for one session as a member of the Legislative Council, in 1865. Later in the same year he received the appointment of police-magistrate, with other Government appointments, for the district of Burke; but before settling down he did a good deal of exploring with the aid of Mr. George Phillips, surveyor, and his accurate estimates of the quality of the land did much towards facilitating its occupation. He remained in the Burke till 1871, when, after surveying the present road from Cunnamulla to St George, he once more took to mining, this time on the tin mines at Stanthorpe. In June, 1872, he was appointed inspector of brands in the Moreton District, and held the office up to the time of his death. In consideration of the distinguished service he had rendered to the colony Parliament a few years ago voted Mr Landsborough a sum of £2000 with which he took up a large selection at Caloundra, where, in a beautiful situation on the Bribie Passage, within sight of the ocean, the old explorer has of late years spent all the time he could spare from his official duties. His death will be a surprise to most people, as his appearance was always that of robust health, and, though well advanced in years, he had by no means the appearance of extreme age. Mrs Landsborough died in Sydney some years ago from illness contracted during their residence at Burketown, but a large family remain to mourn the loss of a father whose name will always be remembered with honour as one of the bravest of our early explorers.

DEATH OF MR. W. LANDSBOROUGH. (1886, March 17). The Brisbane Courier (Qld. : 1864 - 1933), p. 5. Retrieved April 27, 2012, from http://nla.gov.au/nla.news-article4483987

Editor's Note – Landsborough was a founding owner of Bowen Downs as in the early 1860 he selected about 36 or so blocks that made up the initial Landsborough's Run. Later in life, he bought Loch Lamerough that was his pastoral property at Caloundra where he died on the 16 March 1886 and was buried there. But 1913, his widow, and second wife, Maria Theresa Carter, who he married in 1873, had him reburied at Toowong Cemetery – Portion 12, Section 55, Grave Number 3. Maria is also buried alongside him when she died in November 1921.

Landsborough was survived by three daughters and three sons. His first wife Caroline Hollingworth Raine died of tuberculosis.

Kanaka Billey – 11 September 1886

Billey[78], a 25 years old South Sea Islander had been in Queensland for about 6 years when he was killed on the 11 September 1886 from a fall from his horse. He was a station hand at Mount Cornish which is where he is buried. Mount Cornish, like many of the stations at this time had numerous South Sea Islanders working for them as labour was scarce during the 1880s.

Llewellyn Lloyd – 27 November 1886

Llewellyn Lloyd[79], born on the 25 November 1886, the child of Richard Carre Lloyd and Isabella, died when he was just 2 days old on the 27 November 1886. His parents were camped on the Thomson River not far from the present day Longreach. (See Jessie Mary Lloyd)

Lydia Mary Bailey – 24 January 1887

Lydia Bailey[80], the daughter of Samuel Bailey and Elizabeth Mary Hitchman, was born at Mt Cornish on the 24 January 1887. She died just 26 days later on the 18 February 1887. Lydia was the eldest sister of Annie Mary – [1888-1898], Lydia Deborah – [1890], Ada – [1891], Elizabeth – [1893-1903], George Henry – [1895], Kate –

78 *Qld Ref 1886/000035*
79 *Qld Ref: 1887/000002 & 1887/000003*
80 *Qld Ref: 1887/C10*

[1897], Samuel William – [1900] and Edward – [1902]. E. R. Edkins and Phoebe Peters buried her at Mount Cornish.

Western Roads – 9 October 1885

WESTERN ROADS.

The following information respecting the water and camps on Western Roads in Central District cannot fail to be of use to travellers, and especially to persons in charge of stock :—

	Miles.
Jericho to Springs, Cobb's Camp	22
Springs to Range Dam—Fisher's	15
Fisher's to Aramac Creek	23
Fisher's to Aramac Town	12
Aramac to Rainburn	13
Rainburn to Reynold's Tank	11
Tank to Sardine Creek	9
Creek to Griffith's Bore	8
Bore to Thompson River, Muttaburra ...	12
Muttaburra to Bangall Creek	6
Creek to Government Dam, Kensington...	17
Government Dam to Bradley's Creek ...	16
Creek to the Darr	18
Darr to Harriet's Creek	15
Creek to Old Vindex	20
Old Vindex to Policeman W.H.	9
W.H. to Winton	8
Aramac to Camoola, water all the way ..	50
Camoola to Cattle Creek	18
Cattle Creek to East Darr...	12
Darr to Kelly's Creek	18
Kelly's Creek to Grass Hut	16
Grass Hut to 8 Mile Bore	8
Bore to Crawford's Creek	15
Crawford's Creek to Old Vindex	10
Old Vindex to Police W.H.	9
Green Tree to Springer's, Alice River ...	10
Springer's to Dixon's	7
Dixon's to Box Flat Springs	18
Box Flat to Friendly Springs	19
Friendly Springs to Stake Yard, Aramac Creek	14
Stake Yard to Township	10
Barcaldine Head Station to Saltern Creek Station Dam	25
From Dam to Coreena Shed, Aramac Creek	24
Shed to Stake Yard	10
Stake Yard to Aramac	10
Aramac to Sheep Station Creek	24
Sheep Station Creek to Rodney Downs...	6
Downs to Beaconsfield	22
Beaconsfield to Rimbah	18
Thence down the Thompson River to Westlands. Water all the way. Westlands to Isisford. Good water about every seven miles, excepting one stage of fifteen miles	65
Isisford to Hughenden, via Muttaburra. Same track as above to Rimbah. Thence up the Thompson River and Landsborough River, via Tower Hill, to Hughenden. Muttaburra to Mount Cornish	9
Mount Cornish to Station Dam	3
Station Dam to Station Dam	4
Dam to Washpool, Cornish Creek ...	14
Washpool to Bowen Downs Shed ...	4
Shed to Bowen Downs	4
Scarbury to Billabong, Thompson River	13
Thence up the River to Muttaburra. Water all the way. Bowen Downs by Reedy Creek, 36 miles. Water all the way...	36

After leaving Reedy Creek very little water is met until reaching the Belyando.

WESTERN ROADS. (1885, October 9). Morning Bulletin (Rockhampton, Qld.: 1878 - 1954), p. 6. Retrieved May 4, 2012, from http://nla.gov.au/nla.news-article52042620

John Barry – 27 January 1887

The senior-constable at Muttaburra reports to the Commissioner of Police that a young man named John Barry[81], twenty-four years of age, died suddenly at Bowen Downs from sun stroke on the 27th January.

MINING NOTES. (1887, February 5). The Capricornian (Rockhampton, Qld: 1875 - 1929), p. 11. http://nla.gov.au/nla.news-article65742554

THE following news is from the Western Champion of Saturday:– On Wednesday the 26th ultimo, a young man named John Barry, aged twenty-one years, who had been doing some repairs to a dam, was smitten with sun-stroke on the road between the head station at Bowen Downs and the washpool. He died about three hours after being taken ill.

THE GARDEN AND THE FIELD. (1887, February 14). Morning Bulletin (Rockhampton, Qld.: 1878 - 1954), p. 5. http://nla.gov.au/nla.news-article52068317

Editor's Note – When John died he had £7 19s 9d to his name which for a 24 year, old labourer, was probably a reasonable amount.

Bowen Downs – 30 August 1887

Bowen Downs. – A correspondent writes under date, 16th August:– shearing is progressing satisfactorily; the wool going away as shorn. 1,450 bales of greasy, and 101 bales of second class having been despatched up to the present time. About 140,000 sheep have been shorn up to to-night. The whole clip is turning our beautifully clean, perfectly free of all seed, and sound and strong. The Rev. G. L. Lester held service here yesterday week. The Munroes and Mrs. and Mr Chapman gave entertainments in the large wool room here last Thursday, Friday, and drew large houses. Nearly 100 attended every night. We had 80 points of rain last Wednesday afternoon and night; it had all the appearances of general rain. There was a bush fire on the run at Crusoe out-station, 25 miles from head station.

[81] *Qld Ref: 1887/C7*

Fortunately only about one dozen sheep got burned, but fully one hundred others were singed, which we consider a let off as there were about 30,000 shorn sheep in the paddock. Mr. Frazer had long back taken the usual precautions of burning patches all over this huge run. We hope to soon have more rain to put green feed in all the burnt country, which would make the sheep safe. Of course, the late rain will do this to a small degree. We anticipate finishing shearing by the end of the month, as we are shearing at the rate of nearly 6000 per diem, or say fully 33,000 per week.

Local and General News. (1887, August 30). The Western Champion (Blackall/Barcaldine, Qld.: 1879 - 1891), p. 2. Retrieved June 6, 2012, from http://nla.gov.au/nla.news-article79730173

George Willis – 7 March 1888

The police have received information from Muttaburra that a man, name unknown, was drowned at Bowen Downs station on Thursday while crossing a creek which was flooded. The police are searching for the body.

The Brisbane Courier. (1888, March 12). The Brisbane Courier (Qld.: 1864 - 1933), p. 4. http://nla.gov.au/nla.news-article3469864

Inquest of George Willis

Court House
Muttaburra
March 12th 1888

Present
J Hamilton Scott P. M.
Magisterial enquiry held touching the death of George Willis[82] at Cornish Creek near Bowen Downs on 7th.
This deponent on oath saith:
My name is Daniel Maker I am a horse driver residing at Bowen Downs I know deceased George Willis by appearance only.

[82] *Qld Ref: 1888/000017*

We were both working in the morning of the 7th inst. deceased came to me for a loan of a horse to go and look for his horses which were across the creek which was in flood.

We were camped at the travellers hut on Bowen Downs head station.

I said can you swim, he said no, I said don't cross this horse as he is pretty rowdy, he said he was going to get a black boy to cross the creek and he would wait on this side. This was about 7 a.m.

He did not turn up to the station at 2 p.m. so I got a horse and rode to look for him. I rode along the creek and could see no sign of him that evening so I came back next morning. I saw the boundary rider bringing in my horse with no bridle on.
I found the tracks of the horse where he went into the creek and must have turned back I found the bridle half a mile from the creek on the road back. I searched all that day for the body but could not find it. I got the blacksmith to make a drag but could not find the body.

Deceased was a single man 19 or 20 years of age his height was bout 5ft 7 or 8 inches, light hair no beard but very slight moustache; he had a white flannel shirt and moleskins trousers and elastic side boots.

Deceased had two horses a riding saddle and pack saddle and some money; I don't know how much.
This is all I know about the matter

Sgn Dan Maher

Taken and sworn before me at Muttaburra March 12th 1888

Court House
Muttaburra
March 16th 1888

Present
J Hamilton Scott P. M.
Magisterial enquiry held touching the death of George Willis.

This deponent on oath saith: My name is John Herbert Rait; I am a sheep hand residing at Crusoe; I did not know deceased George Willis. On the morning of Friday 9th inst I rode out with Cameron the horse-breaker at Bowen Downs and a black boy to look for his body.

We took the boat at Bowen Downs where it had been left by those who had been looking for the body previously, we went half a mile down the creek in the boat; out attention was called to the body by the black boy.

The body was lying across a log with the face down in the water we then sent the boy to get the spring cart from the station but on second consideration we changed our mind and decided not to shift the body till the police came next day.

The body was found about half a mile down the creek from the stud paddock fence about 2 miles from the Bowen Downs Station.

The body was dressed in a pair of moleskins trousers and what looked like a white flannel shirt and boots.

Sgn John H Rait

Taken and sworn before me at Muttaburra

March 16th 1888 J Hamilton Scott P. M.

Court House
Muttaburra
March 20th 1888

Present

J Hamilton Scott P. M.

Magisterial enquiry held touching the death of George Willis

This deponent on oath saith:

My name is William Quilter; I am a police constable stationed at Muttaburra; I did not know the deceased George Willis; I remember 9th inst I went to look for the body of a man named George Willis reported to be drowned. The body had been found when I got there by Mr. Cameron and a black boy.

I was shown the body by a man named John Ph…… and another whose name I do not know; the body was in the creek (Cornish Creek); it was on a lot of rubbish; was face downwards; it was dressed in moleskins trousers, white flannel shirt and elastic side boots.

We removed the body to land and I examined it and found no marks of violence; the face was disfigured by being in the water for so long; the man's height was bout 5ft 8in fair hair moustache only.

We buried the body about half a mile from where it was found about three miles from the Bowen Downs head Station.

I searched the body and found two pounds two shillings. I brought it in and handed it to the Senior Constable who is agent for the curator of intestate estates.

Sgn William Quilter

Taken and sworn before me at Muttaburra

March 20th 1888 Sgt Hamilton Scott P. M.

Editor's Note – Elastic Side Boots – There are several Australian companies manufacturing boots – Blundstone (perhaps the original dating back to 1870), Rossi Boots (established in 1910 and still manufactured in Australia) and R. M. Williams.

http://en.wikipedia.org/wiki/Australian_work_boot

James Morgan – 12 July 1888

The Late Fatal Accident – In reference to the unfortunate occurrence which resulted in the death of an old man last week, the magistrate holding the inquest received a letter from Mr. E R Edkins, of Mount Cornish, in which the following additional particulars are contained concerning the deceased. His name was James Morgan[83], and he had been in the service of the owners of

[83] *Qld Ref: 1888/000080*

Mount Cornish for the last 20 years. He was 65 years of age. On the 9th of this month the deceased cashed in Muttaburra an order on the station for £21, and two days afterwards he received a cheque for £15 18s. 1d., the balance wages due to him. He then stated to be was going to Rockhampton, and informed some people that he had sent his money on to that place. On the next day when he was killed only seven pounds was found upon deceased. He was supposed to have some money in the bank, and had made a will leaving his property to his sister, a resident in London. The inquiry was closed on Saturday, and the depositions forwarded to the Attorney-General.

Local and General News. (1888, July 24). The Western Champion (Blackall/Barcaldine, Qld.: 1879 - 1891), p. 2. Retrieved May 27, 2012, from http://nla.gov.au/nla.news-article79709291

Killed by a Coach

Killed by a Coach. — On Thursday evening at about 8 p.m. as the Aramac coach was entering Barcaldine, the driver, Walter Smith, discovered that he had lost his only passenger from the inside of the coach. He delivered the mails without loss of time, and immediately informed Mr. Webster (Cobb's agent) of what bad occurred. It was at once surmised that the passenger, who had been intoxicated, had fallen out of the coach and had met with a serious accident. The matter was at once reported to the police, but Sergeant Livingstone, for the reason probably that he had no horses in the paddock, said that nothing could be done until the morning. Mr. Webster, however, got a spring cart and started, Mr. Dixson, driver of the Blackall coach, driving the cart, and Mr. Smith riding a saddle horse. Before leaving the yard, constable Carmody came down and said if Cobb & Go. would provide a horse he had instructions from the Sergeant to help in the search. After proceeding about four miles on the Aramac road, the party found the man of whom they were in search. It was a very cold night, and the poor fellow was lying on the track covered with blood, and naked from his waist up wards. His leg was broken, his chin cut and bruised, and all the skin peeled off his chest, as if he had been dragged for some distance. About 160 yards away the police picked up his shirts and coat rolled together as if they had been dragged over his head, he was conscious when the party reached him, and said he would be right if he had a blanket. The men lifted him into the spring cart, and Mr. Webster and constable Carmody taking off their coats made him us comfortable as possible. He was brought into town at 10 o'clock, and taken to Dr. Willis' surgery, and from there to the hospital, where, not with standing that the Doctor did all he could to restore animation, the unfortunate man died within half-an-hour. Death was caused by shock to the system, accelerated by excessive loss of blood and exposure to the cold. At a magisterial inquiry held on Saturday before Mr. Campbell, the above facts were elicited. Deceased booked at Muttaburra by the name of Morgan; he was drinking frequently on the road, and brought a bottle of whisky with him from Aramac, which he refused to give up to the driver. Walter Smith looked in the coach occasionally and deceased seemed to be all right. He last saw him at the ten-mile gate from Barcaldine, and did not miss him from the coach until it arrived in town. Deceased was between 60 and 65 years of age, and had been employed until recently on an outstation of Mount Cornish. He had a watch and £7 in notes in the pocket of his clothes. The inquiry was adjourned for a week, in order to obtain further particular from the manager of Mount Cornish to supply information required by the Registrar. In the Court Mr. Willis drew attention to what he considered was neglect on the point of the police in not requesting a medical man to attend the search party. He could not say it for certain but it was probable the man's life might have been saved if a doctor had been with the party when the man was found, and the hemorrhage could have been stopped and animation restored.

Local and General News. (1888, July 17). The Western Champion (Blackall/Barcaldine, Qld.: 1879 - 1891), p. 2. Retrieved February 25, 2013, from http://nla.gov.au/nla.news-article79709275

Barcoo Extract – With reference to my paragraph last week respecting the Bev. Mr. Lester's work in the Mitchell district, I am requested to state that in all probability the support accorded would be such as to warrant the erection of churches both at Aramac and Muttaburra. Subscription lists are now open, and are being already freely responded to. Of course the buildings will not be of an elaborate character, but will answer the purpose for years to come.

THE BARCOO. (1888, August 3). Morning Bulletin (Rockhampton, Qld.: 1878 - 1954), p. 3. Retrieved September 23, 2014, from http://nla.gov.au/nla.news-article52019322

Narrow Escape – 11 August 1888

A Narrow Escape. – On Saturday last, the 11th August, a man named John Andrews, who had been working for Mr. Abel Stott, at the Bowen Downs washpool, saved himself from perishing of thirst by setting fire to the grass in one of the Bowen Downs sheep paddocks, six miles from the head station. He was found by the Manager, (Mr. S. P. Fraser) and a horse breaker (Wm. Cameron) about three quarters of an hour after the fire started staggering at the head of it in a most deplorable condition, and at the point of death. Two men were dispatched for water as fast as their horses could carry them; a dam fortunately being only about 1½ miles away. Immediately water was given him he rallied sufficiently to speak, before that he was unconscious. After a little time he was conveyed into the head station where he now remains in a very weak state, but recovering slowly. It appears John Andrew had started from Bowen Downs for Tuaburra out station on Tuesday 7th, and took the wrong road, and wandered about the paddocks between the fences from that time until he was found without a single drink. He showed wonderful judgment in igniting the grass, and the tact of his doing so saved him his life. There were 40,000 ewes and lambs in the paddock, and a high wind blowing, but the station hands managed to get the fire out by 8 p.m. without the loss of a sheep. The poor fellow before lighting the fire had sufficient sense to pick upon a bare place for himself.

Local and General News. (1888, August 14). The Western Champion (Blackall/Barcaldine, Qld.: 1879 - 1891), p. 2. Retrieved May 4, 2012, from http://nla.gov.au/nla.news-article79709371

Harry Morant – False Pretences

ROCKHAMPTON POLICE COURT.

THE FALSE PRETENCE'S CASE.

Harry Morant, the young fellow to whom we alluded vaguely last week as having been charged with obtaining money from a man named Samuels, at Muttaburra, by means of false pretences, was again brought up in custody. Senior-Sergeant Love produced the warrant which had been issued at the instance of Samuels, and which was signed by the Police Magistrate at Muttaburra. The warrant was issued on the 18th of October, 1888. Mr. Lukin: It does not say where the offence was committed. I shall have to remand you to Muttaburra, Morant. Defendant: It is very hard indeed on me, and it has caused me a lot of inconvenience, I suppose it is no use my giving you any particulars of the case? Mr. Lukin: Not the slightest. All I have to do is to remand you to Muttaburra. Defendant: Very well. I was in Muttaburra with Samuels for a long time, and we had a disturbance. I suppose this is the outcome of it. Mr. Lukin: I cannot help it. You are remanded to Muttaburra.

ROCKHAMPTON POLICE COURT. (1889, January 1). Morning Bulletin (Rockhampton, Qld.: 1878 - 1954), p. 5. Retrieved September 24, 2014, from http://nla.gov.au/nla.news-article52274299

Tuesday January 15th 1889

Before the Police Magistrate – Harry Morant

False Pretences – Plea: Not Guilty

Minute:

The prosecutor asked the prisoner whether the piebald mare he sold to Joseph Samuels is the same piebald mare he sold to J H Grimshaw.

The prisoner admitted that the mare was the same.

Joseph Samuels on his oath states: I am a storekeeper residing at Arrilalah. I know the prisoner. I remember the 27th day of April last year; I purchased a piebald mare branded JP near shoulder from the prisoner. I paid the prisoner for the mare £5 by a cheque, cash £2.8/- and goods £2.12/-. The prisoner gave me a receipt for the mare. [Receipt tendered Exhibit 1]. The prisoner told me that the mare was his property. If I had known that the mare was the property of another person I would not have bought it. Since I purchased the mare, she was claimed by Mr Grimshaw of Ambo Station. Mr Grimshaw sued me in the Small Debts Court for the value of the mare, and I was ordered by the bench to give back the mare to Grimshaw or the value of it £12. The mare is now on the road up to be handed over to Mr Grimshaw.

To the Prisoner: I remember seeing you in Muttaburra and asked you if you had a harness horse for sale. You said you had a piebald mare; you could sell me running at Ambo. I went out to Ambo the same night. The horses you spoke to me about were not in and I rode on the next day. You waited a day after me at Ambo but I do not know what your intention was I was at Ambo about two months after that. I was in Muttaburra during the race times. On neither occasion did Mr Grimshaw claim the mare.
I did not have the piebald mare on either occasion when I was in Muttaburra. I did not tell Mr Grimshaw that I had purchased them are from the prisoner.

The prisoner delivered the mare to me himself at Arrilalah.

Joseph Samuels

Taken and sworn before me at Muttaburra fifteenth day of January 1889 Charles A M Morris Pros.

John Henry Grimshaw on his oath states: I am overseer at Ambo Station. I know the prisoner I remember the 20th March last year I purchased four horses from the prisoner that day and received delivery of two. There was a piebald mare amongst the horses I purchased from the prisoner and the one I took delivery of. I paid prisoner £20 by cheque on QN Bank Muttaburra. The prisoner gave me a receipt for the horses. [Receipt tendered Exhibit 2]. I afterwards heard from the Police at Arrilalah that prisoner had disposed of the piebald mare to Mr Samuels of Arrilalah. After I received the information, I laid claim to the mare as my property. Mr Samuels refused to hand on over the mare on the grounds that he had purchased the mare. I afterwards summoned him for the mare or the value of £12 and the Bench ordered the mare to be handed back to me. I never authorized the prisoner to sell the mare to Mr Samuels or any other person.

I could not swear that I sent you a wire asking you to return Loan. If I used the word 'Loan' in the telegram it must have referred to the £20. I remember you coming to Ambo with three horses. You said you had lost money and asked me for £20 for the horse. I was aware that it was your intention to join George King at Isisford and going South with him. I don't recollect your leaving the horses as security for £20. I was aware you did not go South. I remember your saying that you had a chance of selling the piebald mare. You were to have both the piebald mare and the brown buck on the understanding that you were to purchase them. I was lead to believe that you would purchase them immediately they were brought in for you. I sent Ryan out to get the horse in for you. I remember you putting the piebald in the harness that day and I jumped beside you. You drove the mare away with my knowledge and consent. I did see you again until you returned to the races in June. I do not remember seeing Samuels during race time. On your return from Arrilalah you told me you had sold the grey and had lost two or three others.

The sale of the horses to me by prisoner was a bon-a-fide sale. I considered the £20 was fair value for them as I did not want them. I bought the horses from the prisoner only to oblige him than because I wanted them. I got the horses into the yard on the understanding that the prisoner would purchase them before he would sell then to anybody else. The prisoner had no authority to sell the piebald before completing the purchase of her. The prisoner did not purchase from me the piebald mare or the other horses mentioned on the receipt. I would have sold back the horses to prisoner and have given a receipt for the £20: I allowed the prisoner to take the horses to Maneroo where he said he had work. I next saw the prisoner on the 18th of June. The prisoner did not tell me he had sold the mare to Mr Samuels – he led me to believe that he had lost the piebald mare. I did not see any receipt for the mare, besides the receipt to Mr Samuels, after he had sold him the mare. When the prisoner dove the horses away I did not consider he had purchased them. When I saw prisoner at the races he said he would pay me for the horses.

J H Grimshaw

Taken and sworn before me at Muttaburra fifteenth day of January 1889 Charles A M Morris Pros.

Judgement

Three months in Rockhampton goal with hard labour.

Charles A M. Morris

Extract - 'Bench Deposition Book' - Police Court Muttaburra

Owen Callan – 27 January 1889

Sydney P Fraser reported the death of Owen Callan[84] a bushman with greyish hair, taken by a sudden illness on the 23 January 1889. Owen is buried in an unknown site on Bowen Downs. He was last

[84] *Qld Ref: 1889/C8*

seen in the company of James Stewart. Sydney P Fraser reported his death.

Police Gazette

Editor's Note – Owen, an Irishman, actually died on the 27 January 1889.

Ah Ching – 13 July 1889

The Bowen Downs' station cook, Ah Ching[85] who was born in China, died on the 13th July 1889 from cirrhosis of the liver although only about 46 years old. He was buried in the Muttaburra Cemetery, in an unknown site. Ernest Goldstiver of Muttaburra was the undertaker.

Resumption – August 1889

Aramac district, open at Court-house, Muttaburra, ten farms on Bowen Downs resumption, Thomson river – four parish of Camoola from 13,000 to 20,000 acres, two at Longway of 10,000 acres each, and four at Goodberry, one of those being 9000 and three 10,000 acres each

(No heading). (1889, August 15). The Brisbane Courier (Qld.: 1864 - 1933), p. 5. http://nla.gov.au/nla.news-page96735

Archibald Douglas – 17 November 1889

Archibald Douglas[86], born in Scotland was found drowned in Cornish Creek on Bowen Downs on the 17 November 1889. He was about 60 at the time of his death. Archibald had been in Queensland for about 40 years before he died, and was buried where he was found by the creek.

[85] *Qld Ref: 1889/C89*
[86] *Qld Ref: 1889/C49*

Elizabeth Chambers – 4 December 1889

Elizabeth Chambers[87] born on the 23rd November 1889 was the daughter of George Chambers and Elizabeth Nye who married on the 23 August 1888. Elizabeth died at Bengall Creek on the 4 December 1889 of convulsions when only 11 days old.

George and Elizabeth went on to have three other children: George Alfred born 2 August 1891 and died on the 4 March 1892, William James born 4 May 1893 and Annie on the 6 January 1896.

[87] *Qld Ref: 1889/C51*

1890s

James Gordon – 22 June 1890

DEATHS.

GORDON. —On the 22nd of June, at Bowen Downs, Queensland, James Gordon[88], infant son of James and Isabella Gordon.

"Better off, but sadly missed; Asleep in Jesus."

Family Notices. (1890, July 7). Morning Bulletin (Rockhampton, Qld.: 1878 - 1954), p. 1. Retrieved February 11, 2014, from http://nla.gov.au/nla.news-article52335408

James Gordon – 22 June 1890 — Bowen Downs Wool Shed

Photo: Judith McClymont

Editor's Note – James Gordon was a three month old baby when he died on the 22 June 1890, from 'water on the brain' at the Bowen Downs Shearing Shed, where he is buried. He was the son of James Gorson and Isabella Crosbie (Crosby).

[88] *Qld Ref: 1890/000016*

Isabella [Crosbie] first married in March 1885 to Richard Baggley Sargent. In 1888, the January birth and August death of their only child, Isabella, was recorded. In March 1888, Richard, who was wardsman at the Muttaburra Hospital, died of typhoid, and is buried (with headstone) in the Muttaburra Cemetery.
In 1889, Isabella married her second husband, James Gordon. James Gordon and Isabella Crosbie (Crosby) went on to have other children: John James born 21 March 1891, Thomas Wallace, born on the 4 July 1893 and died 18 March 1897 at Barcaldine, Isabella born 4 March 1898, then twins Agnes and Mary born on 8 March 1901.

John Francis Cameron – 30 October 1890

SUICIDE THROUGH DRINK.

(By Telegraph) Brisbane November 3

The police have received information from Blackall that John Francis Cameron[89], the Manager of Bimbah Station, committed suicide on Monday by taking poison, as the result of a three days drinking bout at Longreach.

SUICIDE THROUGH DRINK. (1890, November 4). South Australian Register (Adelaide, SA 1839 - 1900), p. 5. Retrieved May 16, 2012, from http://nla.gov.au/nla.news-article47262803

Suicides. – Mr. J. Cameron overseer at Bimbah out-station, Mount Cornish, committed suicide on Monday by taking strychnine. No cause can be assigned for the rash act. The deceased has been rather eccentric for some time past. He was a very old resident, and respected by all who know him. Last evening at 10.30 a report reached the police that a man had suicided at the carrier's camp by taking poison. Upon going to the locality the body of a dead man, together with a dead dog, was found lying on some bullock yokes; remains of a bottle of strychnine and a partly used bottle of beer, was found at hand. Deceased, who was a carrier named Henry C. Eckel[90], is a married man and leaves a wife and family.

89 *Qld Ref: 1890/000031*
90 *Qld Ref: 1890/000092*

The Barcoo and Mitchell (Q.). (1890, November 22). Australian Town and Country Journal (NSW: 1870 - 1907), p. 16. Retrieved May 7, 2012, from http://nla.gov.au/nla.news-article71184713

Editor's Note – John was the son of Alexander Cameron and Catherine Cameron. Henry Conrad was the son of Henry Eckel and Maria Khal.

Campbell Turner – 7 March 1891

Fatal Accident to a Somnambulist at Rockhampton.

A lamentable accident happened early on Saturday morning at the Criterion Hotel, Rockhampton, by which a promising young man named Campbell Turner[91], 26 years of age, and overseer at the Bowen Downs station, lost his life. Turner, who was the nephew of Mr. F. B. Fraser, of Bowen Downs, only arrived by train from Barcaldine on Friday night, and was just recovering from an attack of low fever. He was en route for Helidon Station, near Toowoomba, where his mother lives, and was to have left on Saturday morning by the Buninyong. He retired to rest about 11 o'clock on Friday night, and at 2.30 on Saturday morning Constable Hogan, who was on duty in Fitzroy Street, heard a sound of moaning near the Criterion, and on proceeding in that direction found Turner lying off the pavement feebly groaning and in an insensible condition. He presented a terrible spectacle, as the blood was oozing from all parts of his body. He was at once conveyed inside the hotel, and Drs. Callaghan and Voss sent for, but Turner only lived an hour. His right leg was smashed in two places, several ribs were broken, and his skull was fractured. It is supposed that bc had walked in his sleep, got over the balustrade of the balcony, and fallen from a height of 30 foot.

Further particulars of the fatal accident at the Criterion Hotel state that Turner was a most temperate man, and one who would not in the least be likely to drink to excess, also that he had been troubled with somnambulism. The balustrade before the

[91] *Qld Ref: 1891/C3525*

Criterion Hotel is over 8 feet high, quite sufficient to avert any accident under ordinary circumstances.

Fatal Accident to a Somnambulist at Rockhampton. (1891, March 11). Warwick Examiner and Times (St. Lucia, Qld.: 1867 - 1919), p. 3. Retrieved May 17, 2012, from http://nla.gov.au/nla.news-article82210867

Editor's Note – Campbell was the son of William Turner and Catherine Macdonald. S P Fraser, of Bowen Downs not F. B. as stated.

Shearers' Dispute – 14 May 1891

Information has been received in Brisbane in reference to the burning of the three out stations on Dillalah run. The unionists came up and camped at the Bowen outstation, turning their horses in the paddock. They then went to the hut and ordered the cook to get breakfast immediately, and to be careful that it was the best he could raise. The cook, who was in great fear about the breakfast, bolted into the scrub as soon as the men had sat down. After breakfast they caught their horses, and four of them rode ahead, taking the stockman with them. After trying to find the cook, those who remained behind are alleged to have set fire to the hut. The other out-stations were burnt down in a similar manner.

THE SHEARERS' DISPUTE. (1891, May 14). The Brisbane Courier (Qld.: 1864 - 1933), p. 6. Retrieved June 4, 2012, from http://nla.gov.au/nla.news-article3526041

Alfred Badke – 3 December 1891

Authority was granted to Mr. A. Badke to effect repairs to the dam at Sardine Creek to the extent of £5, and to act as caretaker, asking a charge similar to that levied at the Government dam at Tuaburra, half of which he will be allowed to retain.

Aramac[?]. (1891, December 29). The Western Champion (Blackall/Barcaldine, Qld.: 1879 - 1891), p. 2. Retrieved June 2, 2012, from http://nla.gov.au/nla.news-article79708103

Alfred Badke[92], the son of Alfred Badke and Elizabeth Ellen Golling, was born at Sardine Creek, on the 25 November 1891 and

[92] *Qld Ref: 1891/000036*

died on the 3rd December 1891 also at Sardine Creek. His parents had four children after Alfred: Thomas Alfred – [1893 – 1893], Thomas Henry – [1895], Minney Ellen – [1896] and Mary Ann – who died on the 17 March 1898. Alfred was a Licensed Victualler.

It is presumed that Alfred was buried at Sardine Creek.

OUR correspondent at Bowen Downs writing on 18th March says:- There is a change in the weather last night, and this morning light rain is falling. The last two or three days have been very hot, from 100 to 105 degrees in the shade. Water was struck yesterday in No. 4 bore at 1,650 ft., about 35,000 gallons daily. Operations will be continued till a larger supply is obtained.

STOCK AND STATION REPORT. (1892, March 22). The Western Champion and General Advertiser for the Central-Western Districts (Barcaldine, Qld.: 1892 - 1922), p. 5. Retrieved October 13, 2012, from http://nla.gov.au/nla.news-article77214488

Murder of a Black Woman – 1892

An aboriginal woman has been found near Bimbah with her head battered in, and the body partially burned.

Murder of a Black Woman. (1892, May 9). Bathurst Free Press and Mining Journal (NSW: 1851 - 1904), p. 2. Retrieved March 31, 2014, from http://nla.gov.au/nla.news-article62733901

Patrick Toohey – 4 June 1892

FATAL OCCURRENCE AT BOWEN DOWNS.

OUR correspondent at Bowen Downs writing on 4th June says:– A man named M. O'Donnell, but whose proper name is supposed to be P. Toohey[93], arrived here a few days ago, and, from his appearance, seemed to be very hard up. He got rations in the usual way, and went to the travellers' hut; he was subject to fits, and it is supposed that while in one of them he fell into the fire and burnt

[93] *Qld Ref; 1892/000018*

his left elbow and hip. He came up to the station and got some dressing for it, and did not seem to mind it much. I am told he was found early on Friday morning lying out in the road with very little covering, and, as Thursday night was very cold, he must have suffered much, as he was quite stiff when carried into the hut. He appeared in an unconscious state, and word was sent to Aramac for police and medical assistance; but, before either arrived, the man died. All that could be done was done, but he never spoke after being carried into the hut. A constable arrived about 1.30 p.m., and viewed the body. A magisterial enquiry was held before S. P. Fraser, Esq., J.P., and the body was decently buried in the afternoon. It is thought he got one of the fits he was subject to, and could not rally.

http://nla.gov.au/nla.news-article77215199 The Western Champion and General Advertiser for the Central-Western Districts (Barcaldine, Qld.: 1892 - 1922), Tuesday 14 June 1892, page 5

Editor's Note – M. O'Donnell, was officially Patrick Toohey, but also went by the name of 'Mad Mick'. He was a vagrant and is buried on Bowen Downs in as unknown grave site. Maybe it is at the Homestead Cemetery.

Ralph Erskine McDonald – 25 June 1892

Sudden Death. – From Bowen Downs comes news of the death of Mr. R. E. McDonald[94], of Fleetwood. It appeared Mr. McDonald had been suffering from a chest complaint for some considerable time, and it is surmised (as he was, alone) that a fit of coughing came on and he died in it.

Barcoo and Mitchell (Q.). (1892, July 23). Australian Town and Country Journal (NSW: 1870 - 1907), p. 16.http://nla.gov.au/nla.news-article71201900

Editor's Note – Ralph is actually buried in the Aramac Cemetery. He was the son of Angus William McDonald and Mary McDonald.

[94] *Qld Ref: 1892/000969*

Annie Oliver – 7 July 1892

A SUSPICIOUS CASE.

On July 6th a man named Oliver, with wife and child, passed Bowen Downs (says our correspondent) and camped on Cornish Creek, at the Tower Hill Crossing. At 10 o'clock the next morning they reported that the child died at 12 o'clock the previous night. Mr. Fraser, J.P., and Dr. Williamson, of Williamson and Thornton, Tower Hill, who had arrived about midday, went to view the body. The Dr. could give no opinion as to cause of death, and the parent's answers not being satisfactory, Mr. Fraser refused an order for burial, and sent a special messenger in to Muttaburra for the Government medical officer.

(Source: http://nla.gov.au/nla.news-article77215458 The Western Champion and General Advertiser for the Central-Western Districts (Barcaldine, Qld.: 1892 - 1922), Tuesday 12 July 1892, page 5)

MAGISTERIAL INQUIRY AT BOWEN DOWNS.

OUR correspondent; writing from Bowen Downs 9th July, says:– Dr. Egan, Government medical officer at Muttaburra, and Sergt. Green of same place, arrived at Bowen Downs on July 8. The doctor held a post-mortem examination on the body of Annie Oliver[95], aged 10 years and 11 months, who died at Bowen Downs on the night of the 6th instant. The next day an inquiry was held before Mr. S. P. Fraser, J.P., conducted by Sergt. Green. The father of the child gave evidence, and the doctor showed that death resulted from peritonitis, the disease being of long standing.

http://nla.gov.au/nla.news-article77215500 The Western Champion and General Advertiser for the Central-Western Districts (Barcaldine, Qld.: 1892 - 1922), Tuesday 19 July 1892, page 5)

Editor's Note – Annie was the daughter of Charles Oliver and Ellen Symes was born in 1881. In Qld BDM, the mother is listed as Ellen Harris[96].

[95] *Qld Ref: 1892/000023*
[96] *Qld Ref: 1881/C6042*

Letter to the Editor: Extract – 16 July 1892

Shearing started at Bowen Downs last week, when 40 workers more than were taken on presented themselves. The telegraph operator is kind enough to say:

In connection with the recent firing of a hay stack at that station the manager believes the fire to be the work of an incendiary and not of union action on the part of the unionists. Which is a sort of "don't drag him in the horse pond", don't you know!

http://nla.gov.au/nla.news-article70862574Worker (Brisbane, Qld.: 1890 - 1955), Saturday 16 July 1892, page 4

David Drummond – 23 August 1892

SUDDEN DEATH. OUR correspondent at Bowen Downs, writing on 26th instant, says:– A man, named David Drummond[97], died suddenly at Caledonia a few days ago. The usual inquiry was held and the police informed.

The Western Champion and General Advertiser for the Central-Western Districts (Barcaldine, Qld. 1892 - 1922) Tuesday 30 August 1892 p 6 Article

Editor's Note – David was born in Scotland and the actual date of death was 23rd August 1892. Birth, Deaths and Marriages says he was a railway guard who supposedly was overcome by 'brain fever'.

Archibald McCullock – 25 September 1892

Death – A lad named Archie McCulloch[98] received injuries at Bowen Downs which resulted in his death in a very simple manner. He was playing leapfrog with others in the shed on September 20 when he slipped and fell, breaking one of his arms just above the wrist. He was taken to Aramac Hospital, where he succumbed on Sunday morning, mortification having set in.

Barcaldine (Q.). (1892, October 8). Australian Town and Country Journal (NSW: 1870 - 1907), p. 15. http://nla.gov.au/nla.news-article71205010

[97] *Qld Ref: 1892/000028*
[98] *Qld Ref: 1892/000032*

Editor's Note – Archibald McCullock, (McCulloch), the son of James McCullock and Elizabeth Dawson, died on the 25th September 1892, is buried in the Aramac Cemetery. Archie as he was known was born in 1878 and had nine siblings: Horatio – 1874-1944, Charles William – 1875-1876, Florence Mary – 1879, Robert Duncan – 1882-1962, born in Blackall aged 81 when he died, Alice Jessie – 1884, Nellie May – 1885, William David – 1888-1930, George Wallace – 1891-1957, Isabel Jeanette – 1894.

Rowland William Clarke – 8 January 1893

DEATH AT MOUNT CORNISH.

A CORRESPONDENT sends the following:– At Mount Cornish, on Sunday last, under circumstances more than usually sad, Master Rollo Clarke[99], nephew of E. R. Edkins, Esq., succumbed to an attack of that dread disease typhoid fever. He had been ailing for three weeks, but no serious result was anticipated till within a few days of his death, and even then great hopes were entertained that he would eventually pull through. However, it was not to be, and the melancholy truth gradually forced itself on his relatives, who were watching him incessantly, that his naturally delicate constitution was unable to battle successfully against the dreadful fever that was rapidly consuming his young life; and in spite of all Dr. Lindsay's efforts, aided by the best and most gentle nursing, the patient gradually sank and passed quietly away. He was in his 17th year, and had been on the station for about eighteen months, during which time his quiet, kindly disposition had made him such a general favorite that his untimely end brought heartfelt sorrow to all; and great sympathy was expressed for Mr. and Mrs. Clarke, who reside in Sydney, and Mr. and Mrs. Edkins, in their sad bereavement. The funeral took place on Monday, when a large party from the station followed the remains to the Muttaburra cemetery, where they were interred.

DEATH AT MOUNT CORNISH. (1893, January 17). The Western Champion and General Advertiser for the Central-Western Districts (Barcaldine, Qld.: 1892 - 1922), p. 6. http://nla.gov.au/nla.news-article77216891

[99] *Qld Ref: 1893/0000002*

Editor's Note – Rowland William was the son of William Clarke and Mary Sophia Edkins, born in 1874 in the Grafton district.

Maud Margaret Eldershaw – 7 February 1893

Maud Margaret Eldershaw[100] was the daughter of Henry Lindefield Eldershaw, a sheep overseer on Bowen Downs, and Margaret McCarron. She married Henry in 1890. Maud died due to convulsions at Crusoe on the 12 February 1893 just 5 days after her birth on the 7 February 1893. Henry and Margaret had an elder daughter Mary Windyer, who was born in 1891.

Walter Robert Shaw – 6 February 1893
Margaret Ann Shaw – 7 February 1893

SINGULAR DEATH OF TWO CHILDREN.

A correspondent, writing from Tuaburra (Bowen Downs) on February 10th, says – J Shaw, wife and family camped near here on Sunday last, on their way to Crusoe. Shaw said two of his children, 3½ years and 16 months old, were not well. On the same night the boy was seized with convulsions, but again seemed better next morning till 2 o'clock, when the little fellow was again seized. His father at once picked the little boy up, and ran for the station, a distance of about one mile; but, before reaching it, the little fellow died. A buggy and horses were at once procured and Shaw drove the family to Muttaburra, also taking the remains of the little boy but, upon reaching the hotel at Sardine Creek, the mother found it was useless to proceed with the second child, as it seemed to get worse. Everything was done for the little sufferer, but without success, and it died on Tuesday morning. The father had just returned from Muttaburra after burying the boy, when he had to

[100] *Qld Ref: 1893/000043*

carry the second child for burial. I understand the doctor is going to hold a post mortem. The parents say the children had been eating castor oil seeds, which are supposed to be poisonous.

SINGULAR DEATH OF TWO CHILDREN. (1893, February 14). The Western Champion and General Advertiser for the Central-Western Districts (Barcaldine, Qld.: 1892 - 1922), p. 5. Retrieved May 23, 2012, from http://nla.gov.au/nla.news-article77217123

Editor's Note – These two children were Walter Robert[101] born on 29th August 1889 dyeing on 6th February 1893 and Margaret Ann[102] born in Longreach on 22nd July 1891 dying on 7 February 1893, were the children of James Gordon Shaw and Margaret Katherine O'Keefe. Other children of the Shaw's were Mary born 12 March 1888 and Lelena born 22 March 1893 and Margaret Catherine born 28 April 1894, dying on 1 February 1895.

James Gordon Shaw [father], aged 64, the son of Jacob Sloane Shaw and Mary Elnew, is buried in the Muttaburra Cemetery after he died on 21 June 1919 from influenza. He was a cook working at the Australian Hotel, Muttaburra.

ARAMAC.

FROM OUR OWN CORRESPONDENT

The weather has been very boisterous of late, with light rains, but they have not been sufficient to fill dams nor thoroughly soak the ground. The total rainfall recorded so far this month is just over one inch. The prospect for this immediate neighbourhood are much brighter than they were two weeks ago.

The stock passings since my last are; 2,400 stud rams from the Meadows to Bowen Downs, Scottish Australian and Investment Company, owners, W. Taylor in charge. Two mobs of sheep crossed the reserve last week for Ambo Downs, travelling for grass and water, Winter Newton and Co., owners, T. H. Huggins and J. Day in charge; owing to rain falling on Ambo Downs, the owners of the sheep wired to the drovers in charge to return with the sheep to Ambo Downs.

[101] *Qld Ref: 1893/000019*
[102] *Qld Ref: 1893/000020*

Bowen Downs mailman reports having picked up a carrier named Robinson, about seven miles on this side of Bowen Downs, suffering from an accident that befell him, while losing his team of bullocks. From what I can hear, the young man (age twenty three), with another carrier, was on his way back from Bowen Downs to Barcaldine. When seven miles from Bowen Downs he proceeded to lose his team of bullocks. The drawing chain hook caught in the calf of his right leg, he tried to free himself, and the bullocks which were attached, became, frightened and started off, dragging the poor fellow some distance before they could be brought to a standstill. He suffered greatly, but is doing well in the Hospital here.

Aramac, 21st March, 1893.

ARAMAC. (1893, March 27). Morning Bulletin (Rockhampton, Qld.: 1878 - 1954), p. 5. Retrieved May 7, 2012, from http://nla.gov.au/nla.news-article52445145

ACCIDENT AT BOWEN DOWNS.

Our correspondent reports on 3rd August:

A young man named J. Forbes met with a nasty accident at Bowen Downs Wash pool on the 1st inst. It appears the young fellow had loaded his gun and afterwards found he had no caps. The Chinaman gardener made one out of a piece of tin, putting the head of a match in it. After capping the gun Forbes put the hammer down, and having his left hand over the muzzle he commenced to bump the gun on the ground, causing it to go off, the whole charge going right through the palm of his hand; five or six pellets lodged in his left cheek, and one went through his left ear. Mr. Astoll at once procured a vehicle and sent the unfortunate sufferer into Muttaburra. It is to be hoped he will soon recover. He had a wonderful escape.

ACCIDENT AT BOWEN DOWNS. (1893, August 8). The Western Champion and General Advertiser for the Central-Western Districts (Barcaldine, Qld.: 1892 - 1922), p. 6. Retrieved May 7, 2012, from http://nla.gov.au/nla.news-article77218492

Shooting Case at Mt Cornish – 7 February 1893

Sub-Inspector Dillon received the following telegram from Senior-Constable Blyton on the 28th ultimo:– "Muttaburra, January 27th, 1893. About 7 p.m. last night, at Mount Cornish station, a man named Edward Kearnan, employed cutting hay, went into the bachelors' quarters under the influence of drink, and was put out by Mortimer King, the head stockman. Kearnan afterwards returned and shot King in the muscle of the right arm with a small revolver. Kearnan has been arrested." Further particulars have been received of this outrage. When the report was made to the police at Muttaburra Senior-Constable Blyton and Constable Quilter at once proceeded to Mount Cornish, where they were informed that Edward Kearnan, who is a hay-cutter, had gone to his camp, about five miles distant. They at once proceeded thither, arriving at the camp about 10.30 p.m. They were informed by Kearnan's mates, Hitchman and Hibband, that he had left about an hour previously; also, he had told them he had shot King, but did not know what injury he had done or he would know what to do. He loaded a Winchester rifle, and when he heard the police coming rode away, taking the rifle with him. The police then went in the direction Kearnan had gone, but being unable to find him returned to the camp. Shortly after returning they saw a man, whom they took to be Kearnan, on foot, come through a fence about 50 yards from the camp. He had a rifle in his hand, and went behind a tree. The police walked towards him, leading their horses. The senior-constable called out, "Is that you Kearnan?" He replied, "Who are you?" The senior-constable said, "I am Blyton." Kearnan replied, "Who the b-y h- are you?" Quilter said, "You know very well who we are." Kearnan said, "You are the police." The senior constable told Kearnan not to be foolish, but to come and give up the rifle. Kearnan then came from behind the tree and walked backwards towards the tent. The police followed him up, and when they were within about 50 yards of him Kearnan grasped the rifle with both hands as if about to take aim, and looking towards Quilter said,

"Don't you b-r do that: you keep back; you can yarn to me, but don't come too near." Blyton again advised Kearnan not to make a fool of himself, but Kearnan still kept walking back-words with the rifle clasped in both hands, ready to fire, the police gradually getting nearer to him. When near the mess table Hibband, who was planted behind a tree, sprang out and secured Kearnan, thus preventing injury being done to anyone. The rifle was found to contain 15 cartridges, and Kearnan is known to be a crack shot. The police then arrested him, and charged him with shooting at King with intent to murder. They then searched the camp and found a small six-chambered revolver, which Kearnan admitted was the one he had shot King with. Five of the chambers were loaded and one discharged. After being arrested Kearnan said, "If any of the jackaroos from Mount Cornish had been with you I would have shot them, and I was nearly shooting you". At the time of the outrage there were about a dozen men around, but no attempt was made by them to disarm Kearnan, he being allowed to proceed to the horse-yard, catch a horse and ride away?

Shooting Case at Mt. Cornish. (1893, February 7). The Western Champion and General Advertiser for the Central-Western Districts (Barcaldine, Qld.: 1892 - 1922), p. 7. Retrieved May 27, 2012, from http://nla.gov.au/nla.news-article77217103

Horse Stealing

ON the 4th June Sergeant Molone started on a most remarkable journey, in connection with a case of horse-stealing, which has attracted considerable attention, as the horses concerned belong to the Barcaldine district. On his journey, the Sergeant picked up a constable at Aramac, who accompanied him all the way. At Bowen Downs, Corinda, Elbe, and Oakley the station managers willingly supplied the Sergeant with fresh horses, which were of great assistance to him in the prosecution of his journey. Some difficulty was experienced from Bowen Downs to Corinda as there was a flood on the main road, but this difficulty was obviated by following a buggy track for about 40 miles by moonlight, which brought the constables to Corinda. There was a difficulty in obtaining fresh horses at Aberfoyle, as Mr. Jardine was short at the time, but this gentle man kindly lent some on his outstation. After accomplishing 225 miles under 36 hours the constables were detained for the evening at Oakley, as no horses were procurable until the morning. The remaining 30 miles to Torrent Creek were done the next morning in three hours. The stolen horses were found, some in possession of the police, some in paddocks. The Sergeant, upon clipping the horses, discovered that several of the brands had been "faked," and that the horses were owned by residents of Barcaldine. Witnesses were procured at Torrens Creek and Pentland, and the offenders were brought before the P.M. at Charters Towers and thence remanded to Barcaldine. On the return journey from Pentland (about 380 miles), the Sergeant traced to the possession of the accused several horses. It was on this journey also that one of the accused was found to be concerned in a case of cattle stealing, which is now being proceeded with at the Police Court, Barcaldine. It is interesting to know that during Sergeant Malone's journey he travelled as a drover, with a long beard and hair of equal length, in company with a bushman, from whom the Sergeant learnt man; interesting particulars about himself and his exploits in the district

A TRIP ACROSS COUNTRY. (1893, July 25). The Western Champion and General Advertiser for the Central-Western Districts (Barcaldine, Qld.: 1892 - 1922), p. 3. Retrieved April 14, 2013, from http://nla.gov.au/nla.news-article77218353

James Magee – August 1893

James Magee's[103] body was found in the Top Paddock of Ambo – an out-station of Mt Cornish. He was a labourer working at Ambo.

He had perished. James was buried at Ambo on the 16 August 1893.

[103] *Qld Ref: 1894/000064.*

James was born in Ireland and was between 60 and 65 years old when he died.

ACCIDENT AT BOWEN DOWNS.

Our correspondent reports on 3rd August:— A young man named J. Forbes met with a nasty accident at Bowen Downs Wash pool on the 1st inst. It appears the young fellow had loaded his gun and afterwards found he had no caps. The Chinaman gardener made one out of a piece of tin, putting the head of a match in it. After capping the gun Forbes put the hammer down, and having his left hand over the muzzle he commenced to bump the gun on the ground, causing it to go off, the whole charge going right through the palm of his hand; five or six pellets lodged in his left cheek, and one went through his left ear. Mr. Astoll at once procured a vehicle and sent the unfortunate sufferer into Muttaburra. It is to be hoped he will soon recover. The lad a wonderful escape.

ACCIDENT AT BOWEN DOWNS. (1893, August 8). The Western Champion and General Advertiser for the Central-Western Districts (Barcaldine, Qld.: 1892 - 1922), p. 6. Retrieved June 22, 2014, from http://nla.gov.au/nla.news-article77218492

Mary Jane Ford – 13 October 1893

DEATH AT BOWEN DOWNS.

OUR correspondent writes under date October 14th:– Mrs. Wm. Ford[104], the wife of an old servant on Bowen Downs, died and was buried yesterday. The poor woman had been ailing for some little time, and Mrs. S. P. Fraser hearing of it, drove to the woolshed (where the Ford family were living) to see how she was. Mrs. Fraser at once saw that the case was serious, and had the patient brought to her (Mrs. Fraser's) house. The Muttaburra doctor was sent for on two occasions, and did all he could. Mr. and Mrs. Fraser gave the most careful and unremitting attention to the patient, watching

---

[104] *Qld Ref: 1893/0000057*

in turn with the poor woman's husband day and night, but in spite of all their care and attention, she breathed her last about 2 p.m. yesterday, and was followed to her last resting place by a large number of the station employees. She leaves a family of seven children, the youngest being quite a baby.

The Western Champion and General Advertiser for the Central-Western Districts (Barcaldine, Qld.: 1892 - 1922), 24 October, 1893: p. 6, http://nla.gov.au/nla.news-article77219441)

Editor's Note – Mrs. William Ford – Mary Jane Ford – was the daughter of Campbell and Margaret Hide. She married William on the 6 November 1877. They have four children registered in Qld. BDM: Thomas – [1883]; Isabella Grace – [1885]; Agnes Mary – [1887]; Richard Gillespie – [1892]. Richard remained in the area as on the 1 September 1915 he enlisted giving Bowen Downs as his place of birth on the 9 April 1893. He was 23 and his occupation was labourer at Bowen Downs. He died on the 2 August 1943 from heart failure and is buried in the North Eastern Section of the Muttaburra Cemetery in Grave No 178. At the time of his death, he was working as a station-hand at Bannockburn Station.

Unknown – 19 October 1893

Unknown male body found about 3 years after death at Tower Hill Creek on Mt Cornish. The body was buried where it was found, on the 19 October 1893.

Charles Brownsey – 26 January 1894

Death from Thirst.

Our Bowen Downs correspondent writes on the 29th January:—On the 27th an old man named Charles Brown, better known as "Old Brownie", formerly a dam-maker, was found dead at the Windmill Dam, about three miles from Mt. Cornish. It was reported to the police and Messrs. Edkins and S. P. Fraser, J.P., and Dr. Lindsay went out and held an enquiry, when it was found the poor old fellow had perished for want of water. He left Bowen Downs a few days ago (he had been spelling for a few days) on his way to

Muttaburra; the distance he would have to travel without water would be from Bowen Downs washpool to Mt. Cornish, say 22 miles. There are lots of men who are running the same risk every day; they have not the means to buy a water-bag, and it is no joke carrying "bluey" over the downs in this weather.

Death from Thirst. (1894, February 6). The Western Champion and General Advertiser for the Central-Western Districts (Barcaldine, Qld.: 1892 - 1922), p. 6. http://nla.gov.au/nla.news-article79731368

Editor's Note – Charles Brownsey[105] an Englishman aged about 65 years died on the Mount Cornish run on the 26 January 1894 and was buried – 27 January 1894 at Mount Cornish.

Joseph Hayton – 9 April 1894

At about four o'clock yesterday morning a man named Joseph Hayton[106] was admitted to the local hospital, after having attempted to commit suicide by cutting his throat with a razor. The unfortunate man called at the Bowen Downs head station carrying his swag, and was supplied by the storekeeper with the usual rations on Saturday morning last. He was met some few miles from the station that afternoon by the Aramac Bowen Downs mailman on the road to town. On Sunday he was discovered with his throat cut about ten miles from the station. Mr. S. P. Fraser at once went out to the place and sent him on into town in charge of Mr. W. H. Wills, the storekeeper, and another man. He did not arrive till four o'clock next morning. Dr. MacDonnell was immediately in attendance. The man is now in a very dangerous condition, and appears to have made a most determined attempt to do away with himself.

Aramac, 13th February, 1894

ARAMAC. (1894, February 17). The Capricornian (Rockhampton, Qld: 1875 - 1929), p. 21. Retrieved June 3, 2012, from http://nla.gov.au/nla.news-article67941039

[105] *Qld Ref: 1894/000021*
[106] *Qld Ref: 1894/000034*

Editor's Note – Joseph Hayton actually died on the 9 April 1894, whether it was a result of the above is not known, but Joseph committed suicide by drowning at Green Hills.

Ah Young – 23 November 1894

Tommy Ah Young[107], aged 30 years old, the son of Tom Chong, a schoolmaster, was the cook at Bowen Downs. He died on the 23 November 1894 of dysentery, at the '29 Mile' on the Corinda – Bowen Downs Road so was buried there.

Angus William McDonald – 28 December 1894
Accident at Bowen Downs.

An occasional correspondent writes on the 4th inst.:— It is with very much regret, a feeling that is joined in by all on this station, that I have to record the sad termination to the painful accident which happened to young Angus McDonald[108], eldest son of Mr. John McDonald, of this station. The accident happened on 21st December last, and on the 28th, at about 11 p.m., the poor lad succumbed to the injuries received. All the attention that could be afforded him was rendered by the officials of the Aramac hospital. Drs. Reid and Lindsay were in close attendance, but had little hope from the first. The lad's afflicted mother watched by him from the first to the last, and saw him pass quietly away. Everyone who knew the deceased regret him, for he was a large-hearted, good and honest young.

Accident at Bowen Downs. (1895, January 15). The Western Champion and General Advertiser for the Central-Western Districts (Barcaldine, Qld.: 1892 - 1922), p. 8. Retrieved May 7, 2012, from http://nla.gov.au/nla.news-article79735683

---

[107] *Qld Ref: 1894/000075*
[108] *Qld Ref: 1895/000005*

McDonalds' Headstones – Aramac Cemetery

[Source: Betty Wakley-Bunkell Doman Name Trust]

> *Editor's Note – Angus was the son of John McDonald and Mary Jonson [Johnson] – born on 2nd March 1876, so was only 19 years old. Angus was the brother of Mary [1874], Ralph Erskine [1878], Ann [1880], Isabella [1882] and John Patrick [1884]. Angus is buried in the Central section of the Aramac Cemetery, Plot 163.*

Margaret Catherine Shaw – 1 February 1895

Margaret[109], the daughter of James Gordon Shaw and Margaret Katherine O'Keefe. James and Margaret married on the 13 January 1887. She was the sister of – Mary [1888], Walter Robert [1889 – 1893], Margaret Ann [1891 – 1893] and Lelena [1893]. She was born at Tablederry on the 28th April 1894 and died just 10 months later from gastric enteritis on the 1st February 1895. She is buried in Muttaburra Cemetery, but her actual grave site is unknown. Margaret Catherine was the third child this family lost at the tender age of under 5 years. [See Walter Robert and Margaret Ann who died February 1893]

[109] *Qld Ref: 1895/000006*

George Edwin Gallogly – 2 February 1895

GALLOGLY. – On the 29th January, at Bowen Downs, the wife of G. B. Gallogly, of a son.

The Brisbane Courier (Qld.: 1864 - 1933) Saturday 9 February 1895 p 4 Family Notices

DEATHS:

GALLOGLY. – On the 2nd February, at Bowen Downs, the beloved infant son of George B. and M. J. Gallogly, aged 4 days.

http://nla.gov.au/nla.news-article3596629

Mr. and Mrs. G. B. Gallogly, of Bowen Downs, went into Aramac on the 22nd of October to celebrate their silver wedding by entertaining their friends on the 28th. A social evening with music, singing and dancing was provided at Mrs. Payne's Marathon Hotel. There were from 20 to 40 of Mr. and Mrs. Gallogly's friends present, including the children. The fun was kept up until a late hour, and was concluded by all hands singing "Auld Lang Syne" and the National Anthem, three cheers for Mr. and Mrs. Gallogly and one for the little Galloglys. The supper was provided by Mrs. Payne, and all the delicacies procurable were in plenty and received due justice. The table was beautifully laid out, and the lovely roses and other flowers were very much admired. Mrs. Payne, who was ably assisted by Mr. B. Duke, deserves credit for the way the supper was served. Mr. Duke also played for both dances and singers. On Tuesday evening the little ones had a party all to themselves. They all seemed to have a real good time, and the affair broke up at about 11 p.m., fully satisfied with the good things put before them. Mrs. Gallogly received several nice little presents to mark the event. The heartiness of the functions testified to the esteem in which Mr. and Mrs. Gallogly are held by everyone. Both have resided in the district for over thirty years, nearly the whole of which, we believe, was spent on Bowen Downs.

Barcaldine And District Budget. (1905, November 6). The Western Champion and General Advertiser for the Central-Western Districts (Barcaldine, Qld.: 1892 - 1922), p. 3. http://nla.gov.au/nla.news-article75611923

Editor's Note – George Edwin Gallogly[110] the son of George Beattie Gallogly and Mary Jane Maclolm was born on the 29th January 1895 and died just 5 days later on the 2nd February 1895 of convulsions. He is buried at Bowen Downs Homestead. He was the third child, having two elder sisters – Georgina Elsie Myre (10-8-1891) and Phyllis Eileen (24-7-1893), and a younger sister, Annie Maria Edith Elvena (4-9-1896). George Beattie Gallogly was the book-keeper at Bowen Downs for over 40 years and was the auditor for the Division of Aramac while F. R. Greenwood was the other Auditor, E. W. Bowyer, Clerk, and Sydney P. Fraser, was the Chairman of the Aramac Division.

John Henry Thomas – 19 July 1895
WHOLESALE POISONING.
The Shearers at Bowen Downs.
One Dead, Several Critical.

(By TELEGRAPH)

BRISBANE, Monday

A telegram from Rockhampton states that a private message has been received stating that two attempts had been made within three days to poison the shearers at Bowen Downs station. On the first occasion eight men were poisoned, and on the second four. Altogether nine men were poisoned. Fortunately a supply of medicine was on hand, or several of them would certainly have died. As it is, three men are still in a critical state; the others are convalescent.

Another message dealing with the same subject, is to the effect that it is suspected that the poisoning was caused by strychnine that had been placed in the bread, meat, and sago puddings.

A letter received from Bowen Downs says that the scenes witnessed at the shed were beyond description; human beings were contorting themselves into all shapes and forms in all directions. One man called Thomas[111] has succumbed. He is unknown; and it

[110] *Qld Ref: 1895/000007*
[111] *Qld Ref: 1895/C24*

is thought that this name is assumed. One Richardson and one of five brothers, all well-known shearers, named Christie Shulz, are said to be in a critical state.

Sergeant Malone and other police have gone post haste to the district. The second death is expected.

http://nla.gov.au/nla.news-article44176482 Barrier Miner (Broken Hill, NSW: 1888 - 1954) Monday 22 July 1895 Page 2 of 4

Editor's Note – Thomas was the son of John Thomas and Emma Richards born in Melbourne Victoria. He was 31 years old when he died.

Dr. Lindsay was the medical officer from Aramac who attended him, while Walter Dickson and S P Fraser witnessed the burial at the Bowen Downs' Wool Shed.

THE BOWEN DOWNS POISONING CASES
THE DEATH OF THOMAS
A SCARE IN THE WEST
ACTION OF THE GOVERNMENT
REWARD OF £2500 OFFERED
(By Electric Telegraph)
(From our Own Correspondents)
BARCALDINE, July 21

A letter received from Bowen Downs station states that Thomas, one of the men poisoned there, and whose death has already been reported, died in frightful agony, his screams being terrible.

ROCKHAMPTON July 21

The poisoning case at Bowen Downs has evidently created a bit of a scare in the West. A firm in town received yesterday a wire from a station requesting them to forward at once antidotes against poisoning by arsenic or strychnine for 200 men. The wire concluded that such supplies will have to be included in every shearing order in future.

The government have decided to offer a reward of £2000 for information which will lead to the conviction of the person who put the poison in the food at Bowen Downs, and the owners of the station have supplemented the amount by offering a reward of £500. The contents of the stomach of the deceased man Thomas have been analysed and found to contain poison. A staff of detectives and other police are at the station, and every effort is being made to discover the means by which the poison was placed in the food.

The Brisbane Courier (Qld.: 1864 - 1933), Wednesday 24 July 1895, page 5

John Henry Thomas – 19 July 1895 — Bowen Downs Wool Shed

Photo: Judith McClymont

[Extract] – Page 301

£2,000 Reward

A Reward of £2,000 will be paid for such information as shall lead to the apprehension and conviction of the person or persons who, on the 16th July, 1895 introduced poison into the food supplied to the men engaged as shearers at Bowen Downs Station, and a Free Pardon will be granted to any person concerned in the crime, not being the principal offender, who shall give such information.

Police Gazette

BARCALDINE, July 21.

An urgent telegram received from Aramac states that forty-nine fresh cases of poisoning occurred at Bowen Downs. This time strychnine is suspected. It is believed the poison was put in meat and sago puddings eaten by the men. There is no suspicion attached to anyone. Only the shearers' mess was affected. A letter received states that the scenes at the shed were beyond description, human beings contorting themselves into all shapes and forms in all directions. A man called Thomas has succumbed. He is unknown, and it is thought his name was an assumed one. Richardson, one of five brothers, and reported to be a son of Mr. V. Richardson, of Hit or Miss Farm, near Barcaldine, and Christie Schultz, both well-known shearers, are very bad. Another death is expected.

Sergeant Malone has passed through here for Bowen Downs. The Aramac and Muttaburra police are already there.

ARAMAC, July 20.

Two attempts have been made to poison the shearers at Bowen Downs. The first time five showed symptoms. A letter received from Bowen Downs states that forty-nine men have been poisoned through the medium of food. The writer says it was dreadful to see the poor fellows suffer, and he never wishes to witness such a scene again, a doctor from Muttaburra was sent for; but he had not arrived when the letter was written. There are a couple of the shearers here, and one intends to take out his wife to cook for him. No clue has been ascertained as to the perpetrator of the deed.

Later:
Two of the shearers have just arrived in town. They report that one of the poisoned men, by name Thomas, has since died. Official news has been received here confirming the reported poisoning, and stating that one death has occurred. The Pastoralists' Association has no definite information.

Barcaldine July 22

[Extract] An official inquiry was commenced at Bowen Downs yesterday into the recent poisoning cases there. Constable Ward arrived at Barcaldine this afternoon from Bowen Downs, which place he left on Saturday evening. He brought with him in sealed packets on a pack-horse samples of the poisoned food, and he proceeds with them to Longreach by to-night's train. Inspector Lamond is expected to arrive to-day, then the samples will be sent to Rockhampton for analysis.

One can hardly believe the poisoning to have been the result of accident on both occasions. It is possible that some strychnine carelessly left about might have become mixed with the flour, or with the salt used in making the bread; but for poison to have been dropped into a sago tin and distributed throughout the food points directly to intentional crime. Mr. Fraser, manager of the station, did all he could to relieve those who were poisoned, and an antic taken in time, followed by a dose of brandy, no doubt did much to counteract the poison.

Barcaldine, July 23

A letter received from Bowen Downs Station states that Thomas, one of the men poisoned there, and whose death has already been reported, died in frightful agony, his screams being terrible.

Rockhampton, July 23

The poisoning cases at Bowen Downs have evidently created a bit of a scare in the West. A firm in town received yesterday a wire from a station in the West requesting them to forward at once antidotes against poisoning by arsenic or strychnine for 200 men. the wire concluded that such supplies will have to be included in every searing order in future.

The government has decided to offer a reward of £2000 for information which will lead to the conviction of the person who put the poison in the food at Bowen Downs, and the owners of the station have supplemented the amount by offering a reward of £500. The contents of the stomach of the deceased man Thomas have been analysed, and found to contain poison. A staff of detectives and other police are at the station, and every effort is being made to discover the means by which the poison was placed in the food.

http://nla.gov.au/nla.news-article70859887 Worker (Brisbane, Qld.: 1890 - 1955), Saturday 27 July 1895, page 2

The Poisoning at Bowen Downs.

By Telegram.
FROM OWN CORRESPONDENT.

Muttaburra, Friday evening.

THE three men arrested on suspicion of having caused the death of James Thomas by poisoning at Bowen Downs were brought up on remand at the police court this morning. On the application of Sub-inspector Galbraith they were further remanded until Monday next. The Police Magistrate notified from the Bench that the trial would take place on that day with closed doors.

The Poisoning at Bowen Downs. (1895, September 10). The Western Champion and General Advertiser for the Central-Western Districts (Barcaldine, Qld.: 1892 - 1922), p. 8. http://nla.gov.au/nla.news-article79760192

MUTTABURRA, Wednesday.

The Bowen Downs poisoning cases were resumed today. Sydney P. Fraser, manager of Bowen Downs, stated that he took possession of the flour and coarse salt after the police had taken samples, and destroyed them by burning. He remembered when the poisoning took place and could swear positively to seeing over 20 men vomiting. He took possession of the sago pudding and handing it to the police. He searched the bake house and burnt about £16 worth of rations, but found no poison. He gave emetics to all the sick men who required them, and gave some to Dickson to give, to the suffers. He only administered emetics at the shearers mess table and did not remember giving emetics to the prisoner Langhorne. He remembered a conversation with the prisoner Bristowe with reference to the poisoning, and he was telling him how to test strychnine poison, and he concluded he knew what he was talking about. After the second poisoning, Bristowe wanted him to send a cablegram home, but he did not do so. He knew Maher as Baxter. He received information from the police with reference to poisoning of the food at Bowen Downs. A letter was produced and read as follows:– "I wish to inform you that 20 men leave the Union camp here to-morrow, to shear at Bowen Downs. If taken on they intend poisoning other labourers' food. I am unable to ascertain the names of the 20 who leave immediately. Have a sharp look out for them and inform the police at the Shed. Signed Patrick Ryan Senior-constable". The witness was severely cross examined by the prisoner, but nothing of importance was elicited. The other cases were adjourned.

MUTTABURRA Thursday

The Bowen Downs poisoning cases were continued at Muttaburra today when further important evidence was given, but it was not allowed to be published. About one-third of the witnesses for the prosecution have been examined.

Telegraphic Intelligence. (1895, September 25). The North Queensland Register (Townsville, Qld.: 1892 - 1905), p. 6. http://nla.gov.au/nla.news-article79285917

BOWEN DOWNS POISONING CASES.

BRISBANE, Monday.

The Bowen Downs poisoning cases were continued at Muttaburra to-day. More important evidence was given, but the police would not allow it to be published yet. Five more witnesses are to be called for the prosecution. The case was further remanded for eight days

BOWEN DOWNS POISONING CASES. (1895, October 1). The Sydney Morning Herald (NSW : 1842 - 1954), p. 5. http://nla.gov.au/nla.news-article14018987

The Bowen Downs Poisoning Cases.

THE cases against the three men charged with causing the death of J. H. Thomas at Bowen Downs by placing poison in the food of the shearers' mess, is now drawing to a close. Several witnesses have been subpoenaed from the southern part of the colony, and the trouble in bringing them to the preliminary investigation at Muttaburra has been very great and expensive. It is expected the case will close to-day. Mr. Richardson, who was so badly poisoned, has been advised to proceed to Rockhampton for change of air and further medical advice. Mrs. Richardson will accompany her son to the coast. Richard Youll, another of the poisoned men, is suffering from paralysis, and has recently been admitted into the hospital at Muttaburra, where he now lies in a precarious condition.

The Bowen Downs Poisoning Cases. (1895, October 22). The Western Champion and General Advertiser for the Central-Western Districts (Barcaldine, Qld. : 1892 - 1922), p. 9. http://nla.gov.au/nla.news-article79761104

Bowen Downs Poisoning Case

BRISTOWE COMMITTED FOR TRIAL.

(By Telegraph from our Correspondent)

MUTTABURRA, October 23

The evidence in the Bowen Downs poisoning cases was concluded today. Thomas York stated that he was shearing at Bowen Downs on the 18th July. Did not recall the exact day they started shearing. After the poisoning he told Bristowe that he (witness) was told by Langhorn, Baxter and himself were going to be arrested. This was three or four days after the poisoning. Bristowe told witness he had seen Sub-inspector Galbraith, and was told it was not true, and the police had not the slightest suspicion against him. The men were in the habit of gambling there, but did not gamble till all hours of the morning, except on Saturday night. Witness did not remember if they were gambling on the night of the 17th July.

Examined by the police, witness said he did not know who told him about Bristowe being arrested, but was certain it was not the police. Bristowe and others were suspected by the shearers a day or two after the poisoning. Bristowe was committed for trial.

http://nla.gov.au/nla.news-article21637522 The Queenslander (Brisbane, Qld.: 1866 - 1939), Saturday 2 November 1895, page 820

Levi Small – 26 July 1895

Death of an Old Identity: OUR Bowen Downs correspondent wrote on the 29th July:– On the 26th inst, one Levi Small[112], better known as "Nobby," died here after a short illness. He was working about the bore water near the woolshed and caught a very severe

[112] *Qld Ref: 1895/000025*

cold, accompanied with some kind of fever. The symptoms were, some people say, those of dengue fever. Mr. Taylor, the overseer here, brought the poor old fellow in on Sunday, the 21st. He was seen by Dr. Lindsay, who prescribed for him, and Mrs. Taylor and others did all they possibly could for him; but he passed away on Friday, about 2.30 p.m., and was followed to his resting place by about 35 people on Saturday. He was a very old servant of this Company, and has been working here for about 16 or 17 years. The last twelve months the deceased had been away prospecting, and only returned a few weeks ago – it would seem to leave his bones where he had worked so long. He certainly died among those who thought a lot of him, for he was liked by all. He was about 89 years of age, and at one time was well known at the Peak Downs copper mines.

The Western Champion and General Advertiser for the Central-Western Districts (Barcaldine, Qld.: 1892 - 1922) Tuesday 6 August 1895 p 10

Accident at Bowen Downs.

ON the 14th instant, Herbert Taylor, son of the head-station overseer at Bowen Downs, was out driving horses with H. Mallon. They got separated somehow, and when Mallon shortly afterwards found young Herbert, his leg was broken half-way between the knee and ankle. He said his mare bolted with him and he got knocked off in the scrub. It is a wonder he was not killed, as the scrub is very thick where the accident occurred. Mallon reported the accident and a buggy was sent out for young Taylor, and he was brought in to the station and afterwards sent to Muttaburra. Dr. Lindsay set the limb, and, as young Taylor is only nine years old, the doctor hopes to have him about again in a few weeks.

Accident at Bowen Downs. (1895, November 26). The Western Champion and General Advertiser for the Central-Western Districts (Barcaldine, Qld.: 1892 - 1922), p. 14. Retrieved May 7, 2012, from http://nla.gov.au/nla.news-article79761772

Arthur Whiting – 8 January 1896

AN inquiry has been held at Longreach into the death of Arthur Whiting[113], who perished on the Camoola road from sunstroke and want of water.

Advertising. (1896, January 21). Warwick Argus (St. Lucia, Qld.: 1879 - 1901), p. 3. Retrieved May 26, 2012, from http://nla.gov.au/nla.news-article76619607

Editor's Note – Arthur was the son of Joseph Whiting and Elizabeth George. He was the brother of Cecil William Curnow – [1877], Joseph Percy George – [died 1879] and Frank Ernst – [1880]. It is presumed he was buried where he was found.

Thomas McCarthy – 15 February 1896

Further particulars concerning the sad drowning case at Camoola Park, says the Longreach Standard of Saturday last, are supplied us by Mr. Pym, who was present when the search party found the remains of the late Mr. Thomas McCarthy[114]. On Saturday morning Mr. McCarthy, in company with the gardener at Camoola Park, crossed the river in a boat near the corner of Edg's selection. On landing Mr. McCarthy caught a horse; and telling the gardener to wait with the boat for his return, rode away to drive some horses out of the paddock, The gardener waited a long time, and Mr. McCarthy not returning by sundown, he supposed that he (Mr. McCarthy) had ridden to Cooney's public house, and started back to the station. It was a very difficult passage in consequence of the trees and strong current, so the gardener after nightfall, striking a fence, tied up the boat and remained where he was until daylight. He then went on to the station and landed there in a rather exhausted condition. Directly he had made his report all the men at the station started out to search for Mr. McCarthy, some going across to the public-house, when it was ascertained that Mr. McCarthy had not been there. The party was joined by men from

[113] *Qld Ref: 1896/000011*
[114] *Qld Ref: 1896/000030*

this place, and the river and billabongs were searched for traces of the missing man and without success. On Monday morning they found the horse with his bridle entangled in the stump of a tree, and following the tracks discovered where he had crossed a billabong. This hole was dragged for some time without success; but later on they found the track again in a shallower place, and here, among some wattle trees, was the body of the drowned man floating on its side in about 3 ft. of water. It was surmised that in trying to head the horses he was driving Mr. McCarthy urged his horse across the water; but the animal raring up, threw his rider and kicked him on the head. Where the tracks were discovered the water was only just deep enough for a swim, there was no current, and a man falling in could easily have saved himself by catching hold of one of the numerous small trees with which the billabong was crowded. The body was much decomposed when brought ashore, and it was buried at the place. The late Mr. McCarthy twenty-eight years of age, although he had been in Mr. Parsons's employ for some time. He was of extremely energetic habits and a great favourite with his employer and those who were associated with him. Mr. McCarthy had no relatives in the colony; but his many friends will be grieved to hear of his sudden and untimely death.

THE FLOODS IN CENTRAL QUEENSLAND. (1896, February 29). The Capricornian (Rockhampton, Qld: 1875 - 1929), p. 28. http://nla.gov.au/nla.news-article70638030

Dora Macartney Miller – 9 April 1896

MILLER.—On the 9th April, at Bimbah, Longreach, Dora Macartney[115], beloved daughter of John Miller, Homestead, aged 21 years. Deeply regretted.

Family Notices. (1896, May 16). The Queenslander (Brisbane, Qld.: 1866 - 1939), p. 921. Retrieved March 31, 2014, from http://nla.gov.au/nla.news-article20448091

[115] *Qld Ref: 1896/C32*

ATTEMPTED SUICIDE.

On Friday last, before Messrs. P. G. Grant, P.M., and A. F. Evans and G. A. Henderson, J.P., James Lambert was charged with the above offence on the 13th December. – Constable Hayes gave evidence that he met the accused in a wagonnette with two men named Chapman and Ward at the latter's camp on the Bimbah road about three miles out of town. Chapman said accused had stabbed himself. Witness saw blood on accused's shirt. He spoke to accused, who said "I tried to do away with myself." He had him conveyed to town, and was present when the doctor examined him. There were four wounds in accused's stomach. The two knives and singlet (stained with blood) produced in Court were taken from accused, who appeared to have been drinking. He arrested the accused on Thursday. – Charles A. Chapman, a travelling saddler, said accused was at his camp on the Bimbah road on the 13th instant. He noticed that accused had been drinking heavily. He saw him go over towards the tucker box. There were two pocket knives on the box, but witness removed them. He next saw accused open the box, and take out a white-handled knife with which he stabbed his stomach. Witness believed the knife produced was the same one. He tried to take the knife from him, but accused made two stabs at him. He did not think accused knew what he was doing, as he appeared to be out of his mind. Accused then stabbed himself with a second knife, when witness threw him to the ground, and wrested it from him. Witness then noticed part of accused's stomach protruding, and blood flowing from the wound. The singlet produced was like the one accused was wearing. – Arthur Ward, laborer, living near Bimbah, said he remembered the 13th instant. On that day he was called to Chapman's camp, where he saw accused sitting on the ground. Chapman was holding him. Accused looked like a man in the horrors. Witness lifted up his singlet, and saw three wounds in his stomach. Chapman and wit ness attended to the wounds, and brought him in to the doctor. – Sergeant Farquharson applied for a remand at this stage, which was granted on the understanding that the case would be heard again as soon as Dr. Hewer returned to town. Bail was allowed the accused on his own reoognisance.

Longreach Police Court. (1895, December 31). The Western Champion and General Advertiser for the Central-Western Districts (Barcaldine, Qld.: 1892 - 1922), p. 9. Retrieved March 31, 2014, from http://nla.gov.au/nla.news-article79762434

Extract: The District Court was opened on Friday Inst by his Honour Judge Miller. Mr. H. E. King was (Crown Prosecutor), and Mr. C. B. Fitzgerald, M.L. was the only barrister present. The solicitors in Court were Messrs. L. Davidson and E. M. P. Pugh Longreach, and Mr. Major, Barcaldine. James Lambert, on bail, was charged with attempting to commit suicide, by slabbing himself with a knife on the 13th of December last, at Bimbah. He pleaded guilty, and was sentenced to one minutes' imprisonment.

LONGREACH. (1896, April 23). Morning Bulletin (Rockhampton, Qld.: 1878 - 1954), p. 5. Retrieved March 31, 2014, from http://nla.gov.au/nla.news-article52506680

Shearing – Bowen Downs – August 1896

Bowen Downs Station, which cut out on the 26th August, shore 312,500 sheep, the weekly average being over 44,600.

QUEENSLAND NEWS. (1896, September 5). Morning Bulletin (Rockhampton, Qld.: 1878 - 1954), p. 5. Retrieved June 2, 2012, from http://nla.gov.au/nla.news-article52515033

James Hammond – 5 December 1896

Sad Case of Drowning.

TELEGRAMS were received from Bowen Downs on Monday stating that a lad named James Hammond[116], who for a considerable time past had been employed at the Champion office, but who was having a spell by taking a round with a hawker, was drowned at Bowen Downs washpool on Saturday. He was seen on the side of the waterhole, which has steep banks, by a neighboring Chinese gardener, and the lad was supposed to have been fishing when he apparently overbalanced himself and fell in. No particulars are yet

[116] *Qld Ref: 1896/000069*

to hand beyond the information that up to the time the messenger was despatched the body had not been recovered. Young Jimmy was a quiet, inoffensive, obliging lad, and was a member of the band of the Barcaldine corps of the Salvation Army, and many will regret his untimely end. Mrs. Hammond has our deepest sympathy in her bereavement.

http://nla.gov.au/nla.news-article79766828 The Western Champion and General Advertiser for the Central-Western Districts (Barcaldine, Qld.: 1892 - 1922) Tuesday 8 December 1896 p 7 Article

The Drowning Case at Bowen Downs.

Our Correspondent at Bowen Downs supplies us with the following particulars of the drowning of the lad James Hammond:– On the 5th instant word was sent to the station that a lad, aged about 16, named James Hammond, or Ah Ming, had lost his life while swimming in the Bowen Downs washpool. Mr. Fraser and others proceeded to the scene of the accident, and made arrangements for the recovery of the body; this was not found till to-day (7th). From what I can gather it appears the young man was swimming across the waterhole to recover a bird that had been shot, and when about half-way across suddenly sunk and was not seen to rise again. It is supposed he was sized with cramps. Word was sent to the police at Muttaburra, and a constable was present when the body was recovered. An inquiry was held before Mr. S. P. Fraser, J.P., and the body was buried under his order. The deceased was travelling with an Indian hawker, and is a son of Ah Ming, or Hammond, a produce dealer of Barcaldine.

http://nla.gov.au/nla.news-article79766867 The Western Champion and General Advertiser for the Central-Western Districts (Barcaldine, Qld.: 1892 - 1922), Tuesday 15 December 1896, page 7

Editor's Note – James Hammond was the son of George Hammond and Mary Lock, the brother of George Henry [1879], Donald Harold [1885], Lieda Ann [1887], Elizabeth [1890 – 1908], Thomas [1893], Louisa [1897], Susan Florence [1899], Elsie Mary [1903].

Michael Lee – 13 March 1897

QUEENSLAND.

(By Telegraph from our Correspondents.)

BARCALDINE, March 24.

On the 18th Instant it was reported at Bowen Downs that the body of a man was discovered on the 16th close to the Seven Mile Yards, on the Corinda-Bowen Downs Road. From an inquiry held by Mr. Fraser, it appears that the remains are those of a man named Michael Lee[117] lately in the employ of Mr. Scott, a drover, who said deceased, was in good health while he was with him. Death had evidently resulted from natural causes. The weather is hot again to-day and clouds are coming up.

QUEENSLAND. (1897, April 3). The Queenslander (Brisbane, Qld.: 1866 - 1939), p. 716. Retrieved February 11, 2014, from http://nla.gov.au/nla.news-article20771477

Found Dead near Bowen Downs.

ON the 16th instant, a man, in the employ of and travelling with Mr. J. M. Niall, reported that the dead body of a man was lying near the road and close to the seven-mile yard on the Corinda-Bowen Downs road. Word was sent to the police at Muttaburra, and a constable arrived early on Wednesday morning, the 17th. Hr. S. P. Fraser, the constable and others went out, examined and then buried the body. On Thursday morning, an enquiry was held before Mr. S. P. Fraser, J.P., from which it appears the man, who was identified as Michael Lee, was lately in the employ of Mr. R. Scott, drover, who said he was in good health while with him, but was ailing before he started from Corinda. It would appear from the position of the body and general surroundings of the camp that the man must have died in his sleep, and without a struggle.

Found Dead near Bowen Downs. (1897, March 30). The Western Champion and General Advertiser for the Central-Western Districts (Barcaldine, Qld.: 1892 - 1922), p. 7. Retrieved April 14, 2013, from http://nla.gov.au/nla.news-article76380450

[117] *Qld BDM Ref: 1897/C31*

Alexander Bell – 1 April 1897

Information was received in Longreach on the 2nd April that Mr. Alexander Bell[118], manager of Camoola Downs, died suddenly on the previous night. Mr. Bell had been for about eighteen months at Camoola, and was much esteemed. He was a strong, apparently healthy man, and it is therefore presumed death was caused by rupture of an aneurism.

CENTRAL DISTRICTS. (1897, April 17). The Queenslander (Brisbane, Qld.: 1866 - 1939), p. 875. Retrieved May 26, 2012, from http://nla.gov.au/nla.news-article20772031

Editor's Note – Alexander was the son of Andrew Bell and Isabella.

Water Struck – No 8 Bore – June 1897

BARCALDINE, June 18. Water has been struck in No. 8 bore, on Bowen Downs, at a depth of 1860 ft. The water is flowing 4in. over the top of the 6in. casing. Boring is being continued in expectation of obtaining a larger supply.

LATEST BY TELEGRAPH. (1897, June 26). The Queenslander (Brisbane, Qld.: 1866 - 1939), p. 1382. http://nla.gov.au/nla.news-article24467301

John Murphy – 23 July 1897

MUTTABURRA.

(FROM OUR OWN CORRESPONDENT.)

The weather here at present is all that could be desired — the days warm and the nights cold, in fact, you require an extra pair of blankets to keep you warm. An old identity named John Murphy[119], aged about sixty years, was found dead at his camp on the 25th July at the Bowen Downs Wool Scour. It appears he was employed on Bowen Downs run for many years past to poison dingoes. On the 22nd July he went to the station to get his usual fortnightly, was last seen alive on the 23rd July by a Chinaman named Jimmy Ah Young.

[118] *Qld Ref: 1897/000029*

[119] *Qld Ref: 1897/000053*

The Chinaman is camped about there. On the 25th July Jimmy did not see Murphy going his rounds, so he went up to his tent and discovered him lying dead. The case was reported to the officer-in-charge of police, and he lost no time in sending out Constable McElhiney to bury the body. An inquiry was held before Mr. S. P. Fraser, J.P., to ascertain the cause of death. The evidence showed that the cause of death was exposure.

MUTTABURRA. (1897, August 7). The Capricornian (Rockhampton, Qld: 1875 - 1929), p. 29. Retrieved June 10, 2012, from http://nla.gov.au/nla.news-article68181941

Amos Brooks – Aramac Cemetery

Photo: Patterson-Kane, Peter & Karen

Amos Brooks – 18 July 1898
Sudden Death at Bowen Downs.

Mr. Amos BROOKS[120], the well-known bootmaker of Aramac, who was shearing at Bowen Downs, has been ill with the influenza epidemic that is going round. He was very bad on Monday and intended going to the doctor the following day, but it was too late

120 *Qld Ref: 1898/C76*

as he died Tuesday night. Much sympathy is felt for him and his family, as he was a man universally respected.

"The Western Champion and General Advertiser for the Central-Western Districts (Barcaldine, Qld.: 1892 - 1922) 26 Jul 1898: 7 <http://nla.gov.au/nla.news-article76385511>.BOWEN DOWNS.

Editor's Note – Amos Brooks, born in Aylesbury UK, the son of James Brooks and Martha Bonwick. He was Rebecca E Hall's husband. He was buried on the 19 July 1898 in the Aramac Cemetery.

Sidney Edwards – 1 August 1898

Sidney Edwards[121], the son of Jacob Edwards, a carpenter and joiner and Harriett, died on the 1 August 1898 at Caledonia although his place of burial is unknown. He was a butcher by trade. Sidney was married to Rosina Cheshire on the 10 November 1883 and they had five children: Rosina Harriet – [1887 – 1881], Beatrice Susan – [1889], Sidney – [1891], Thomas William – [1893] and Daisy Rachel – [1895].

TUABURRA, AN OUTSTATION OF BOWEN DOWNS.

Tuaburra, an outstation of Bowen Downs Station, 1898

John Oxley Library, State Library of Queensland Negative number: 18613

[121] *Qld Ref: 1898/000078*

Bowen Downs – 2 August 1898

SHEARING progressing well here (writes our special correspondent on the 23rd ult.). The nights are very cold, and a lot of the men are suffering with a kind of influenza, which, in some cases, has caused the patients to seek the hospital, and in one case proved fatal, namely, Mr. A. Brooks, well-known in Aramac as shoemaker. Brooks was shearing here, but complained before starting of pains in the chest. He contracted the epidemic and it settled on his chest in form of a severe cough. Nobody thought he was so far gone, as it shortly proved, for after a week's illness he expired on Monday evening, 18th inst. Mr. S. P. Fraser received a message from Aramac through his telephone, 42 miles distant, wishing Brooks' remains to be conveyed to Aramac. They accordingly left here in a coffin for Aramac, arriving there on Tuesday night. It is very fair to say that no work was done on the Tuesday out of respect for deceased. – The reading room and library is an established fact now, thanks to the working of the committee, especially Mr. J. Breton, secretary. The manager of Bowen Downs, Mr. S. P. Fraser, is likewise entitled to the thanks of everybody for the willing spirit in which he took it up and did all he could to make it a success. For the benefit of other places I will mention how quick a place can be provided and with what material. The walls consist of old wool packs, the roof is of iron, three tables have sitting accommodation for 50 men. It is premature, but I hope to see the day that all sheds – in fact, all places where men congregate in numbers – will have substantial accommodation for purposes of this sort. There is no doubt it is a death-blow to gambling. The room is lighted with six kerosene lamps, obtained from Meacham & Leyland, and you can see several games of chess, draughts, dominos, and cribbage, also whist – all intellectual games here. There is a weekly supply of some 50 newspapers. The library consists of nearly 100 volumes, mostly obtained by contributions from the men; but I must mention that Messrs. Brown & Booker and C. J. Kingston, of Aramac, also Mr. W. Kewley, of Longreach, contributed very handsomely in the shape of books. A debating club in connection with the reading room is also in progress. – The past week has been a very eventful one, as something unusual has taken place every evening. On Monday evening Mr. Brooks died; Tuesday, the members for Leichhardt and Mitchell, also the Rev. M. Webster, of Barcaldine, addressed the men; on Wednesday and Thursday, Professor Smith, a herbalist, gave concerts and sold some pills; on Friday, Mr. Langston, organiser, A.W.U., visited here; and to wind the week up on Saturday night a gentleman of the Sandown type showed us how to handle shots, weights and bars of iron, and his better-half did a bit of boxing with him.

A CORRESPONDENT was good enough to wire us from Muttaburra on Wednesday that "Jack O'Mohoney was beaten by Madam Salvator in four rounds at Bowen Downs woolshed." As "Jack" has the reputation of being a bit of a bruiser, it says a lot for the lady, but perhaps he was gallant enough not to exhibit his best form.

A CORRESPONDENT writing on the 24th July, says that the death of Mr. Amos Brooks gave the men a great shock, in as-much as he actually died standing up; ten minutes previous to his death he was walking about. A great many men are still laid up with colds, and some cases have become so serious as to necessitate a visit to Aramac and Muttaburra hospitals. A buggy and horses are now stationed here to take our sick men to the hospital. The reading room is in full swing, and is crowded nightly. It seems to have done away entirely with the "Nap" school, and the "Two-Up" games usually carried on to a pretty tune here. – Shearing is going on well, and it will take six or seven weeks to "cut, out" yet. Mr. Scott, the overseer, is having really good work done, which you rarely see in a large shed, as it is very difficult to get 70 really good machine hands together. The Wolseley machines are doing better all-round work this year than they ever did previously.

Round the Sheds. (1898, August 2). The Western Champion and General Advertiser for the Central-Western Districts (Barcaldine, Qld: 1892 - 1922), p. 7. http://nla.gov.au/nla.news-article76385584

William Neville – 13 December 1898

Muttaburra Mems.

FROM OUR OWN CORRESPONDENT.

On Monday morning, 1st inst. it was reported to the police by two boys named James Toole and James Ah Que that whilst riding in a paddock on Mount Cornish station, about eight miles from here, they had found the dead body of a man near the Thomson River. Sergeant Blyton and Constable Miller, accompanied by Dr. Townley, proceeded with the boys to where they had seen the corpse, which was found to be that of a man apparently about 60 years of age. Dr. Townley made an examination of the body, and as death was evidently due to natural causes, the police buried the man near where he was found. From papers found on him his name would seem to be William Nevill[122], a travelling plumber or tinsmith. His saddles and pack were at the foot of a tree near where the deceased lay and his horses were hobbled within sight. His property was taken charge of by the police. From the dried up state of the body the man must have been dead about three weeks.

Muttaburra Mems. (1899, January 10). The Western Champion and General Advertiser for the Central-Western Districts (Barcaldine, Qld: 1892 - 1922), p. 11. http://nla.gov.au/nla.news-article75670743

Thomas Farie Gray-Buchanan – 27th April 1899

MUTTABURRA, May 3. News has been received that a selector named Buchanan[123] at Eastfield, Tower Hill Creek, accidentally shot himself with a rifle. An inquiry will be held.

QUEENSLAND NEWS. (1899, May 6). The Capricornian (Rockhampton, Qld: 1875 - 1929), p. 19. Retrieved May 22, 2012, from http://nla.gov.au/nla.news-article68212556

[122] *Qld Ref: 1898/000003*

[123] *Qld Ref 1899/003203*

Thomas Farie Gray- Buchanan – Aramac Cemetery

[Source: Betty Wakely-Bundell Domain Name Trust]

In the will of Thomas Farie Gray-Buchanan, late of Eastfield, near Muttaburra, grazier, deceased, application on the part of Francis Hamilton Bradon Turner, of Rockhampton, manager of Dalgety and Company, the duly constituted attorney of Lieutenant-Colonel James Ross Gray-Buchanan, of Eastfield, Cambuslang, Scotland, the sole executor and legatee named in the will, that the sureties to the bond for the administration of the estate be dispensed with, and that the costs of the application be paid out of the estate. Mr. T. P. Barrymore (from the office of Messrs. Rees R. and Sydney Jones) appeared in support of the application. Order: Adjourned till Friday.

[No heading]. (1899, November 29). Morning Bulletin (Rockhampton, Qld.: 1878 - 1954), p. 7. Retrieved May 22, 2012, from http://nla.gov.au/nla.news-page5087908

Editor's Note – Thomas Farie Gray Buchanan, the son of James Ross Gray-Buchanan and Kate Farie, actually died on the 27 April 1899 at the age of 24 years. He was born in Glasgow on the 27 July 1875, and is buried in the Aramac Cemetery, Row 8 Plot 169: Id: 186.

1900 – 1910

James Campbell – 1 January 1901
and
Isaac Alton [Olsten] – 1 January 1901

On New Year's Day a man named James Campbell, but better known as "Dirty Scotty", died suddenly at Crusoe, where he was camped. The police went out and buried him. The sum of £27 odd was found on him. Another man, Isaac Olsten[124] by name, was found dead on the boundary fence between Towall and Ambo. He hung his swag in a tree and seems to have gone away looking for water, as there was a small billy alongside the dead body, which was about a mile from where the swag was left. From his appearance the man must have been dead four or five days when found. Charles Rienstra, who was cooking at McCarthy's Exchange Hotel, was taken suddenly ill on the afternoon of the 11th inst. He was taken to the hospital and died at half-past five the following morning. The cause of death was heat apoplexy.

Muttaburra Mems. (1901, January 15). The Western Champion and General Advertiser for the Central-Western Districts (Barcaldine, Qld.: 1892 - 1922), p. 9. Retrieved May 27, 2012, from http://nla.gov.au/nla.news-article76565031

Editor's Note – James Campbell[125], a shearer, from Scotland, died on the banks of Cornish Creek at Crusoe where he was camped.

Isaac Alston, as he was named in Qld BDM, is presumed to be buried where he was found on the boundary between Towall and Ambo.

Charles Rienstra, born in Holland, died on the 4 January 1901, aged about 50 years and is buried in the Muttaburra Cemetery, but the actual grave site is unknown.

[124] *Qld Ref: 1901/000009*
[125] *Qld Ref: 1901/C10*

MUTTABURRA.
(From Our Own Correspondent.)
The sad news of the death of Her Most Gracious Majesty the Queen, which was received this week, cast quite a gloom over the town. The sorrow at the intelligence appeared to be unbroken.

Several showers fell during the week, registering the meagre total of 0.16in., when 'according to appearances as many inches should have fallen. Reports from the surrounding stations to hand are are equally disappointing.

The 8000 sheep depastured on Mount Cornish for so long are now making a start for home. Mr. Martin is in charge. Mount Cornish is very heavily stocked from different holdings in the district, being occupied as relief country. Unless rain falls within a very short period heavy losses will be experienced thereon.

A mob of 150 horses, the property of Messrs. Edkins, Campbell, and Co., of Bimbah has, passed through last week, en route for Malboona, whither they are going for grass.

Our Progress Association has at length awakened to a sense of its duly. I hear a meeting is to be held on Monday. I was beginning to think that this body had outlived its usefulness.

Muttaburra, 26th January, 1901.

MUTTABURRA. (1901, February 2). The Capricornian (Rockhampton, Qld.: 1875 - 1929), p. 27. Retrieved September 24, 2014, from http://nla.gov.au/nla.news-article68250618

James Langan – 4 March 1901

LONGREACH, March 8.

A man named James Langon[126], sixty-seven years of age, committed suicide at Bimbah last night. Langon, who had previously been working at Crossmore, came to Bimbah, where Mr. R. H. Edkins gave him work. Nothing out of the common was noticed, but last night Langon was missed. A search was made and his swag and other articles were found in the river and then the body was found.

[126] *Qld Ref:1901/C27*

Langon was subject to hallucinations in regard to a will which he said gave a wrongful disposal of some property. At Christmas he was locked up here for his own protection.

QUEENSLAND NEWS. (1901, March 6). Morning Bulletin (Rockhampton, Qld.: 1878 - 1954), p. 5. Retrieved October 13, 2012, from http://nla.gov.au/nla.news-article52727288

Editor's Note – The Qld BDM register states that James was born in Ireland and was about 55 years old not 67 as stated in this article.

Mark Caulfield – 28 July 1901

Mark Caulfield[127] was 69 years old when he committed suicide by taking laudanum on the 28 July 1901. The site of his grave on Bowen Downs is unknown like many of those who died in the early development of this country they were buried where they died.

[Extract] Bowen Downs commenced lamb-marking a few days ago, and Culloden is ready to start. Culloden commences to shear on the 1st September, and Rockwood starts on the 1st August. I am unable to give the number to be shorn at these stations. Bowen Downs commences on September 1st, when they will shear 160,000 sheep.

Muttaburra Memos. (1901, July 30). The Western Champion and General Advertiser for the Central-Western Districts (Barcaldine, Qld.: 1892 - 1922), p. 12. Retrieved May 2, 2012, from http://nla.gov.au/nla.news-article76568083

Nathaniel Buchanan – 23 September 1901

QUEENSLAND PIONEERS.

Nat Buchanan.

(By John E. Bennett).

Nat Buchanan had probably a high claim to the title of the greatest of all Australian drovers.

[127] *Qld Ref: 1901/000055*

He was born near Dublin, in 1826, and arrived in Australia with his people six years later. His brothers, Frank and Andrew answered the lure of the gold of California, but scratched in vain for the yellow metal and were forced to work their passage home again. In 1859, the year of separation, Nat joined with Landsborough and explored the Fitzroy and Belyrando Rivers country, in search of suitable properties for grazing. As a result of these efforts, Bowen Downs the largest station in Australia, was founded and run by a company comprising: Landsborough, Buchanan and others.

It fell to Buchanan's lot, as an experienced drover, to bring the stock up the Western rivers and across to Bowen Downs, in order to stock it, and these first excursions occupy a large page in the development of the Australian pastoral Industry.

In 1863 he married Katherine Gordon, sister of the famous Gordon Brothers, whose careers were so indissoluble associated with that of Buchanan in after years. Mrs. Buchanan deserves to go down in history as one of the great women pioneers of Australia, for she accompanied her husband to the station, which was then on the outskirts of settlement, and there lived with him through all the trials of the times.

In 1871, Buchanan took up land on the Bellinger River, in New South Wales, the "beautiful Bellinger". He found, however, that the area was too restricted for one of his leanings, and he took up land in the North once more at Rocklands.

In the interim, he had explored much of the Gulf country and had acquired vast holdings, but a sudden drop in values had left him almost penniless. That was prior to his selection on the Bellinger.

Towards the end of the 1870s, commenced the famous aeries of long distance droving feats that has made him famous.

The first major one was from Travers and Gibson's station at Aramac, across what is now the Northern Territory to Glencoe Station. The party carried 12 months' supplies of food in three drays and carried by 60 horses. Burketown was then a deserted village, and from Cloncurry they had to traverse 1,000 miles into which white men had never been.

Buchanan, prince of bushmen, as Captain Mackay called him, used to push ahead to choose each night's camp and to select the best water holes, or to find the only waterholes where water was scarce. As for himself on these journeys, it was said that he seldom drank water and could last longer than most men without fluid of any kind whatsoever. The Gordon Brothers were members of the outfit.

They crossed the McArthur near where Borroloola now stands. While Buchanan was ahead some miles looking for further supplies, one of the men was killed by the blacks, being decapitated as he stood over the campfire. Apart from that there were no casualties, and actually more cattle than the party started out with were delivered, because some of the calves born on the road were saved.

The Gordons remained on Glencoe, but Buchanan returned to explore the country South-east of Daly Waters.

In 1881, he performed a remarkable feat by driving 20,000 cattle from Queensland across to Glencoe, on behalf of those great pioneers of the cattle industry, C. B. Fisher and Maurice Lyons. Although the cattle were delivered safely, with scarcely the loss of a single beast, they went down in their hundreds afterwards to something contracted on the property, and, we are told, the survivors never thrived at all.

For the next three years or so, Buchanan was engaged on these long drives with cattle for North Australia. In 1883, he stocked Wave Hill Station from Bowen Downs, and in the same year drove a mob of 4000 beasts from Richmond, near Hughenden, across to the Ord River in Western Australia.

Looking back over those years we find that he was the first man to travel stock to the Barkly Tableland, the Northern Territory, Victoria River or the Ord River in Western Australia.

An even greater feat was to follow. In 1890, he took a trial shipment of bullocks to Singapore in order to test what was thought might be an excellent outlet for the stations of Northern Australia. The animals brought £8 per head, expenses came to £5 per head. The ring of dealers in Singapore opposed the move, and no further trade took place.

Two years later came the big disaster of 1892, when failures on the stations were the order of the day. With a mob from the Ord River, Buchanan started west for some where beyond Hall's Creek. They crossed the Lower Fitzroy beyond the King Leopold Ranges, which they penetrated, passed along in the vicinity of Ninety Mile Beach to Marble Bar in Western Australia. From there they struck across towards the upper waters of the Fortesque, found a track through the Hamersley and Ophthalmia Ranges, lying between that river and the Ashburton, and dominated by Mt. Bruce, a 4000 feet peak, on to the head waters of the Ashburton, crossing that river to the Gascoyne, thence to the Upper Murchison, where the mob was safely handed over, after a journey of 1,800 miles along an unknown way, later called Buchanan's track.

In 1894, Buchanan lost Wave Hill through the financial crash and, at nearly 70 years of age, was engaged to find a way for the South Australian Government from Sturt Creek to the Barkly Tableland. His only companion was a black boy, whom he had to handcuff to a heavy camel saddle to prevent him running away, for a portion of the journey. The journey, despite great handicaps, was eventually completed, and Buchanan retired to the Tamworth district, where he spent the remnants of his savings in purchasing a lucerne farm, which he worked until his death in 1901. It is of interest to note that Andrew Buchanan, as far back as 1882, fashioned a sheep-shearing machine.

QUEENSLAND PIONEERS. (1938, August 16). Townsville Daily Bulletin (Qld.: 1885 - 1954), p. 7. Retrieved June 10, 2012, from http://nla.gov.au/nla.news-article62168595

Thomas Henry Coyne – 8 January 1902
Death at Bowen Downs.

Our Bowen Downs correspondent writes as follows – On the 6th inst. an old servant of this station passed away rather suddenly in the person of poor old Tom Coyne[128], who was stationed at Crusoe outstation. He had been complaining for some time past of a pain in the chest, especially after any exertion. This was put down to indigestion, but apparently Tom knew better, for on the above date he was lying under the verandah, and felt the end coming, for he called his wife and little children around him and said, "You will soon have no daddy", bade them all good-bye, and with one gasp lay back dead. Mrs. Coyne was quite alone, when fortunately a traveller turned up who went to Muttaburra and gave information. The sad news was wired to Mr. S. P. Fraser on the 9th, and he started at once for Crusoe. In the meantime the traveller returned to Crusoe and dug the grave. A coffin was taken out by the police, and poor old Tom was laid in his last resting place. Mr. Fraser arrived just as Mrs. Coyne and her family were returning from the burial, and he tells me their grief was heartrending. It is under stood that heart failure was the cause of death. Coyne leaves a wife and four little children to mourn him, the eldest of which is only 10 years of age. Great sympathy is expressed for them here. I think Coyne was well-known in Barcaldine, as he used some years ago to drive small lots of fat sheep from here.

http://nla.gov.au/nla.news-article76363254 The Western Champion and General Advertiser for the Central-Western Districts (Barcaldine, Qld.: 1892 - 1922) Monday 20 January 1902

Editor's Note – Thomas Henry was the son of Patrick Coyne and Ellen McLoughlin dying on the 8 January 1902. He married Mary Nestor in 1889 and they had the following children according to Qld BDM: Annie – 1892, Thomas Henry – 1893, Agnes Margaret – 1896, Mary – 1898 and both Annie (1899) and Agnes (1902) were enrolled in the Muttaburra School. Crusoe was an out-station of Mt Cornish.

[128] *Qld Ref: 1902/C17*

Aramac Marsupial Board – 7 June 1902

ARAMAC.

(From Our Own Correspondent.)

The following nominations were received in the election of members of the Aramac Marsupial Board: — E. R. Edkins, Mount Cornish; S. P. Fraser, Bowen Downs; A. G. Niall, Aramac; J. McAuliffe, Stagmount; and W. Williams, Stainburn. This being the exact number required, the gentlemen named here declared elected. The new Board will meet on the 13th of June.

ARAMAC. (1902, June 7). The Capricornian (Rockhampton, Qld: 1875 - 1929), p. 47. http://nla.gov.au/nla.news-article68273383

Jeremiah O'Brien – 7 January 1903

MUTTABURRA.

(From Our Own Correspondent.)

I have to report the death, on the evening of the 5th instant, at Cornish Creek, twelve miles from here, of Jeremiah O'Brien[129], a well-known and respected employee of Bowen Downs. He came into Muttaburra for the Christmas and New Year holidays and left on the 4th instant intending to go back to work at Potosi. He fell a victim to heat apoplexy.

MUTTABURRA. (1903, January 19). Morning Bulletin (Rockhampton, Qld.: 1878 - 1954), p. 5. Retrieved May 31, 2012, from http://nla.gov.au/nla.news-article52975051

Editor's Note – Jeremiah, born in Clonakilty, Cork, Ireland, was a 36 year old labourer when died from heat apoplexy after suffering for 3 days. He was buried on the 8 January 1903 on Cornish Creek, Muttaburra by James Keogh. A Magisterial inquiry was held at Muttaburra on the 9 January, 1903 by Peter Cunningham Gorrie, J.P.

Jeremiah was not married and had lived in Queensland for about 19 years.

Qld BDM – Death Certificate

[129] *Qld Ref: 1903/C3*

Ah Sue – 17 January 1903

A Chinaman named Ah Sue[130], gardener, Mount Cornish, met his death there a few days ago. He was on top of a windmill and, being struck by the fan, fell to the ground, a distance of 30 ft., and broke his neck.

MUTTABURRA. (1903, January 22). Morning Bulletin (Rockhampton, Qld.: 1878 - 1954), p. 7. http://nla.gov.au/nla.news-article52978452

Editor's Note – Ah Sue is buried at Mount Cornish, but the actual grave site is unknown.

Ah Gow – 8 February 1903

Ah Gow[131] a cook at Mt Cornish died on the 8 February 1903 from 'old age' at the age of 72 years old. He was buried at Mt Cornish although the actual site unknown.

Mary McDonald – 20 July 1904

DEATH.

McDONALD — At Aramac Hospital, on 20th July, Mary[132], wife of John McDonald, overseer at Reedy Creek, Bowen Downs.

Family Notices. (1904, August 8).The Western Champion and General Advertiser for the Central-Western Districts (Barcaldine, Qld.: 1892 - 1922), p. 6. http://nla.gov.au/nla.news-article75607119

Editor's Note – Mary was buried in the Central section (Plot 163) of the Aramac Cemetery on the 20 July 1904. Mary was 58 years old. John and Mary's children were Mary, Angus William, Ralph Erskine, Ann, Isabella and John Patrick. She was the daughter of Patrick Johnston and Ann Kelly. John, Her husband and Ralph their son is also buried in the Aramac Cemetery.

[130] *Qld Ref: 1903/000007*

[131] *Qld Ref: 1903/000012*

[132] *Qld Ref: 1904/C25*

Edward Ketia Russell – 15 October 1904

DEATH OF .MR. E. K. RUSSELL.

The death of Mr. H. K. Russell[133], formerly manager of Bowen Downs Station, and later, with his brother, Mr. Charles Russell, merchant, Townsville, took place at the Royal Mail Hotel, Tingalpa, early on Saturday morning, says the "Brisbane Courier" of the 18th instant. About nine years ago Mr. Russell brought his family to Brisbane, and he was for some time with Messrs. A. B. Webster, Mary Street, after which he was associated with the firm of Messrs. Armand, Ranniger, and Co., indent agents, from which he retired two years ago. The deceased was a member of the Balmoral Divisional Board for three years, during; two years of which he occupied the position of chairman. His death was due to a paralytic seizure about a fortnight ago, and from which he did not regain consciousness. Mr. Russell is survived by two married daughters and two sons

DEATH OF MR. E. K. RUSSELL. (1904, October 21). Morning Bulletin (Rockhampton, Qld.: 1878 - 1954), p. 4. Retrieved May 31, 2012, from http://nla.gov.au/nla.news-article53021526

Editor's Note – Edward Keira Russell was the son of Samuel Russell and Mary Croaker. He married Elizabeth Adams and had the following children: Annette Lydia – 3 October 1873, Samuel Keira – 27 September 1875, Charles William – 21 October 1877, Ernest Arthur – 2 September 1879 and Mary Louisa – 27 June 1881. Edward Keira was actually the book-keeper at Bowen Downs
Edward Russell is buried in the Toowong Cemetery Portion 1, Section 29, Grave 2.

John McDonald – 20 December 1904

The Late Mr. John McDonald.

Mr. John McDonald[134], overseer at Reedy Creek, an out-station of Bowen Downs, passed away about 3 p.m. on Tuesday, the 20th inst. Mr. McDonald was an old identity in this and the Barcoo district, he arriving on the Barcoo in the early '60s. He was an overseer on

[133] *Qld Ref: 1904/002877*
[134] *Qld Ref: 1905/C4*

Bowen Downs from '69 to '75, and again from '82 up to the time of his death. The deceased complained last Sunday morning, and a few hours before his death felt he was much better. He was resting in a hammock when he quietly expired. His body was taken into Aramac last evening, where he will be laid beside his wife, who pre-deceased him just five months. Much sympathy is felt for his family.

Bowen Downs, Dec. 2lst, 1904.

The Late Mr. John McDonald. (1905, January 2). The Western Champion and General Advertiser for the Central-Western Districts (Barcaldine, Qld.: 1892 - 1922), p. 3. http://nla.gov.au/nla.news-article75608574

Edward Roland Edkins – 14 August 1905

DEATH.

EDKINS – On the 14th August, at his residence, Willandra, Napier Street, Drummoyne, Sydney, Edward Roland Edkins, late of Mount Cornish, from effect dengue fever, aged 65 years.

Family Notices. (1905, September 14). The Brisbane Courier (Qld.: 1864 - 1933), p. 4. From http://nla.gov.au/nla.news-article19409503

THE LATE MR. E. R. EDKINS

"Alone the Line", writing in the "Northern Miner" on the 25th of August, says:–

I have before me as I write, a telegram from W. H. L. Thornton. Unfortunately it came when I was away from my home, and the sad news was told late. It reads "Edkins dies Sydney, forty-three years mates, grand man. Thornton".

Well might the last words – "grand man" – be written for Roley Edkins was one of Nature's noblemen. Quoting the words of my telegram to the "Miner", he was a king among men. He was the in-personation of kindness and goodwill to his fellow-men – a man to whose character harshness was impossible. He was a man of strict integrity, whose word in all dealing in stock was bond, and in the past when Mount Cornish was in the heyday of its prosperity, his stock trade was great.

I do not know accurately in what year he came to the North. It was, I believe, 1863, and he was then on the Tableland with

Gibson at Cargoon, and there yet remains the old log hut originally built by him. A year or so later he joined Towns and Co., and set up the boiling works on the Albert at Burketown. In November last year I was in that locality about Beames Brook and saw the remains of "Edkins' Yards". I brought home with me an old splice of the No. 6 wire they used then for fences, and have it here as I write. From Albert in 1866 he took cattle to Victoria, and to him belongs the honour of having been the first to travel stock on the 2000 mile on this route that so many men have followed since. Somewhere about this year, on his return from Melbourne, the boiling works on the Albert, and pretty well the whole country in the Gulf, was abandoned, and I have told you of the good man who is gone fetching pigs from the boiling works across the Gilbert. There are many others who could tell Roland Edkins's early days up there much better than I, Sawtell, yet living Byrimine came with him from Victoria. John Rankin, too, yet resident at Rockhampton, was with him fetching the pigs and there selling them to the Chinamen rushing to the Gilbert diggings.

In 1872 he and his good wife, and their first baby, now R H Edkins, of Longreach came to the Mud Hut on the Thomson River, the embryo of Mount Cornish, and from there, where the good name of Edkins will be honoured whilst the present generation lives, and afterwards, for in the words of the telegram he was a "grand man."

Bushmen, drovers, aye even the vagabonds of the road, respected the name of Edkins. Many years ago a "bad case" drover was detailing his villainies to me, telling of how he had robbed a station of cattle by going back on to the run after having got delivery, and picking up bush cattle and adding them to his mob, and so he talked away. I knew he had droved from Mount Cornish and suggested he had played the same game there. He was adamant at once. "No! Oh No!" he said, "a man who'd take Edkins down would be a bad ---, and you know I'm not that". Bad enough as he was, he respected the man whom death had robbed us of. In his district Edkins was often judge between litigants – a judge who sat without robes or wig, and often under a tree whilst his quart pot simmered. He thought out the merits of each man's case, and disputes over stock transactions involved large sums of money, yet so great was the knowledge and confidence in the character of the man that his decisions were final.

During his management Mount Cornish developed into one of the finest pastoral properties in Australia; but the droughts of 1882 to 1886, and then years later told appalling tales, and no doubt, to, these worries made inroads in his constitution, for he was not a very old man, nor was he infirm in any way. He was a man who lived an even life, and loved his home; and in old days that home was a rare one, even though a mud hut was but the dwelling. And now, after all these years, the reaper has come, and never in his track has he left more sorrow. He had taken from among us one who has nobly fought the battles of the cattle man, and who has at last gone out of life, taking with him the goodwill of his fellow-man and many, as they read of his death, will follow along behind their cattle sadly thinking of the good deeds of the "good man" who is gone.

THE LATE MR. E. R. EDKINS. (1905, August 31). Morning Bulletin (Rockhampton, Qld.: 1878 - 1954), p. 5. Retrieved May 31, 2012, from http://nla.gov.au/nla.news-article53049058

THE LATE MR. E. R EDKINS.

Mr. P. B. Gordon, in a letter in the "Brisbane Courier" of Monday, last, says: "Many old Queenslanders will feel regret that nothing more than a mere passing notice has been taken of the death of Mr. E. R. Edkins, for many years the popular manager of Mount Cornish Station. I was, perhaps, the oldest acquaintance of Mr. Edkins in Queensland. I knew him in the early sixties, when he succeeded the late Mr. W. Cunningham, as manager for Mr. Sheridan, of the Taramiah station on the north bank of the Murray. Mr. Edkins was then a mere lad, scarcely twenty years of age. His mother and sister resided on the station with him. The whole of the station management under him was spick and span and every calf branded up within two months of its birth. When the great emigration set in for the north of Queensland in 1863, Mr. Edkins joined Messrs. Cunningham, Hann, and others in taking up country in the north, and, after several vicissitudes, settled down as manager of the extensive herd of Mount Cornish, which, under his able management, was developed into the best herd without exception in Australia. During the long drought the gradual decrease of the herd by death told on his health, and on the last occasion of my meeting him in Brisbane, some months ago, he was only the shadow of his former self. The memory of Rolley Edkins will find a warm place in the hearts of many old Queenslanders, and in none more so than in that of the writer."

THE LATE MR. E. R. EDKINS. (1905, September 23). The Capricornian (Rockhampton, Qld: 1875 - 1929), p. 17. http://nla.gov.au/nla.news-article72007231

RESEAL OF PROBATE.

Reseal of probate of the Will of Edward Rowland Edkins, formerly of Mount Cornish, but lately of Drummoyne. New South Wales, grazier, has been granted to Edwina Marion Elkins, of Drummoyne, widow. The personality was sworn at under the value of £3,501.

RESEAL OF PROBATE. (1908, August 3). Morning Bulletin (Rockhampton, Qld.: 1878 - 1954), p. 5. Retrieved June 8, 2012, from http://nla.gov.au/nla.news-article53155142

A few days ago, Mr. J. E. Smith, The Stock Inspector, returned from a fairly lengthy trip. He had to go to Bowen Downs in order to inspect 12,000 wethers which are going to Bourke, and while away he also inspected a lot of 8,000 purchased off various places by Mr. J. K. Lomax, of Boatman. He saw Mr. E. Carter's Nonda sheep, which were shorn in Barcaldine, going to Aberfoyle. Mr. Smith came back by Mount Cornish and Crossmore. Now that motor bicycles are a proved success out here – Mr. W. Rhodes came up from Tocal, nearly sixty miles, in a shade over three hours – the

Stock Department could do worse than provide its inspectors with the machine, for it would mean a tremendous caving in time.

LONGREACH. (1905, September 19). Morning Bulletin (Rockhampton, Qld.: 1878 - 1954), p. 7. Retrieved October 13, 2012, from http://nla.gov.au/nla.news-article55809622

Boyd Dunlop Morehead – 30 October 1905

DEATH OF THE HON. B. D. MOREHEAD.

The death of the Hon. Boyd Dunlop Morehead[135], M. L. C., which occurred yesterday shortly before 6 o'clock in the evening; removes from our midst one who in time has played a prominent and important part in public affairs. He had been suffering from a serious illness during the past ten days, and was under treatment in a private hospital. Yesterday afternoon his condition became critical, and Drs. Taylor, Hardie, and Hawkes were summoned. At ten minutes to 6 he passed away, death resulting, it is stated, from an attack of apoplexy. The late Hon. B. D. Morehead was one of the ever-increasing band of native-born Australians who have won a place in our political life. He was born in Sydney on the 24th August, 1843, and received his preliminary education there. At the age of 16 years he visited Scotland, and there received an additional eighteen months' tuition. Returning to Sydney, Mr. Morehead went first to the Grammar School, and then to the Sydney University, where he studied at the same time as Sir Samuel Griffith, Chief Justice of Australia. From the University Mr. Morehead joined the Bank of New South Wales, where he received a sound training in financial matters. Pastoral pursuits next claimed his attention for some time, and he first visited Queensland in 1866 as station inspector for the Scottish Australian Investment Company. In 1873 he was instrumental in founding the firm of B. D. Morehead and Co. (now Moreheads Limited). He was first returned to the Queensland Legislative Assembly as a representative of the Mitchell district in 1872, and he served that constituency for a number of

[135] *Qld Ref: 1905/B6119*

years. In 1880 Mr. Morehead was allocated the portfolio of Postmaster-General in the McIlwraith Ministry. Three years later he contested the Fortitude Valley seat without success, but was shortly afterwards returned for Balonne. Mr. (now Sir Samuel) Griffith was returned to power, and Mr. Morehead sat in Opposition under his old leader, whose place he took in the House as Leader of the Opposition during Mr. McIlwraith's absence in England. Mr. Morehead himself visited the old country in 1880, and on his return the following year he was elected leader of the Opposition. In 1888, again under the Premiership of Sir Thomas McIlwraith, Mr. Morehead took the portfolio of Colonial Secretary. In 1889 Sir Thomas McIlwraith retired, and Mr. Morehead became Premier, with the portfolios of Chief Secretary and Colonial Secretary. The Morehead Ministry held office until August, 1890. After another visit to the old country, Mr. Morehead was appointed a delegate to represent this State on the Federal Council. In 1893 he was offered the post of Agent-General in London, but declined for private reasons. During this same year Mr. Morehead was again returned for Balonne. In 1890 he was called to a seat in the Legislative Council, where his extensive knowledge of the State and of the pastoral industry has proved of considerable service. His life has been marked by considerable activity and usefulness to the State of Queensland, and amongst other positions he has occupied it may be mentioned that Mr. Morehead was a member of the Liquor Commission in 1900, and with Sir Arthur (then Mr.) Palmer, he represented Queensland at the Intercolonial Conference in Sydney in 1881.

DEATH OF THE HON. B. D. MOREHEAD. (1905, October 31). The Brisbane Courier (Qld.: 1864 - 1933), p. 4. Retrieved May 30, 2012, from http://nla.gov.au/nla.news-article19417203

Editor's Note – Boyd was born in Sydney on the 24 August 1843 and was 62 years old when he died in Brisbane. He was the son of Robert Archibald Morehead and Helen Buchanan Dunlop. He is buried in the Toowong Cemetery Portion 12; Section 49; Grave number 6.

He was only 23 years old when he became the manager of Bowen Downs in 1866 remaining in this position until July 1871. His first wife Annabella Campbell nee Ranken died before him, but he was survived by his second wife Ethel Seymour who he married at Brisbane on 3 April 1895. There were seven daughters from his first marriage and one by his second.

Boyd Dunlop Morehead

Toowong Cemetery: Portion 12, Section 49, Grave 6

Alfred Maddern – 13 January 1906

FAITHFUL UNTO DEATH.

Brisbane, Saturday.

A boundary rider on Crusoe run, Muttaburra, discovered the dead body of a man on the road between Crusoe and Hardington, and recognised it as that of a man whom he had given food and directions to water about a mile distant. The body was found half a mile from the water, and beside it was the body of a dog, which had evidently stayed by its master till it died. There was nothing on it to identify the body.

FAITHFUL UNTO DEATH. (1906, January 27). Barrier Miner (Broken Hill, NSW: 1888 - 1954), p. 4. Retrieved June 1, 2012, from http://nla.gov.au/nla.news-article44490451

MUTTABURRA.

(From Our Own Correspondent.)

Constable Keogh, who had been investigating the circumstances attending the death of the man at Crusoe last week, returned on Saturday after examining and burying the body. A boundary rider employed on Mount Cornish told the constable that he saw the deceased, on the 11th instant, and there appeared to be nothing wrong with him then. As he had neither water nor food, the boundary rider gave him some water and what lunch he had with him. There was nothing on or near where the body was found to enable it to be identified.

MUTTABURRA. (1906, January 27). Morning Bulletin (Rockhampton, Ql.: 1878 - 1954), p. 5. http://nla.gov.au/nla.news-article53060699

Editor's Note – This was Alfred Maddern[136] whose body was found in the paddock about 7 miles from the Crusoe homestead – an out-station of Mt Cornish.

The actual burial site is unknown but as stated in the article he was buried where he was found.

John Fergus – 28 February 1906

John Fergus[137] was the son of John Fergus and Mary Ann Murdock, aged about 73 years, when he died from an asthma attack on the 28 February 1906. His actual grave site is on Bowen Downs but the exact site is unknown.

John Thomas Campbell Ranken – 22 March 1907

DEATH OF MR. T. C. RANKEN.

ROCKHAMPTON, March 22.

A private telegram was received from Goulburn to-day announcing the death of Mr. J. T. C. Ranken[138], who was for some years manager

[136] *Qld Ref: 1906/000015*
[137] *Qld Ref: 1906/000026*
[138] *NSW Ref: 1265/1907*

of B. D. Morehead's business at Rockhampton. Mr. Ranken was a brother-in-law of Mr. Morehead. He came to the district in the very early days, and lived for many years at Mount Cornish station. He was aged 68 years.

DEATH OF MR. T. C. RANKEN. (1907, March 23). The Brisbane Courier (Qld.: 1864 - 1933), p. 6. http://nla.gov.au/nla.news-article19481240

[Extract] A Trance

It is fresh in the memory of old westerners when Readford purloined a mob of Mount Cornish cattle and drove them to Adelaide and sold them. His subsequent trial at Roma, and the circumstances connected with his acquittal are well known. This occurred in the early seventies, when Mr. J. T. C. Ranken was engaged on Bowen Downs. He and some others started after the cattle stealers. Mr. Ranken, however, had but recently suffered from an attack of fever and ague, and it would appear that he had not sufficiently recovered to warrant his undertaking such a perilous journey as that of pursuing cattle stealers. A day or two after they started his horse fell with him, and Mr. Ranken was apparently stunned. The men picked him up and brought him back to the out-station. For several days he lay motionless, and the majority of the men present concluded that he was dead. But one fellow said he had grounds for believing the patient lived. The others were sure he was dead, and suggested that the body be buried. The old man drew their attention to the fact that rigor mortis had not as yet supervened, and it was decided to hold over the burial. A very lucky decision, for on the ninth day Mr. Ranken aroused from his lethargy, much to the astonishment of the men in the hut. Mr. Ranken soon recovered after his lengthened repose.

THE CENTRAL WEST. (1898, November 14). Morning Bulletin (Rockhampton, Qld.: 1878 - 1954), p. 6. Retrieved June 3, 2012, from http://nla.gov.au/nla.news-article52542099

Martin Leslie – 20 August 1907

An elderly man named Martin Leslie[139], an employee at Mount Cornish Station, had a very painful experience on Thursday week. He fell from a horse and dislocated his shoulder, and in addition was very badly bruised. From Thursday evening until Saturday, when he was found, he was without food. On Sunday he was brought in to the hospital by Mr W. H. Langdon, who picked him up, and is improving.

MUTTABURRA. (1907, August 24). The Capricornian (Rockhampton, Qld.: 1875 - 1929), p. 32. Retrieved September 19, 2014, from http://nla.gov.au/nla.news-article68899035

Editor's Note – Martin, who was born in England, actually died from the above indecent. He fractured his right rib and punctured his lung as well as the shoulder injury. He was delivered in to the Muttaburra hospital on the 19 August with Dr Mary C DeGaris attending to him. But, he died on the 20 August.

Constable W J Sterne, Muttaburra Police, certified his death in writing. He was buried in the Muttaburra Cemetery on the 21 August with Sam Clemesha as the undertaker, and A W Clemesha and W Byrne as witnesses.

Charles Franklin – 25 July 1908

A Pitiful Death.

LONGREACH. August 10.

Sub-Inspector Quilter received a report in regard to the finding of the dead body of Charles Franklin, on Eastfield, Mt Cornish boundary. Charles Franklin was caretaker of Eastfield, and was living by himself. On the 23rd ultimo, Mr. Camp, the Prairie to Muttaburra mailman, left a note asking Franklin to meet him at a certain gate on the following day, with a roan mare which was running there, but Franklin did not turn up. Four days later Mr. South, a carrier, saw a horse with a saddle on running in Eastfield. He reported the matter at Crusoe, an out-station of Mt. Cornish, with the result that Thomas Firth was sent to search for Franklin.

139 *Qld Ref: 1907/C43*

On the 30th ultimo he found Franklin's body, it was evident that deceased had died a lingering death. He had been thrown from his horse and had not moved from the spot. At his feet was a hole five inches deep which he had kicked up, and at his head the ground was torn up to a depth of 6 inches he had done this with his hands. Round him the grass had been burnt away, as he had evidently set fire to it in the hope of attracting attention, but the grass did not burn to any great extent. When Constable Crane saw the body it was very much decomposed, but so far as he could see there were no marks of violence. The deceased had scratched on his match-box "Charles Franklin, born, Limerick 1848". Running in the paddock with Franklin's horse was Camp's roan mare.

A Pitiful Death. (1908, August 11). The Northern Miner (Charters Towers, Qld.: 1874 - 1954), p. 7. Retrieved May 31, 2012, from http://nla.gov.au/nla.news-article80295234

DEATH IN THE BUSH.

Sub-inspector Quilter is in receipt of a wire from Sergeant Duffy, of Muttaburra, stating that the Mount Cornish stockmen while out mustering, found the dead body of an elderly boundary rider named Charles Franklin on the Mount Cornish and Eastfield boundary (states the Longreach correspondent of the "Courier" on July 31). From appearances the horse must have rolled over Franklin about a week ago. The horse and saddle were found in a paddock. Constable Crane has gone out to investigate the matter and bury the body.

DEATH IN THE BUSH. (1908, August 13). Cairns Morning Post (Qld.: 1907 - 1909), p. 5. http://nla.gov.au/nla.news-

Editor's Note – Charles Franklin[140] was born in Ireland about 60 years ago and was buried, where he was found, on the Mount Cornish and Eastfield boundary on the 1 August 1908.

[140] *Qld Ref: 1908/C58*

Mathew Healy – 23 May 1909

The many friends of Matt Healy[141] were shocked to hear that he had been found dead in his bed at Bowen Downs on Sunday morning last. Matt had been suffering from influenza, but no one expected that the attack would prove fatal. He was a very fine character, and the country would be the gainer if a few more of his sort were to be found, as he was universally respected, and by his intimates very highly esteemed.

http://nla.gov.au/nla.news-article77629162The Western Champion and General Advertiser for the Central-Western Districts (Barcaldine, Qld.: 1892 - 1922) Saturday 29 May 1909

Editor's Note – Mathew was aged 47 and was buried at Bowen Downs Homestead.

Tommy Ah Won – 13 April 1910

I wired you about the death of the Malay cook[142], which occurred rather suddenly at Mt Cornish yesterday, morning. It seems he had been ailing for some time with heart disease and indigestion, for which he had been treated, however, without avail. Yesterday morning, while attending to his duties as cook, he fell down in a faint, and although restoratives was at once administered, he never regained consciousness. Constable J. Rowan, who went to the Station to investigate, reports there were no. suspicious circumstances in connection with his death, and he made arrangements for the burial of the deceases.

Muttaburra Notes. (1910, April 19). The Northern Miner (Charters Towers, Qld.: 1874 - 1954), p. 6. Retrieved October 13, 2012, from http://nla.gov.au/nla.news-article80248052

Editor's Note – It is presumed that the Malay cook was Tommy Ah Won who died 13 April 1910 at Mount Cornish. He was about 50 years old.

---

141 *Qld Ref: 1909/000033*
142 *Qld Ref: 1910/000019*

William Cox – 2 July 1910

(Q.), Thursday.

William Cox, employed on Bowen Downs, was killed, owing to a horse running him against a tree.

The Sydney Morning Herald (NSW 1842 - 1954) 8 Jul 1910: 11. <http://nla.gov.au/nla.news-article15195726

FATAL RIDING ACCIDENT

I am just in receipt of news of a sad accident having occurred at Reedy Creek, an outstation of Bowen Downs, resulting in the death of a young man named William Cox[143]. It appears that he with a couple of other employees were returning to the head station from one of the paddocks, Cox being some distance in front of the others, when the latter unknown to him started racing, with the result that they cannoned into the unfortunate man, who was thrown and killed instantly. Mr. S. P. Fraser went out and held a magisterial inquiry and ordered his burial. The depositions have been forwarded to the Crown Law Offices. Aramac, July 4th, 1910

(Source; The Western Champion and General Advertiser for the Central-Western Districts (Barcaldine, Qld.: 1892 - 1922) 9 Jul 1910: 10. http://nla.gov.au/nla.news-article75677216)

Editor's Note – William, was the son of Ralph Cox, who was a blacksmith, and Ellen Kelly.

His parent erected a natural sand-stone head stone with the carved information on it at Reedy Creek between the Homestead and Shearing Shed. He was only 22 when the accident happened.

William Schofield – 7 July 1910

DEATH. SCHOFIELD. – In the Muttaburra Hospital, on the 6th July, William Schofield[144], 60 years of age, for many years blacksmith and wheelwright at Bowen Downs.

The Western Champion and General Advertiser for the Central-Western Districts (Barcaldine, Qld: 1892 - 1922) Saturday 16 July 1910 p 5 Family Notices

143 *Qld Ref: 1910/000040*

144 Qld Ref: 1910/000043

Editor's Note –William, born in Lancashire England, was about 59 years old when he died of acute heart failure. He was the son of George Schofield and Hannah Halstead.

William is buried in Muttaburra Cemetery but the actual grave site is unknown.

Edwina Edkins – 17 August 1910

DEATH OF MRS. E. R. EDKINS.

The news received in Brisbane yesterday that Mrs. E R. Edkins, widow – of the late Mr. E R. Edkins, who was for many years associated with pastoral pursuits in Queensland, and, among other stations managed Mount Cornish for so long, died in Sydney early yesterday morning. The deceased lady was very widely known throughout the State, where she had a large number of friends. Mrs. Edkins was the first white lady in the Gulf, and during her residence at Mount Cornish the station was really an open house. The news of her death will be received with very widespread regret.

DEATH OF MRS. E. R. EDKINS. (1910, August 18). The Brisbane Courier (Qld.: 1864 - 1933), p. 7. http://nla.gov.au/nla.news-article19651194 article39410785

1911 – 1950

Frederick Goodman – 21 April 1911

A sad drowning fatality occurred at Bowen Downs last Friday (our Muttaburra correspondent telegraphs). It appears that an old age pensioner named Fred Goodman[145], aged 78 years, who had been on Bowen Downs for about 20 years, went fishing at Flannigan's water hole, on Cornish Creek, about two miles from the head station. As he had not returned at 9 p.m., a party went in search of him, and as his clothes were found on the bank of the waterhole it was surmised that he had done what he usually did when his line got caught, which was to go in and release it. His body was found on Saturday in the waterhole, after dragging. Constable Crane was sent out to investigate the matter, and Mr. S. P. Fraser, J.P., manager of Bowen Downs, held an inquiry.

The Queenslander (Brisbane, Qld.: 1866 - 1939) 29 Apr 1911: 39. http://nla.gov.au/nla.news-article22292328

Editor's Note – Fredrick Goodman was the son of Benjamin Goodman.

Horses Took Fright And Bolted – April 1911

Mr. Archie Norton, who has been for many years on Bowen Downs station, was coming into town when for some unaccountable reason the horses took fright and bolted. The brake coming off and getting in between the spokes smashed them, and Mr. Norton fearing a bad accident threw himself out with the result of a dislocated shoulder, which he pluckily put back himself. It was fortunate for him that another station hand was riding in and came across him so that he could ride on to Mount Cornish and get a

[145] *Qld Ref: 1911/000022*

conveyance to bring Mr. Norton to town. He is now on the high road to recovery.

Muttaburra Notes. (1911, April 29). The Western Champion and General Advertiser for the Central-Western Districts (Barcaldine, Qld.: 1892 - 1922), p. 10. Retrieved June 2, 2012, from http://nla.gov.au/nla.news-article75681203

Bowen Downs – 6 May 1911

Our correspondent wrote on the 29th April:– Mr. S. P. Fraser, who has been manager of Bowen Downs for 29 years, started for Saltern Creek to-day, to take up the management for the S. A. I. Co., who recently purchased this property. Prior to Mr. Fraser leaving, the employees, to the number of 24, presented him with a nice little cheque as a token of their esteem. Mr. Fraser intends to purchase a gold watch, which he will have suitably inscribed to remind him of his long sojourn at Bowen Downs.

At Bowen Downs. (1911, May 6). The Western Champion and General Advertiser for the Central-Western Districts (Barcaldine, Qld.: 1892 - 1922), p. 9. Retrieved May 30, 2012, from http://nla.gov.au/nla.news-article75681311

Archibald McNiel – 29 January 1912

A man named Archie McNiel[146] a fencer working for Mr. Harold Seattle at North Crusoe, cut his throat on Monday morning. He had been about eight weeks in town having a spree but seemed all right when he went back to work again two days ago. However, he was evidently suffering from delirium tremens when he committed the rash act. Constable Crane went out to investigate and performed the last solemn rites.

MUTTABURRA NOTES. (1912, February 12). Townsville Daily Bulletin (Qld.: 1885 - 1954), p. 8. Retrieved September 21, 2013, from http://nla.gov.au/nla.news-article58827871

Inquest:

[146] *Qld Ref: 1912/C10*

Statement by Harold Beattie, fencer of North Crusoe near Muttaburra
Harold Beattie on duty sworn, Crusoe, Fencer of North Crusoe near Muttaburra.

I had a man named Archibald NcNeil in my employ as a fencer from about the 15/7/1911 to the 3/12/1911. He was a very decent chap and a good worker. He came to Muttaburra on the 3/12 last to consult a doctor. He told me he was suffering from a bad shoulder. He returned to my camp on the 23/1/1912. He told me no he was allright on return to camp. He had two bottles of Whisky with him. He drank the two bottles up to the 24th. On the 27th he developed systems of the DT's about 10 pm on the night of the 27th he came to me and said the police were after him. He had a rifle. He asked me to sleep in the tent with him as he was afraid. On the 28th he had the DT's again and on the morning of the 29th very bad. He picked up the rifle but put it down again and I hid it. I wanted to go for help but did not want to leave him {only McNeil and Beattie at camp}. About 10 am on the 29th I went into the tent and tried to stop him cutting his throat with a razor, but he gashed it two or three times. {The cut was six inches wide and three inches deep and cut his jugular vein}. He was standing but fell on his face in a pool of blood. There was blood all over the tent. He was dead. I caught my horse and rode ten miles to Crusoe for help. North Crusoe was thirty miles from Muttaburra. Harold Beattie and Constable D. Crane buried remains on North Crusoe. Brother George at Ilfracombe and Edward at Isisford.

<u>Inquest Findings</u>
Archibald McNeil, fencer, 68/1912. Deceased committed suicide by cutting his throat with a razor at North Crusoe on the 29th January 1912. On the 27th he was suffering delirium tremors and about 10am on the 29th he ended his life. He was in Muttaburra from the 2/12/1911 to 22/12/1912 and during that time, he was drinking heavily. Nothing suspicious. No post Mortem

Editor's Note – Archibald was the son of John McNiel and Bridget.
Source: McNeil Family <keithmcneil@optusnet.com.au>

Joseph Rohan – 19 April 1912

A sad Accident occurred last Monday on Brookwood Station run Jos Rohan[147], a boundary rider living at the wool shed, failed to respond to a telephonic call late on Monday night a consequence of which next morning the overseer rode over and found that the hut bad not been occupied the previous night. In the light of this circumstance the police were at once communicated with, and Constable D. Crane left town to organise a search party, who picked up the deceased's tracks a short distance from the shed and followed them to paddock No. 1 Western, Shortly after entering the paddock, and close to the boundary fence between Kensington Downs and Brookwood, one of the searchers spied a riderless horse, which, however, galloped away; in the pursuit they came upon the deceased man's dog. The sagacious animal at once commenced to bark, and led the party at a hand gallop to a water-hole filled by the bore drain, Rohan was found lying face downwards In about 3 ft of water. I am informed by the officer, who was in charge, that from the tracks the cause of the fatality was evident. The horse had been ridden into the .water in order, to give it a drink; the ground was boggy at this particular place and the horse, in plunging, had unseated lite rider, Rohan, who was in a weak state at the time, must have been stunned by the fall and was drowned. The horse tracks show that it had walked straight through the water-hole after the deceased fell. The news of the death came as a shock to many, as only last Saturday, Rohan, who has been in the district some 23 years, was in town to record his vote. The body was interred on Brookwood Station by Constable Crane.

---

[147] *Qld Ref: 1912/C2554*

MUTTABURRA NOTES [?]. (1912, May 10). The Northern Miner (Charters Towers, Qld: 1874 - 1954), p. 6. Retrieved September 21, 2013, from http://nla.gov.au/nla.news-article79092347

Editor's Note – Joseph was the son of Peter Rohan and Johanna Tribey

Arthur Gould Towers – 24 December 1914

Arthur Towers[148], was a boundary rider at Fujiama (Leichhardt) walked out to catch the coach, and perished. He died beside the road between Barcaldine and Aramac and his grave is right beside the road. Arthur, about 70 years old.

Gladys Forde – 5 January 1916

Gladys Forde[149] the daughter of Michael Joseph Forde and Mary Margaret Black, died on 5th January 1916, just 15 hours after her birth. Michael and Margaret had six other children – Michael George [died 1915], George Michael [died 1919], Florrie [died 1925], and John Joseph [died 1961], and Kathleen Mary [born 1914]. Gladys' burial site is unknown, but maybe on Bowen Downs, but her brother George Michael is buried in Aramac Cemetery, actual site also unknown.

FIRES AND HEAVY RAINS IN QUEENSLAND.

Mr. Frank Young, of Adelaide, received the following telegram from Longreach (Q.). On Tuesday (says the "Register"): Maneroo practically burnt out; 200,000 acres Evesham burnt; large area Darr River surrounded by fire at Manningham – last three days. The first started at Mount Cornish, burnt about 70 miles Landsborough River to other side of Evelyn Downs. Several holdings wiped out. Heavy loss of stock. Large area of Saltern Creek burnt. Mr. Jones,

148 *Qld Ref: 1915/C14*
149 *Qld Ref: 1916/C19*

manager of Saltern Creek, included among men burnt to death. "Big fires at Alpha, Jericho district. Scattered storms last week put most of the fires out. Raining steadily, up to 2in. in this district; every appearance of setting in. Eighty points at Manfred; still raining. One to 3½ in Blackall, still raining. Two and a half inches at Alpha".

FIRES AND HEAVY RAINS IN QUEENSLAND. (1918, November 7). Barrier Miner (Broken Hill, NSW: 1888 - 1954), p. 2. Retrieved May 2, 2012, from http://nla.gov.au/nla.news-article45460471

Andrew John Phillips – 27 April 1920

Andrew Phillips[150] (Phillipp), the 30 year old head-stockman on Bowen Downs, was drowned while he was trying to cross Cornish Creek near the Bowen Downs Bridge on 27 April 1920.

Sydney Pechey Fraser – 8 April 1923

Probates of the wills of the following estates have been granted to the Union Trustee Company of Australia, Ltd during the last week – Sydney Pechey Fraser[151], of Clayfield, Brisbane, gentleman, £12,594;

PERSONAL. (1923, June 16). The Brisbane Courier (Qld.: 1864 - 1933), p. 11. Retrieved May 30, 2012, from http://nla.gov.au/nla.news-article20628266

Editor's Note – Sydney was the son of Thomas Hiram Fraser and Emma Francis, born 28 December 1848. Sydney managed Bowen Downs from 1882 until 1911.

Sydney is buried in the Toowong Cemetery Portion 18 Section 120 Grave 10/11, along with his wife Jane Margaret.

[150] *Qld Ref: 1920/C1653*
[151] *Qld Ref: 1923/B39517*

Sydney Perchy Fraser – Jane Margaret Fraser

Toowong Cemetery: Portion 18, Section 120, Grave 6

George Beattie Gallogly – 12 December 1925

The death occurred in the Aramac District Hospital on December 12 of Mr. George B. Gallogly, of Barcaldine, at the age of 80. Mr. Gallogly was a Past Master of the Aramac Masonic Lodge, having filled the chair in 1890-1900, and again in 1904-5. He was initiated into the order with the late Mr. S. P. Fraser, P.M., P.D.G.J.W., manager of Bowen Downs, of which station Mr. Gallogly had been book-keeper for 43 or more years, this constituting him the oldest employee, and longest in service on any station in the Central-West. Deceased was accorded a Masonic funeral. He is survived by his widow and three daughters.

OBITUARY. (1925, December 26). The Queenslander (Brisbane, Qld.: 1866 - 1939), p. 19. Retrieved May 26, 2012, from http://nla.gov.au/nla.news-article25109491

Editor's Note – George, the son of George John Gallogly and Mary Ann Andrews, is buried in the Aramac Cemetery.

Jane Margaret Fraser – 13 August 1934

Mrs. Jane Margaret Fraser[152], widow of Mr. Sydney P. Fraser, who died in Brisbane recently, was 92 years of age. Her husband managed Bowen Downs station, near Aramac, for over 20 years, and afterwards at Saltern Creek station, near Barcaldine, for 11 years. In 1917 Mr. Fraser retired from Saltern Creek station, and there after lived in Brisbane with his family until his death in the year 1923. Mrs. Fraser, during her residence on Bowen Downs and Saltern Creek stations, took a leading part in all charitable, and deserving objects and in social functions. For the last 17 years she has been totally blind, but maintained her interest in current events. She left one son. Mr. Harold Fraser, of Rankin, Aramac; and three daughters, Mrs. J. M. Gray Buchanan, of Kitchener Road, Ascot; Mrs. Colin Butler, of Tallyabra, Quilpie; and Miss May Fraser, of Bayview Terrace, Clayfield, Brisbane.

Obituary. (1934, August 30). The Queenslander (Brisbane, Qld.: 1866 - 1939), p. 8. Retrieved May 31, 2012, from http://nla.gov.au/nla.news-article23338812

Editor's Note – Jane Margaret was the daughter of William Turner and Catherine Cameron. She is buried in the Toowong Cemetery along with her husband Sydney Peachy Fraser who died on the 8 April 1923.

John George Cockburn – 15 April 1935

Mr J. G. Cockburn

The death occurred in the Mater Misericordiae Hospital, Brisbane, on April 15, of Mr J. G. Cockburn[153], of Bowen Downs, Aramac. Mr

[152] *Qld Ref: 1934/B25020*
[153] *Qld Ref: 1935/B27362*

Cockburn recently went to Brisbane for medical attention, and as he appeared to be progressing satisfactorily, his death was unexpected.

Deceased had been associated with the Scottish Australian Investment Co. Ltd., for about forty years, coming from Ferlees, in the St George district, to Bowen Downs as manager about twenty years ago. At his death he also controlled, for his company, Eastmere, Baracorah, and the Champion Block.

In the Yalleroi district Mr Cockburn was an amateur rider and a cricketer in his younger days. He took a keen interest in amateur racing in the Muttaburra and Aramac districts, his colours being carried to victory in a large number of races. For about eight years he was president of the Muttaburra Amateur Turf Club. For the past five years Mr Cockburn had been vice-president of the Aramac Hospital, and was a committeeman for several years prior to that.

He is survived by his widow, who resided at Bowen Downs, and who at present is with her daughter at Nalemba, one son Thomas (Bowen Downs) and a daughter (Mrs L. V. Seaton Palemba)

MR J. C. COCKBURN. (1935, April 25). The Central Queensland Herald (Rockhampton, Qld. : 1930 - 1956), p. 24. Retrieved June 1, 2012, from http://nla.gov.au/nla.news-article72385276

John George Cockburn

Toowong Cemetery: Portion 22 Section 1, Grave 6

Obituary

MR. J. G. COCKBURN

The death occurred in the Mater Hospital, Brisbane, early on Monday morning of Mr. J. G. Cockburn, of Bowen Downs, Aramac. Mr. Cockburn recently went to Brisbane for medical attention, and was progressing satisfactorily, his death, which occurred in his sleep, being unexpected. Deceased had been associated with the Scottish Australian Investment Co. Ltd. for about 40 years, coming from Fernlees in the, St. George district to Bowen Downs as manager about 20 years ago. At his death he also controlled, for his company, Eastmere, Barcoorah and the Champion Block in the Yalleroi district. Mr. Cockburn was a keen amateur rider and a cricketer in his younger days. He took much interest in amateur racing in the Muttaburra and Aramac districts, his colours being carried to victory in a large number of races. For about 8 years he was president of the Muttaburra Amateur Turf Club. For the past 5 years Mr. Cockburn had been vice president of the Aramac Hospital, and was a committeeman for several years prior to that.

He is survived by his widow, who resided at Bowen Downs, and who at present is with her daughter at Nalemba, one son, Tom (Bowen Downs) and daughter (Mrs. L. V. Seaton, Nalemba).

Obituary MR. J. G. COCKBURN. (1935, April 18). The Longreach Leader (Qld.: 1923 - 1938), p. 9. http://nla.gov.au/nla.news-article37252930

Editor's Note – John George was the son of David Cockburn and Julia Anne Downing. In 1908 John married Maude O'Keeffe. He was manager of Bowen Downs from 1911 until his death in 1935. He is buried in the Toowong Cemetery Portion 22, Section 1 Grave Number 6. He was 65 years old when he died. His son Jack Aylmer who was born on 19 July 1911 and died on the 17 October 1939 is also buried with his father at Toowong.

CHANGE IN MANAGERS SCOTTISH INVESTMENT CO.

ARAMAC, Friday

Consequent on the death of Mr. J. G. Cockburn[154], the late manager of Bowen Downs, Barcarooh, Eastmere and Champion, a general

[154] *Qld Ref: 1935/B27362*

shuffle has taken place in the ranks of the staff of the Scottish Investment Co. Mr. J Conway Langdon, formerly of Champion, but more recently of Eastmere, has been appointed to the management of Bowen Downs and Barcoorah. Mr. George Steiglitz, of Champion, has been transferred to Eastmere as manager. Mr. Neville Toogood, late overseer of Bowen Downs, has been promoted to the managership of Champion.

CHANGES IN MANAGERS. (1935, June 22). The Longreach Leader (Qld.: 1923 - 1954), p. 12. Retrieved June 25, 2012, from http://nla.gov.au/nla.news-article39316613

William Taylor

Aramac Cemetery: Section Central, Grave 219
Photo: Lesley Cowper

William Taylor – 10 June 1938

MR. WILLIAM TAYLOR

Mr. William Taylor[155], aged 87 years, a very old resident of the Aramac district passed away peacefully at his home in Aramac yesterday morning. He was upwards of 50 years overseer on Bowen

[155] *Qld Ref: 1938/C1265*

Downs station. He is survived by his wife and a grown up family of daughters. Each of his two sons, predeceased him. The funeral left his late residence at 5 o'clock yesterday afternoon. Rev. R. Johnston of the Church of England officiating at the graveside.

OBITUARY. (1938, June 11). The Longreach Leader (Qld.: 1923 - 1938), p. 16. Retrieved June 4, 2012, from http://nla.gov.au/nla.news-article37547431

Editor's Note – William was the son of John Taylor and Mary Farrell. William married Ellen O'Brien in 1881 and they had the following children: Anney, Lucy Maud, William Herbert, John. John, the son, died when only about 29 days old in 1888, from bronchitis and is buried in the Muttaburra Cemetery – site unknown.

Appendix

Bowen Downs Managers

1861 – September 1866	Nat Buchanan
1866 – July 1870	Boyd Dunlop Morehead
1870 – September 1871	Alfred K Thomas
1871 – September 1875	Robert Kerr
1875 – November 1881	Aynslie J Elliott
1881 – 1882	Edward K Russell
1882 – June 1911	Sydney P Fraser
1911 – September 1935	John G Cockburn
1935 – 1963	James C Langdon
1963 – January 1973	Brian L Braithwaite
1973 – April 1978	Roger W Tapp
1978 – November 1998	Andrew Cowper

Mount Cornish really only had the one manager Edward Roland Edkins and he moved there in 1872 and then left in 1903 when it was sold to New Zealand and Australia Land Company.

Surveys of Runs 1864

Crown Lands Office,
Brisbane, 23rd April, 1864.

PAYMENT FOR SURVEY OF RUNS.

THE Licensees and Lessees of the undermentioned Runs are hereby required to pay forthwith into the Treasury the amounts specified in connection with their respective Runs, in accordance with the provisions of the 49th clause of the Act 27 Victoria No. 17.

Attention is called to the said clause, which declares that unless payment is made within six months after notification in the *Government Gazette*, all the rights and interests of such defaulters shall be forfeited.

E. W. LAMB,
Chief Commissioner of Crown Lands.

Lessee or Licensee.	Name of Run.	District.	Area in Square Miles.	Amount. £ s.
James Thomas Allan	Windeyer Creek	Mitchell	25	7 10
Ditto	Enniskillen Downs	"	100	30 0
Ditto	Enniskillen South	"	100	30 0
Chas. B. Dutton and Archd. F. Dutton	Tambo	"	49	14 14
Ditto	Hebel	"	49	14 14
Chas. B. Dutton and Archd. F. Dutton	Carrangarra	"	49	14 14
Ditto	Hebel	"	49	14 14
Ditto	Carrangarra	"	49	14 14
Berkelman and Lambert	Greendale	"	86	25 16
J. T. Allan and partners	Springblock	"	50	15 0
Ditto	Recovered	"	100	30 0
Ditto	Return	"	100	30 0
H. S. Herden and W. [illegible] Manning	Northampton	"	50	15 0
Ditto	Caerthedine	"	70	21 0
Ditto	Llangynidr	"	100	30 0
Ditto	Pentwyn	"	75	22 10
Ditto	Goordinnah	"	48	14 8
Ditto	Brynderwin	"	70	21 0
Ditto	Hawarden	"	25	7 10
Ditto	Glen Usk	"	25	7 10
Ditto	Brynmawr	"	25	7 10
John Rule and Dyson Lacy	Bellalaad	"	48	14 8
Ditto	Inglerry	"	144	43 4
Ditto	Coreena	"	96	28 16
Henry Daglish	Evebell	"	96	28 16
Ditto	Bowdale	"	96	28 16
William Landsborough	Budgerega	"	100	30 0
Ditto	Crossmoor	"	96	28 16
Ditto	Balang	"	96	28 16
Ditto	Bowen Downs	"	96	28 16
Ditto	Betawong	"	96	28 16
Ditto	Bangal	"	100	30 0
Morehead and Young	Acacia Downs	"	50	15 0

http://nla.gov.au/nla.news-article1258147 - The Brisbane Courier (Qld.: 1864 - 1933), Wednesday 27 April 1864, page 1

Editor's Note – area measurement is in square miles

District of Mitchell – 1893

The Electoral District of Mitchell.

To JOHN CAMERON, Esq., Kensington Downs.

DEAR SIR.—
We, the undersigned Electors and Ratepayers of the Mitchell District, have much pleasure in requesting that you will allow yourself to be nominated as a Candidate for the representation of this District at the forthcoming General Election.

Awaiting your reply, which we trust may be favorable,

We are, Dear Sir,
Yours sincerely,

C. B. Inman, Corona
Francis Campbell, Corona
G. A. Masey, Corona
J. C. Thompson, Corona
Thomas O'Donoghue, Corona
H. C. Richardson, Corona
R. A. Hopkins, Wellshot
W. G. Fitzpatrick, Wellshot
R. Fowler, Wellshot
T. H. Cann Cargill, Wellshot
F. M. Munro, Wellshot
John Mackenzie, Landsborough
S. Fairbairn, Beaconsfield
James Inglis, Beaconsfield
W. R. Anderson, Beaconsfield
R. H. Botterill, Barenya
W. W. de Eodyn, Landsborough Downs
C. H. Leoyahn, Landsborough Downs
R. J. Craig, Landsborough Downs
John Morrow, Landsborough Downs
Wm. Lamond, Landsborough Downs
J. M. Wetherill, Landsborough Downs
R. Robinson, Landsborough Downs
P. O'Shea, Landsborough Downs
S. J. Hill, Katandra
Fred E. Weinholt, Katandra
G. Libby, Katandra
R. Burns, Katandra
William Moore, Katandra
E. Robinson, Katandra
W. Libby, Katandra
John Shiel, Katandra
G. F. Lewis, Katandra
G. F. Mackichan, Katandra
W. Duisey, Katandra
J. R. Jardine, Aberfoyle
James Humphreys, Aberfoyle
H. Murray-Prior, Aberfoyle
J. H. Huskinson, Aberfoyle
J. M'Lucas, Aberfoyle
Morris Murray-Prior, Aberfoyle
W. H. Pincombe, Silsoe
V. W. Buckland, Silsoe
Fred John Bolton, Silsoe
Robert K. Lane, Vergemont
R. J. N. Burrowes, Strathdarr
John B. Cramsie, Strathdarr
A. Louis de Sailly, Strathdarr
Aubrey Betstead, Strathdarr
A. Ayling, Longreach
G. A. Innes, Rockwood
George Meecham, Rockwood
Wallace Stuart, Rockwood
G. E. Stuart, Rockwood
H. F. Stuart, Rockwood
William Orr, Rockwood
John Mitchell, Rockwood
William Orr, Rockwood
John Mitchell, Rockwood
H. J. Stuart, Rockwood
A. J. Scott, Rockwood
James Leslie, Lerida
W. J. Hutchinson, Corinda
James Tolson Jun., Corinda
S. Macfarlane, Corinda
Robert Christian, Lammermoor
C. B. Craig, Lammermoor
W. H. Dunne, Lammermoor
M. J. Whitty, Lammermoor
T. E. Speeding, Uanda
C. G. Williams, Uanda
W. H. Dunne, Uanda
Samuel Saunders, Uanda
Thomas Knox, Evesham
Arch. M'Eachern, Evesham
W. W. Lockwood, Evesham
James Cochrane, Longreach
C. W. Wedgwood, Longreach
R. J. Wedgwood, Longreach
J. Samuels, Longreach
E. Rees, Longreach
P. D. Forrest, Longreach
J. M. Savage, Longreach
Thomas J. Nolan, Longreach
Henry Ellis, Longreach
H. F. Cahill, Longreach
David Cannon, Longreach
H. U. Rickards, Longreach
A. R. Brown, Saltern Creek
William Williams, Saltern Creek
W. J. Simpson, Saltern Creek
J. K. Cudmore, Tara
K. D. L. Cudmore, Tara
A. D. Alexander, Vermont
Sydney Casey, Newstead
Henry J. Sealy, Barcaldine Downs
Joe Kilpatrick, Barcaldine Downs
James Forrest, Barcaldine Downs
William Price, Landsborough
Thomas Swan, Landsborough
John Clarke, Landsborough
Phillip Penny, Landsborough
John W. Crawley, Landsborough
David Beattie, Landsborough
J. S. Henderson, Marchmont
Charles Blume Jun., Camoola
F. H. Kessler, Longreach
Geo. Meacham, Longreach
—. Leyland, Longreach
A. E. H. Reid, Longreach
E. G. Blume, Bexley
Francis Cory, Longreach
Edward F. Pyne, Mount Cornish
E. R. Edkins, Mount Cornish
Oscar Buncke, Barcaldine
Geo. H. Miller, Barcaldine
James Meacham, Barcaldine
James Leyland, Barcaldine
Geo. P. Shakspeare, Barcaldine
C. A. Fattorina, Saltern
A. J. Coldham, Dunraven
James Muir, Darr River Downs
Wm. Shaw, Darr River Downs
G. E. Krell, Darr River Downs
C. E. Douglass, Darr River Downs
C. P. Shawe, Darr River Downs
E. Belcher, Stainburn
W. H. Looker, Stainburn
R. V. Looker, Stainburn
Henry Stanley, Stainburn
W. W. Sale, Summer Hill
Simon Lockhart, Kingsborough
Joseph J. Lockhart, Kingsborough
Angus Lockhart, Kingsborough

Angus Lockhart, Kingsborough
L. E. Tuckerman, Aramac
Allan P. Gairdner, Clare
A. W. Macalister, Aramac
Sam Payne, Marathon Hotel, Aramac
Alexander Cameron, Aramac
C. J. Inman, Aramac
James Brown, Aramac
Henry Humberstone, Aramac
James M'Whannell, Rodney
Wm. Walker, Aramac
Joseph Grant, Aramac
William Henderson, Aramac
Geo. G. Grey, Aramac
John M'Auliffe, Powelin
Geo. Porter, Aramac
E. W. Bowyer, Aramac

J. W. Booker, Aramac
Edward Morley, Aramac
R. G. M'Lean, Aramac
Robt. J. Calder, Aramac
M. Macalister, Leichhardt
J. K. Cameron, Aramac
W. Lowther, Aramac.

Dawnie, Toowoomba,
27th February, 1893.

To the Electors of the Mitchell.

GENTLEMEN,—
In reply to your flattering and numerously-signed Requisition, I have now much pleasure in signifying my willingness to comply with your request, and allow myself to be nominated at the forthcoming Election as a candidate for the representation of your District in Parliament.

I am, Gentlemen,
3- Very faithfully yours,
JOHN CAMERON.

The Western Champion and General Advertiser for the Central-Western Districts (Barcaldine, Qld. : 1892 - 1922), Tuesday 18 April 1893, page 4 http://nla.gov.au/nla.news-article77217660

Electoral Roll – 1893

Bowen Downs- Electoral 1893			
Surname	**First Name**	**Qualifications**	**Address**
Day	James	Residence	Ambo
Harris	Samuel	Residence	Ambo
Hitchman	Henry	Residence	Ambo
Kneen	Joseph	Residence	Ambo
Macgoffin	Richard	Residence	Ambo
Parsons	Charles	Residence	Ambo
Price	James	Residence	Ambo
Wealsh	John	Residence	Ambo
Baldwyn	William	Residence	Bangall Creek
Blythe	William	Residence	Bangall Creek
Gauld	Michael	Residence	Bangall Creek
Robinson	James J	Residence	Bangall Creek
Walker	Edward	Residence	Bangall Creek
Alexander	William	Residence	Bowen Downs
Banks	Bernard Thomas	Residence	Bowen Downs
Bowie	John	Residence	Bowen Downs
Brown	John	Residence	Bowen Downs
Cameron	William	Residence	Bowen Downs
Castle	William	Residence	Bowen Downs
Coyle	John	Residence	Bowen Downs
Daly	Timothy	Residence	Bowen Downs
Dessilly	Harold	Residence	Bowen Downs
Dickson	Walter	Residence	Bowen Downs
Edmonds	Charles John	Residence	Bowen Downs
Eldershaw	Henry L	Residence	Bowen Downs
Fair	Richard Edward	Residence	Bowen Downs
Forrest	Frank	Residence	Bowen Downs
Fraser	Sydney P	Residence	Bowen Downs
Fraser	Charles	Residence	Bowen Downs
Fraser	George Kenneth	Residence	Bowen Downs
Gallogly	G B	Residence	Bowen Downs
Gleeson	Mark	Residence	Bowen Downs
Gleeson	William	Residence	Bowen Downs
Hall	John	Residence	Bowen Downs
Hill	Peter	Residence	Bowen Downs
Johnson	Daniel	Residence	Bowen Downs

Bowen Downs- Electoral 1893			
Surname	**First Name**	**Qualifications**	**Address**
Kennedy	Archibald	Residence	Bowen Downs
King	James	Residence	Bowen Downs
Marriott	Frank	Residence	Bowen Downs
Marsden	Henry	Residence	Bowen Downs
McMaster	John	Residence	Bowen Downs
Milkins	Robert	Residence	Bowen Downs
Miller	Edward G A	Residence	Bowen Downs
O'Brien	Jeremiah	Residence	Bowen Downs
Pearson	George	Residence	Bowen Downs
Philip	George Thomas	Residence	Bowen Downs
Roland	Edward	Residence	Bowen Downs
Rosser	Henry	Residence	Bowen Downs
Sayers	Joseph	Residence	Bowen Downs
Schofield	William	Residence	Bowen Downs
Scott	William	Residence	Bowen Downs
Small	Levi	Residence	Bowen Downs
Small	Richard Charles	Residence	Bowen Downs
Soldson	Alfred	Residence	Bowen Downs
Tayler	William	Residence	Bowen Downs
Walker	William Lester	Residence	Bowen Downs
Walker	Samuel Lindsay	Residence	Bowen Downs
White	Michael John	Residence	Bowen Downs
White	James	Residence	Bowen Downs
White	Charles	Residence	Bowen Downs
Horn	Frederick	Residence	Bradley's Creek
Blume	Charles	Residence	Camoola
Chandler	John Winter	Freehold	Camoola
Edge	Shadrach	Freehold	Camoola
Grimshaw	John Henry	Leasehold	Camoola
Hill	James Roland	Residence	Camoola
Beattie	Thomas	Residence	Corindah
Blakeley	Matthew	Residence	Corindah
Boylan	Thomas	Residence	Corindah
Brand	James	Residence	Corindah
Cameron	Neil	Residence	Corindah
Hutchinson	William John	Residence	Corindah
Kelly	John	Residence	Corindah

Bowen Downs- Electoral 1893			
Surname	**First Name**	**Qualifications**	**Address**
Smith	William John	Residence	Corindah
Stott	William Edward	Residence	Corindah
Thom	Donald	Residence	Corindah
Tolson	James	Leasehold	Corindah
Tolson	Francis	Residence	Corindah
Tolson	James jnr	Residence	Corindah
Augstein	Charles Edward	Residence	Cornish
Barns	Augustus	Residence	Crusoe
Bell	John	Residence	Crusoe
Micklethwaite	Richard Spenser	Residence	Crusoe
Hall	David	Residence	Goodberry
Bailey	Samuel	Residence	Mount Cornish
Bailey	George	Residence	Mount Cornish
Banks	Samuel Westfried	Residence	Mount Cornish
Barrett	Walter James	Residence	Mount Cornish
Edkins	Edward R	Residence	Mount Cornish
Gordon	Alexander	Residence	Mount Cornish
Hay	Montague Grey	Residence	Mount Cornish
Heuston	Patrick	Residence	Mount Cornish
Lloyd	John Payne	Residence	Mount Cornish
Macgoffin	James	Residence	Mount Cornish
Maginnis	Robert	Residence	Mount Cornish
Norton	James Albert	Residence	Mount Cornish
Palmer	Charles Steveson	Residence	Mount Cornish
Philips	Frank James	Residence	Mount Cornish
Pym	Edward	Residence	Mount Cornish
Robertson	Alfred Selwyn	Residence	Mount Cornish
Schofield	George Alfred	Residence	Mount Cornish
McDonald	John	Residence	Reedy Creek
Cooney	Thomas	Residence	Sardine Creek
Gollins	Edward	Residence	Sardine Creek
Gollins	William Thomas	Residence	Sardine Creek
Wright	J Gill	Residence	Scarrbury
Haynes	Charles	Residence	Tablederry
Rhodes	James	Residence	Towal

Index – By Surname

Index – By Surname			
Surname	**Name**	**Date Death**	**Occupation**
Ah Ching		1889/07/13	Cook
Ah Gow		1903/02/08	Cook
Ah Sue		1903/01/17	Gardener
Ah Won	Tommy	1910/04/13	Cook
Ah Young		1876/10/13	Shepherd
Ah Young	Tommy	1894/11/25	Cook
Alston [Olsten]	Isaac	1901/01/01	Traveller
Ambrose	Benjamin	1877/08/1	Labourer
Apii	Polynesian	1878/01/30	Labourer
Baba	Polynesian	1878/02/14	Labourer
Badke	Alfred	1891/12/3	Born Sardine Ck
Bailey	Lydia Mary	1887/01/24	Child
Barkley	Charles	1870/05/3	Hut-keeper
Barney		1865/09	Teamster
Barry	John	1887/01/26	Dam Repairer/Fencer
Bell	Alexander	1897/04/01	Manager
Bender	Henry Joseph	1885/06/01	Child
Bennett	Isabella	1876/01/06	Child
Billey	Kanaka	1886/09/11	Stockman
Billy The Cook		1882/7/25	Cook
Brooks	Amos	1898/07/18	Boot-maker / shearer
Brown	Captain	1884/< March	Labourer
Brownsey	Charles	1894/01/26	Dam-maker
Buchanan	Nathaniel	1901/09/23	Manager / Drover
Burns	Thomas	1871/04/30	Labourer
Butler	Annie Augusta	1882/01/19	Wife & Mother
Cain	Infant [Female]	1882/02/24	Child
Callan	Owen	1889/01/27	Bushman
Cameron	Donald	1881/01/16	Baker
Cameron	John Francis	1890/10/30	Manager - Bimbah
Campbell	James	1901/01/01	Shearer

Index – By Surname			
Surname	**Name**	**Date Death**	**Occupation**
Cann	John	1883/04/12	Stockman
Carr	James	1875/09/22	Stockman
Casey/Ceasey	John	1878/01/22	
Caulfield	Mark	1901/07/28	
Chambers	Elizabeth	1889/12/04	Child
Chiverton alias Redstone		1871/09/29	Carpenter
Clarke	Rowland William	1893/01/14	Stockman
Cleg	Thomas	1880/10/29	Traveller
Coaton	Ann	1885/04/02	House-wife
Cockburn	John George	1935/04/15	Manager - Bowen Downs
Cornish	Edward Brooking	1866/10/27	Pastoral inspector
Cox	William	1910/07/02	Stockman
Coyne	Thomas Henry	1902/01/8	General Servant
Cozens alias Frenche		1866/06	Chainman
Crisp	Sherwin	1869/11/25	Labourer
Daley	Lankey	1883/12	Labourer
Davis	Herbert Cecil	1871/09/	Stockman
Donohue	Maurice	1862	Drover
Douglas	Archibald	1889/11/17	Bushman
Dowling	Patrick	1885/02/23	Stockman
Drummond	David	1892/08/23	Railway Guard
Drury	Ernest T	1880/10/27	Labourer
Durdon	William Henry	1876/12/06	General Servant
Edkins	Edward Roland	1905/08/14	Manager Mt Cornish
Edkins	Edwina	1910/08/17	House-wife
Edwards	Sidney	1898/08/01	Butcher
Eldershaw	Maud Margaret	1893/02/12	Child
Elliott	Aynslie John	1881/11/09	Bowen Downs Manager
Erhardt	Thomas	1879/03/23	Labourer
Faleny	Jeremiah	1883/10/14	General Servant
Fergus	John	1906/02/28	Labourer
Fitzgerald	Martin	1869/02/11	Carter

Index – By Surname			
Surname	**Name**	**Date Death**	**Occupation**
Flood	Sydney	1871/07	
Ford	Mary Jane	1893/10/13	House-wife
Forde	Gladys	1916/01/05	Child
Franklin	Charles	1908/07/25	Care-take - Eastfield
Fraser	Sydney Pechey	1923/04/08	Manager - Bowen Downs
Fraser	Jane Margaret	1934/08/13	House-wife
Gallogly	George Edwin	1895/02/02	Child
Gallogly	George Beattie	1925/12/12	Accountant - Bowen Downs
Gilmour	James Merry	1874/06/10	Sub-Inspector Native Mounted Police
Goodman	Frederick	1911/04/21	Pensioner
Gordon	James	1890/06/22	Child
Gormely	John	1876/06/04	Labourer
Graham	Archibald Drummond	1883/06/02	Stockman
Gray-Buchanan	Thomas Farie	1899/04/27	Grazier
Guild	Mary	1870/11/09	Child
Hammond	James	1896/12/05	Hawker Assistance
Harrison	Margaret Alice	1882/04/11	Child
Harting [Hartwig] [Halting]	John	1884/05/12	Carrier
Hayton	Joseph	1894/04/09	Traveller
Healy	Arthur	1885/04/15	Child
Healy	Mathew	1909/05/23	Overseer
Hohn [Hahn]	Louis	1873/06/04	Working Man
Innes	William	1876/09/24	Shepherd
Jeffray	Alexandra	1877/11/09	Labourer - Mt Cornish
Kanaka		1876/11/13	General Servant
Kanaka	Harry	1876/12/08	Labourer
Keating	Michael	1884/12/20	Shearer
Kennedy	Frederick John Clarence	1883/12/04	Child
Landsborough	William	1886/03/16	Manager Bowen Downs / Drover

Index – By Surname			
Surname	**Name**	**Date Death**	**Occupation**
Langon	James	1901/03/07	Labourer
Lee	Michael	1897/03/13	Drover
Leslie	Martin	1907/08/20	Labourer
Lidder	Charles	1873/05/24	General Servant
Lloyd	Jessie Mary	1885/09/20	Child
Lloyd	Llewellyn	1886/11/27	Child
Lolbassie	Polynesian	1878/05/04	Labourer
Mackay	Charles Douglas	1871/10/17	Overseer Bowen Downs
Maddern	Alfred	1906/01/11	Boundary Rider
Magee	James	1893/08	Labourer
Maggs	George	1876/10/26	Shepherd
Maier	Frederick	1872/08/13	Shepherd
Matow	Polynesian	1876/04/08	Labourer
McCarthy	Thomas	1896/02/15	Sheep Overseer
McCulloch	Archibald	1892/09/25	Youth
McDonald	Ralph Erskine	1892/06/25	Manager - Fleetwood
McDonald	Angus William	1894/12/28	Stockman
McDonald	Mary	1904/07/20	House-wife
McDonald	John	1904/12/20	Overseer
McFetridge	William	1876/03/31	Drover
McLean	Neil	1876/08/29	Horse driver
McLean	George Horseman	1878/02/17	Child
McNeely	Robert	1864/11/20	Overseer - Tower Hill
McNiel	Archibald	1912/01/29	Fencer
Meredith	Llewellyn A	1864/11/20	Land Owner
Miller	Dara Macartney	1896/04/09	
Morehead	Boyd Dunlop	1905/10/30	Manager / Premier Qld
Morgan	James	1888/07/12	General Servant
Murphy	John	1897/07/23	Dingo Poisoner
Murray	Hugh	1880/08/12	Shearer
Navoren	Polynesian	1876/04/22	Labourer
Neville	William	1898/12/13	Plumber - tinsmith
Nicholls	George Jonathon	1864/04/01	Labourer - Bowen Downs

Index – By Surname			
Surname	**Name**	**Date Death**	**Occupation**
Nicholls	Ethel Maria	1864/04/01	Wife
Nicholls	Harriet	1876/08/14	
Nicholson	Thomas	1876/01/14	Dam Sinker
O'Brien	Jeremiah	1903/01/07	General Servant
O'Hea	William	1876/09/12	Reporter
Oliver	Annie	1892/07/07	Child
Phillips [Phillipp]	Andrew John	1920/04/27	Head-stockman
Pryor	Gideon	1880/03/31	Bushman
Quinn	James	1881/08/14	Drover
Ranken	John T Campbell	1907/03/22	Stockman
Rattray	Robert	1883/09/17	Stockman
Raynor	John Henry	1880/10/07	Traveller
Roberts	Robert	1884/12/28	Labourer
Robins	William	1873/03/27	Shepherd
Rohan	Joseph	1912/04/19	Boundary rider
Russell	Edward Ketia	1904/10/15	Book-keeper Bowen Downs
Sammy	Sammy	1871/09/21	Shepherd
Schaumbach	Martin	1882/09/	Cook - Bushman
Schofield	William	1910/07/07	Blacksmith - Wheelwright
Shaw	Walter Robert	1893/02/6	Child - Died Sardine Creek
Shaw	Margaret Ann	1893/02/7	Child - Died Sardine Creek
Shaw	Margaret Catherine	1895/02/01	Child
Shield	James	1880/03/18	Child
Small [Smale]	Levi	1895/07/26	Labourer
Taylor	William	1938/06/10	Sheep Overseer
Thomas	John Henry	1895/07/19	Shearer
Toohey [O'Donell]	Patrick [Alias Mad Mick]	1892/06/04	Traveller
Towers	Arthur Gould	1914/12/24	Boundary Rider
Trouson [Tronson]	Edward Albert	1874/03/01	Ex-Constable
Turner	Campbell McDonald	1891/03/07	Overseer Bowen Downs
Ung	Yee	1885/12/17	Gardner - Mt Cornish
Unknown	Shepherd	1864	Shepherd

Index – By Surname			
Surname	**Name**	**Date Death**	**Occupation**
Unknown	Blackfellow	1876/06	
Unknown		1885/07	
Unknown	Aboriginal woman	1892/05	
Unknown		1893/10/19	
Vaillant/Valliant	Reginald	1876/03/01	Chemist
Vern	Charles Hugo Frederick	1866/05/12	Looking employment
Welsby / Wilkie	Thomas Scott Willamson	1878/02/01	Pianist
White	Mary	1885/11/26	Child
Whiting	Arthur	1896/01/08	Traveller
Williams	Frederick	1866/08/09	Traveller
Willis	George	1888/03/07	Labourer

Index – By Cause of Death

Index – Cause of Death			
Surname	**Name**	**Date Death**	**Cause of Death**
Billy The Cook		1882/7/25	
Buchanan	Nathaniel	1901/09/23	
Cockburn	John George	1935/04/15	
Donohue	Maurice	1862	
Edkins	Edward Roland	1905/08/14	
Edkins	Edwina	1910/08/17	
Edwards	Sidney	1898/08/01	
Fraser	Sydney Pechey	1923/04/08	
Fraser	Jane Margaret	1934/08/13	
Gallogly	George Beattie	1925/12/12	
McDonald	Mary	1904/07/20	
Miller	Dara Macartney	1896/04/09	
Ranken	John T Campbell	1907/03/22	
Unknown		1893/10/19	
McDonald	Angus William	1894/12/28	Accident
Ford	Mary Jane	1893/10/13	Ailing for some time
Fergus	John	1906/02/28	Asthma
Morehead	Boyd Dunlop	1905/10/30	Attack of apoplexy
Jeffray	Alexandra	1877/11/09	Blood poisoning - knife fight
Durdon	William Henry	1876/12/06	Burns
Kanaka	Harry	1876/12/08	Burns
Lloyd	Jessie Mary	1885/09/20	Burnt in Camp-fire
Ah Ching		1889/07/13	Cirrhosis of Liver
Chiverton alias Redstone		1871/09/29	Congestion of Lung
O'Hea	William	1876/09/12	Consumption
Eldershaw	Maud Margaret	1893/02/12	Convulsions
Gallogly	George Edwin	1895/02/02	Convulsions
Harrison	Margaret Alice	1882/04/11	Convulsions
Healy	Arthur	1885/04/15	Croup
McLean	George Horseman	1878/02/17	Croup
Shield	James	1880/03/18	Croup

Index – Cause of Death			
Surname	**Name**	**Date Death**	**Cause of Death**
Keating	Michael	1884/12/20	Delirium tremens
Lolbassie	Polynesian	1878/05/04	Disease of liver
Maggs	George	1876/10/26	Dropsy
Ambrose	Benjamin	1877/08/1	Drowned
Cann	John	1883/04/12	Drowned
Douglas	Archibald	1889/11/17	Drowned
Goodman	Frederick	1911/04/21	Drowned
Hammond	James	1896/12/05	Drowned
Phillips [Phillipp]	Andrew John	1920/04/27	Drowned
Pryor	Gideon	1880/03/31	Drowned
Willis	George	1888/03/07	Drowned
McCarthy	Thomas	1896/02/15	Drowned / Horse Accident
Ah Young	Tommy	1894/11/25	Dysentery
Baba	Polynesian	1878/02/14	Dysentery
Matow	Polynesian	1876/04/08	Dysentery
Navoren	Polynesian	1876/04/22	Dysentery
Robins	William	1873/03/27	Dysentery
Vaillant/Valliant	Reginald	1876/03/01	Dysentery
Nicholson	Thomas	1876/01/14	Excessive drinking
Murphy	John	1897/07/23	Exposure
Toohey [O'Donell]	Patrick [Alias Mad Mick]	1892/06/04	Exposure
Ah Sue		1903/01/17	Fell from a Mill
Turner	Campbell McDonald	1891/03/07	Fell Pub Veranda
Barkley	Charles	1870/05/3	Fever
Dowling	Patrick	1885/02/23	Fever
Gormely	John	1876/06/04	Fever
Williams	Frederick	1866/08/09	Fever
Small [Smale]	Levi	1895/07/26	Fever - Dengue Fever
Cornish	Edward Brooking	1866/10/27	Fever - Gulf
Landsborough	William	1886/03/16	Fever - Gulf
Burns	Thomas	1871/04/30	Fever & other causes

Index – Cause of Death			
Surname	**Name**	**Date Death**	**Cause of Death**
Unknown	Blackfellow	1876/06	Flogged
Shaw	Margaret Catherine	1895/02/01	Gastric enteritis
Ah Won	Tommy	1910/04/13	Heart Disease
Campbell	James	1901/01/01	Heart Disease
Carr	James	1875/09/22	Heart Disease
Coyne	Thomas	1902/01/8	Heart Disease
Crisp	Sherwin	1869/11/25	Heart Disease
Harting [Hartwig] [Halting]	John	1884/05/12	Heart Disease
Innes	William	1876/09/24	Heart Disease
McDonald	Ralph Erskine	1892/06/25	Heart Disease
McDonald	John	1904/12/20	Heart Disease
Murray	Hugh	1880/08/12	Heart Disease
Nicholls	Harriet	1876/08/14	Heart Disease
Quinn	James	1881/08/14	Heart Disease
Schofield	William	1910/07/07	Heart failure
O'Brien	Jeremiah	1903/01/07	Heat apoplexy
Kennedy	Frederick John Clarence	1883/12/04	Heat Exhaustion
Billey	Kanaka	1886/09/11	Horse Accident
Cox	William	1910/07/02	Horse Accident
Flood	Sydney	1871/07	Horse Accident
Franklin	Charles	1908/07/25	Horse Accident
Graham	Archibald Drummond	1883/06/02	Horse Accident
Kanaka		1876/11/13	Horse Accident
Lidder	Charles	1873/05/24	Horse Accident
Leslie	Martin	1907/08/21	Horse Accident
Drummond	David	1892/08/23	Horse Accident - brain fever?
Rohan	Joseph	1912/04/19	Horse Accident - Drown
McLean	Neil	1876/08/29	Horse Accident - Internal rupture
Butler	Annie Augusta	1882/01/19	Illness
Bender	Henry Joseph	1885/06/01	Infant

Index – Cause of Death			
Surname	**Name**	**Date Death**	**Cause of Death**
Cain	Infant [Female]	1882/02/24	Infant
Chambers	Elizabeth	1889/12/04	Infant
Forde	Gladys	1916/01/05	Infant
Lloyd	Llewellyn	1886/11/27	Infant
White	Mary	1885/11/26	Infant
Faleny	Jeremiah	1883/10/14	Inflammation
Brooks	Amos	1898/07/18	Influenza
Healy	Mathew	1909/05/23	Influenza
Rattray	Robert	1883/09/17	Internal Injuries
Gilmour	James Merry	1874/06/10	Jaundice
Ung	Yee	1885/12/17	Laryngeal
Fitzgerald	Martin	1869/02/11	Liver disease
McCulloch	Archibald	1892/09/25	Mortification Set in - broken arm
Nicholls	George Jonathon	1864/04/01	Murder / Suicide
Nicholls	Ethel Maria	1864/04/01	Murder / Suicide
Ah Young		1876/10/13	Murdered
Unknown	Aboriginal woman	1892/05	Murdered
Raynor	John Henry	1880/10/07	Murdered - Stabbed - Penetrated heart
Maier	Frederick	1872/08/13	Murdered by Black -Tambo
Barney		1865/09	Murdered by Blacks
Cozens alias Frenche		1866/06	Murdered by Blacks
Davis	Herbert Cecil	1871/09/	Murdered by Blacks
Mackay	Charles Douglas	1871/10/17	Murdered by Blacks
McFetridge	William	1876/03/31	Murdered by Blacks
McNeely	Robert	1864/11/20	Murdered by Blacks
Meredith	Llewellyn A	1864/11/20	Murdered by Blacks
Sammy	Sammy	1871/09/21	Murdered by Blacks
Unknown	Shepherd	1864	Murdered by Blacks
Vern	Charles Hugo Frederick	1866/05/12	Murdered by Blacks
Morgan	James	1888/07/12	Murdered in robbery
Neville	William	1898/12/13	Natural causes

Index – Cause of Death

Surname	Name	Date Death	Cause of Death
Lee	Michael	1897/03/13	Natural causes - Inflammation, pneumonia
Ah Gow		1903/02/08	Old Age
Taylor	William	1938/06/10	Old Age
Russell	Edward Ketia	1904/10/15	Paralytic seizure
Alston [Olsten]	Isaac	1901/01/01	Perished
Brown	Captain	1884/< March	Perished
Cameron	Donald	1881/01/16	Perished
Casey/Ceasey	John	1878/01/22	Perished
Daley	Lankey	1883/12	Perished
Maddern	Alfred	1906/01/11	Perished
Magee	James	1893/08	Perished
Towers	Arthur Gould	1914/12/24	Perished
Trouson [Tronson]	Edward Albert	1874/03/01	Perished
Unknown		1885/07	Perished
Welsby / Wilkie	Thomas Scott Willamson	1878/02/01	Perished
Whiting	Arthur	1896/01/08	Perished
Brownsey	Charles	1894/01/26	Perished - want of water
Oliver	Annie	1892/07/07	Peritonitis
Elliott	Aynslie John	1881/11/09	Phthisis – Wasting away
Thomas	John Henry	1895/07/19	Poisoned
Guild	Mary	1870/11/09	Poisoned - Accidently
Shaw	Walter Robert	1893/02/6	Poisoned - Accidently
Shaw	Margaret Ann	1893/02/7	Poisoned - Accidently
Apii	Polynesian	1878/01/30	Poisoned wound - leg
Badke	Alfred	1891/12/3	Premature Baby
Bell	Alexander	1897/04/01	Rupture of an aneurism
Gray-Buchanan	Thomas Farie	1899/04/27	Shooting Accident
Hohn [Hahn]	Louis	1873/06/04	Starvation
Callan	Owen	1889/01/27	Sudden Illness
Cameron	John Francis	1890/10/30	Suicide
Caulfield	Mark	1901/07/28	Suicide

Index – Cause of Death			
Surname	**Name**	**Date Death**	**Cause of Death**
Cleg	Thomas	1880/10/29	Suicide
Drury	Ernest T	1880/10/27	Suicide
Erhardt	Thomas	1879/03/23	Suicide
Hayton	Joseph	1894/04/09	Suicide
Langon	James	1901/03/07	Suicide
McNiel	Archibald	1912/01/29	Suicide
Schaumbach	Martin	1882/09/	Suicide
Barry	John	1887/01/26	Sun Stroke
Bennett	Isabella	1876/01/06	Thrush
Clarke	Rowland William	1893/01/14	Typhoid Fever
Coaton	Ann	1885/04/02	Typhoid Fever
Roberts	Robert	1884/12/28	Unknown
Gordon	James	1890/06/22	Water on Brain
Bailey	Lydia Mary	1887/01/24	Whooping Cough

Index – By Grave Location

Index – By Grave Location				
Surname	Name	Date Death	Grave Location	Age
Nicholson	Thomas	1876/01/14	20 Mile Creek - Mt Cornish - Bowen Down Rd	
Ah Young	Tommy	1894/11/25	29 mile Corindah & Bowen Downs Rd	
Alston [Olsten]	Isaac	1901/01/01	Ambo and Towall Boundary	
Chiverton alias Redstone		1871/09/29	Aramac Cemetery	23 years
Gallogly	George Beattie	1925/12/12	Aramac Cemetery	80 years
McDonald	Mary	1904/07/20	Aramac Cemetery	
Vaillant/Valliant	Reginald	1876/03/01	Aramac Cemetery	
Gormely	John	1876/06/04	Aramac Cemetery	60 years
Innes	William	1876/09/24	Aramac Cemetery	65 years
McDonald	John	1904/12/20	Aramac Cemetery	
Nicholls	Harriet	1876/08/14	Aramac Cemetery	32 years
Brooks	Amos	1898/07/18	Aramac Cemetery	
Taylor	William	1938/06/10	Aramac Cemetery	88 years
Welsby / Wilkie	Thomas Scott Willamson	1878/02/01	Aramac Cemetery	43 years
Gray-Buchanan	Thomas Farie	1899/04/27	Aramac Cemetery	24 years
McDonald	Angus William	1894/12/28	Aramac Cemetery - Central 163	18 years
McCulloch	Archibald	1892/09/25	Aramac Cemetery - Unknown	14 years
Williams	Frederick	1866/08/09	Aramac Creek	
Flood	Sydney	1871/07	Aramac Creek	
Cozens alias Frenche		1866/06	Aramac Creek	
Vern	Charles Hugo Frederick	1866/05/12	Aramac Creek - Thomson River Area	
Maier	Frederick	1872/08/13	Aramac Creek Station	28 years
O'Hea	William	1876/09/12	Aramac Station	28 years
Billy The Cook		1882/7/25	Bangall Creek	25 years

Index – By Grave Location				
Surname	**Name**	**Date Death**	**Grave Location**	**Age**
Durdon	William Henry	1876/12/06	Belltopper Creek - Bowen Downs Road	
Kanaka	Harry	1876/12/08	Belltopper Creek - Bowen Downs Road	
Chambers	Elizabeth	1889/12/04	Bengall Creek	20 days
Miller	Dara Macartney	1896/04/09	Bimbah	21 years
Butler	Annie Augusta	1882/01/19	Bimbah	
Unknown	Aboriginal woman	1892/05	Bimbah	
Cameron	John Francis	1890/10/30	Bimbah	
Langon	James	1901/03/07	Bimbah	67 years
Schaumbach	Martin	1882/09/	Bimbah	
Unknown		1885/07	Bowen Down - Clermont Road	
Lolbassie	Polynesian	1878/05/04	Bowen Downs	
Maggs	George	1876/10/26	Bowen Downs	54 years
Matow	Polynesian	1876/04/08	Bowen Downs	
Navoren	Polynesian	1876/04/22	Bowen Downs	
Robins	William	1873/03/27	Bowen Downs	40 years
Burns	Thomas	1871/04/30	Bowen Downs	
Brown	Captain	1884/< March	Bowen Downs - Paddock - Stainburn Road	65 [60]years
Trouson [Tronson]	Edward Albert	1874/03/01	Bowen Downs - Beaconsfield Run	28 years
Douglas	Archibald	1889/11/17	Bowen Downs - Cornish Creek	60 years
Willis	George	1888/03/07	Bowen Downs - Cornish Creek	
Mackay	Charles Douglas	1871/10/17	Bowen Downs - Cornish Creek	29 years
Oliver	Annie	1892/07/07	Bowen Downs - Cornish Creek - Tower Hill Crossing	10 years 11 mths
Phillips [Phillipp]	Andrew John	1920/04/27	Bowen Downs - Cornish Creek Bridge	30 years

Index – By Grave Location				
Surname	**Name**	**Date Death**	**Grave Location**	**Age**
Goodman	Frederick	1911/04/21	Bowen Downs - Cornish Creek -Flannigan's Water Hole	78 years
Ford	Mary Jane	1893/10/13	Bowen Downs - Homestead	
Gallogly	George Edwin	1895/02/02	Bowen Downs - Homestead	5 days
Toohey [O'Donell]	Patrick [Alias Mad Mick]	1892/06/04	Bowen Downs - Homestead	
Small [Smale]	Levi	1895/07/26	Bowen Downs - Homestead	89 years
Harting [Hartwig] [Halting]	John	1884/05/12	Bowen Downs - Homestead	
Healy	Mathew	1909/05/23	Bowen Downs - Homestead	47 years
Gilmour	James Merry	1874/06/10	Bowen Downs - Homestead	42 years
Barney		1865/09	Bowen Downs - Homestead	
Apii	Polynesian	1878/01/30	Bowen Downs - Homestead	
Donohue	Maurice	1862	Bowen Downs - Homestead - Original	
Cameron	Donald	1881/01/16	Bowen Downs - Marathon	55 years
Sammy	Sammy	1871/09/21	Bowen Downs - Out station	30 years
Lee	Michael	1897/03/13	Bowen Downs - Seven Mile Yards	
Murray	Hugh	1880/08/12	Bowen Downs - Shearing Shed	
Thomas	John Henry	1895/07/19	Bowen Downs - Shearing Shed	
Gordon	James	1890/06/22	Bowen Downs - Shearing Shed	3 months
Graham	Archibald Drummond	1883/06/02	Bowen Downs - Tuaburra	19
Fergus	John	1906/02/28	Bowen Downs - Unknown	73 years

Index – By Grave Location				
Surname	**Name**	**Date Death**	**Grave Location**	**Age**
Baba	Polynesian	1878/02/14	Bowen Downs - Unknown	
Crisp	Sherwin	1869/11/25	Bowen Downs - Unknown	
Forde	Gladys	1916/01/05	Bowen Downs - Unknown	16 hours
Fitzgerald	Martin	1869/02/11	Bowen Downs - Unknown	48 years
Ah Young		1876/10/13	Bowen Downs - Unknown	
Davis	Herbert Cecil	1871/09/	Bowen Downs - Unknown	
Guild	Mary	1870/11/09	Bowen Downs - Unknown	2 years 9 mths
Callan	Owen	1889/01/27	Bowen Downs - Unknown	35 years
Caulfield	Mark	1901/07/28	Bowen Downs - Unknown	
Roberts	Robert	1884/12/28	Bowen Downs - Unknown	
McLean	George Horseman	1878/02/17	Bowen Downs - Wash Pool	6 weeks 1 day
Hammond	James	1896/12/05	Bowen Downs - Wash Pool	16 years
Murphy	John	1897/07/23	Bowen Downs - Wash Pool	60 years
Barry	John	1887/01/26	Bowen Downs - Wash Pool	24 years
Pryor	Gideon	1880/03/31	Bowen Downs - Wash Pool Lagoon	37 years
Rohan	Joseph	1912/04/19	Brookwood Shearing Shed	
Nicholls	George Jonathon	1864/04/01	Bullock Creek	33 years
Nicholls	Ethel Maria	1864/04/01	Bullock Creek	40 years
Edwards	Sidney	1898/08/01	Caledonia	43 years
Drummond	David	1892/08/23	Caledonia	
McCarthy	Thomas	1896/02/15	Camoola Farm - Thomson River	28 years
Bell	Alexander	1897/04/01	Camoola Farms	
Whiting	Arthur	1896/01/08	Camoola Rd - 14 miles Longreach	
Drury	Ernest T	1880/10/27	Coreena Station	
Carr	James	1875/09/22	Cornish Creek	30 years
O'Brien	Jeremiah	1903/01/07	Cornish Creek - 12 miles Muttaburra	

Index – By Grave Location				
Surname	**Name**	**Date Death**	**Grave Location**	**Age**
Unknown	Shepherd	1864	Cornish Creek - Duck Pond Creek	
Eldershaw	Maud Margaret	1893/02/12	Crusoe	5 days
Campbell	James	1901/01/01	Crusoe	
Coyne	Thomas	1902/01/8	Crusoe	
Maddern	Alfred	1906/01/11	Crusoe - 7 miles from homestead	60-65 years
Cornish	Edward Brooking	1866/10/27	Darlinghurst Sydney	44 years
McDonald	Ralph Erskine	1892/06/25	Fleetwood	
Ranken	John T Campbell	1907/03/22	Goulburn	68 years
Hayton	Joseph	1894/04/09	Green Hill - Unknown	
Erhardt	Thomas	1879/03/23	Landsborough River	
Towers	Arthur Gould	1914/12/24	Leichhardt - beside Barcaldine Road	70 years
Shield	James	1880/03/18	Mount Cornish	6 days
Ah Won	Tommy	1910/04/13	Mount Cornish	50 years
Unknown		1893/10/19	Mount Cornish - Tower Hill Creek	
Casey/Ceasey	John	1878/01/22	Mount Cornish - 9 miles from homestead	50 years
Ah Sue		1903/01/17	Mt Cornish	
Billey	Kanaka	1886/09/11	Mt Cornish	
Lidder	Charles	1873/05/24	Mt Cornish	20 years
Faleny	Jeremiah	1883/10/14	Mt Cornish	47 years
Ah Gow		1903/02/08	Mt Cornish	72 years
Brownsey	Charles	1894/01/26	Mt Cornish	
Bennett	Isabella	1876/01/06	Mt Cornish	11 days
Coaton	Ann	1885/04/02	Mt Cornish	33 years
Bailey	Lydia Mary	1887/01/24	Mt Cornish	26 days
Raynor	John Henry	1880/10/07	Mt Cornish - 10 Mile Dam	45-50 years
Neville	William	1898/12/13	Mt Cornish - 8 miles east Muttaburra	60 years

Index – By Grave Location				
Surname	**Name**	**Date Death**	**Grave Location**	**Age**
Harrison	Margaret Alice	1882/04/11	Mt Cornish - Ambo	3 months
Cain	Infant [Female]	1882/02/24	Mt Cornish - Ambo	1 day old
Rattray	Robert	1883/09/17	Mt Cornish - Ambo	23 years
Lloyd	Jessie Mary	1885/09/20	Mt Cornish - Ambo - No Name Creek	10 years 11 mths
Magee	James	1893/08	Mt Cornish - Ambo - Top Paddock	
Healy	Arthur	1885/04/15	Mt Cornish - Bangall Creek	1 year 11 mths
Dowling	Patrick	1885/02/23	Mt Cornish - Bradley's Creek	26 years
White	Mary	1885/11/26	Mt Cornish - Bradley's Creek	6 days
Kanaka		1876/11/13	Mt Cornish - Budgeragar	
Barkley	Charles	1870/05/3	Mt Cornish - Eastern side Thomson River	41 years
Franklin	Charles	1908/07/25	Mt Cornish - Eastfield Boundary	60 years
Ambrose	Benjamin	1877/08/1	Mt Cornish - Marathon	
McLean	Neil	1876/08/29	Mt Cornish - Marathon	
Hohn [Hahn]	Louis	1873/06/04	Mt Cornish - Marathon	
Unknown	Blackfellow	1876/06	Mt Cornish - Police Barracks	
Morgan	James	1888/07/12	Mt Cornish - Unknown	65 years
Leslie	Martin	1907/08/20	Muttaburra Cemetery	50 years
Schofield	William	1910/07/07	Muttaburra Cemetery - Grave 25	59 years
Clarke	Rowland William	1893/01/14	Muttaburra Cemetery - Grave 71	17 years
Cann	John	1883/04/12	Muttaburra Cemetery - Old Cemetery	
Cleg	Thomas	1880/10/29	Muttaburra Cemetery - Old Cemetery	60 years
Ah Ching		1889/07/13	Muttaburra Cemetery - Unknown	46 years

Index – By Grave Location				
Surname	**Name**	**Date Death**	**Grave Location**	**Age**
Shaw	Margaret Catherine	1895/02/01	Muttaburra Cemetery - Unknown	9 months
Ung	Yee	1885/12/17	Muttaburra Cemetery - Unknown	
Shaw	Walter Robert	1893/02/6	Muttaburra Cemetery - Unknown	$3^1/_2$ years
Shaw	Margaret Ann	1893/02/7	Muttaburra Cemetery - Unknown	16 months
McNiel	Archibald	1912/01/29	North Crusoe	
Daley	Lankey	1883/12	Reedy Creek - Aramac Rd - Sandy Creek	
Cox	William	1910/07/02	Reedy Creek - Between Homestead - Shearing Shed	22 years
McFetridge	William	1876/03/31	Road 180 miles north Mount Cornish	22 years
Elliott	Aynslie John	1881/11/09	Rockhampton	33 years
Turner	Campbell McDonald	1891/03/07	Rockhampton	26 years
Badke	Alfred	1891/12/3	Sardine Creek Dam	9 days
Jeffray	Alexandra	1877/11/09	Scarbury	
Kennedy	Frederick John Clarence	1883/12/04	Scarbury	7 Years
Bender	Henry Joseph	1885/06/01	Scarbury	9 Months
Keating	Michael	1884/12/20	Stainburn Downs	
Quinn	James	1881/08/14	Stainburn Road	50 years
Edkins	Edward Roland	1905/08/14	Sydney	
Edkins	Edwina	1910/08/17	Sydney	
Buchanan	Nathaniel	1901/09/23	Tamworth	75 years
Lloyd	Llewellyn	1886/11/27	Thomson River Longreach	2 days
Cockburn	John George	1935/04/15	Toowong Cemetery Brisbane	66 years
Fraser	Sydney Pechey	1923/04/08	Toowong Cemetery Brisbane	75 years
Fraser	Jane Margaret	1934/08/13	Toowong Cemetery Brisbane	92 years

Index – By Grave Location				
Surname	**Name**	**Date Death**	**Grave Location**	**Age**
Morehead	Boyd Dunlop	1905/10/30	Toowong Cemetery Brisbane	62 years
Landsborough	William	1886/03/16	Toowong Cemetery Brisbane	61 years
Russell	Edward Ketia	1904/10/15	Toowong Cemetery Brisbane	
McNeely	Robert	1864/11/20	Tower Hill Creek	
Meredith	Llewellyn A	1864/11/20	Tower Hill Creek	30 years